Original Land Titles in Delaware

Commonly Known as

The Duke of York Record

Being An Authorized Transcript From the Official Archives of the State of Delaware, and Comprising the Letters Patent, Permits, Commissions, Surveys, Plats and Confirmations by The Duke of York and Other High Officials, From

1646 to 1679.

Printed by Order of the General Assembly of the State of Delaware.

CLEARFIELD

Originally published
Wilmington, Delaware, 1903

Reprinted for
Clearfield Company, Inc. by
Genealogical Publishing Co., Inc.
Baltimore, Maryland
1997

International Standard Book Number: 0-8063-4697-3

Made in the United States of America

AUTHORIZATION.

This edition of one thousand copies of the Duke of York Record was printed by authority of the General Assembly of the State of Delaware, expressed in the following joint resolutions:

Joint Resolution in relation to printing the Book in the Recorder's office at Dover, known as the Duke of York Record.

WHEREAS, There is now in the office of the Recorder of Deeds at Dover, one volume in manuscript, of the Dutch grant of lands from the year A. D. 1646 to the year 1657 inclusive, and of the Duke of York's grant of lands in Delaware from the year 1657 to 1680 inclusive; and

WHEREAS, Said volume contains much valuable information which should be preserved, and is of much value to the State, and age has already made much of the writing imperfect, and some of the written pages are deficient, having been destroyed by the British when New Castle was captured during the Revolutionary War; therefore, be it

Resolved by the Senate and House of Representatives of the State of Delaware in General Assembly met:

That a committee of two on the part of the Senate and a committee of three on the part of the House be appointed to have said volume printed for the use of the State.

Approved March 16, A. D. 1899.

Committee
- On part of Senate,
  - SAMUEL M. KNOX,
  - ELISHA H. F. FARLOW.
- On part of House,
  - DAVIS H. FRAZIER,
  - JAMES W. ROBERTSON,
  - FRANCIS J. MCNULTY.

In pursuance of this authority the committee advertised for proposals as follows:

PROPOSALS FOR STATE PRINTING.

Sealed proposals for printing, binding, and delivering 500 copies of the Duke of York's Records, from the year 1646 to 1679, will be received by the Chairman of the Legislative Committee for the publication of the same, as ordered by Joint Resolution of the General Assembly, approved March 16, 1899, directed to Harrington, Delaware, will be received until November 11, 1899. Fifty of said copies to be bound in sheep. Said Records to be printed on 55 lb. paper, in octavo, in long primer type, so as to contain at least 45 lines to the page.

The bids will be presented to the Joint Committee, which reserves the right to reject any or all bids. The next General Assembly will provide payment for warrant.

D. HENRY FRAZIER, Chairman.
P. O. Harrington, Del.

Nov. 1, 1899.

After due consideration of the bids submitted, the committee awarded the contract to The Star Publishing Company, of Wilmington, Del., as appears from the subjoined letter:

STATE OF DELAWARE.
HOUSE OF REPRESENTATIVES.

Dover, Nov. 13, 1899.

Mr. J. B. Bell, President Star Publishing Co.

Sir: I herewith notify you the committee appointed by the recent Legislature have awarded to you the contract for printing, compiling, indexing and binding five hundred copies of the Records of the Duke of Yorke as per Resolution passed by said body, at the price of $625.00.

Very respectfully yours,
FRANCIS J. McNULTY,
Secretary of Committee.

For reasons which it is not necessary here to state, it was impossible for the contracting printers to secure the manuscript volume of the Duke of York Record until November, 1902, and at the session of the General Assembly which convened January 6, 1903, the following joint resolution was adopted:

Be it Resolved by the Senate and House of Representatives of the State of Delaware in General Assembly met:

That a committee of one on the part of the Senate and two on the part of the House be and the same is hereby appointed for the purpose of supervising the printing of the Duke of York Records, authorized by a previous Legislature, and the same committee is hereby authorized and directed to procure the printing of five hundred (500) additional copies of the said Records at a cost for the additional copies not to exceed the sum of three hundred and seventy-five dollars ($375).

Approved A. D. Feb. 27, 1903.

Committee
- On part of Senate: FRANCIS J. McNULTY,
- On part of House: ABRAHAM L. TYRE, WILLIAM H. GEHMAN, JR.

Under the authority of this resolution, the committee gave the following order:

Dover, March 9, 1903.

To The Star Publishing Co., Wilmington, Delaware.

Gentlemen: You are hereby authorized to print five hundred (500) additional copies of the Duke of York Record for the sum of three hundred and seventy-five dollars ($375).

WM. H. GEHMAN, JR.,
ABRAHAM L. TYRE,
FRANCIS J. McNULTY.

Original Land Titles of Delaware

Commonly Known as

The Duke of York Record.

(Note.—The numerals appearing in parenthesis throughout the text indicate the manuscript pages of the Record.)
Note.—Page 1 of the Record is in Old Holland Dutch, the translation being on the following page. This printed transcript begins, therefore, with page 2 of the Record, being the translation of page 1.)

No. 1.

(2)
We Willem Kieft, Director General, and Councilors, in the name of the High and Mighty Lords the States General of the United Netherlands, of his Highness of Orange, and of the Honorable Lords Directors of the Privileged West India Company residing in New Netherland, Witness and declare hereby that we on the day of the date hereinafter mentioned have granted and permitted to Abraham Planck, Symon Root, Jan Andriesen and Pieter Harmensen to, settle on the South River of New Netherland, and take possession of the lands situate on the said river obliquely opposite to the Islet called 't Vogele Lant (the Birds' Land), of which lands they are authorized to appropiate to themselves One hundred Morgen, * to establish there four Farms or Plantations and begin to cultivate the same within a year from this date, or sooner if it be possible, on pain of losing this their grant. Upon condition that the aforesaid persons, or such as might get their grant, acknowledge the Honorable Lords Directors aforesaid as their Lords and Patrons under the sovereignty of their High Mightinesses, and provided they willingly sumbit themselves to all such charges and duties as by the aforesaid Lords are already or still shall be determined upon. Constituting therefore aforesaid Abraham Planck, Symon Root, Jan Andriesen and Pieter Harmensen, to take, in our place, real and actual possession of the aforesaid One hundred Morgen land, giving them full power, authority and special command to accept, cultivate and use the aforesaid land, situate in the aforesaid South River, as they do their own patrimonial lands and effects; we the

*A "Morgen" was equal to about three acres.—Translator.

grantors, in our aforesaid capacity, not having, holding or reserving in the least any part, claim or authority of and to the aforesaid One hundred Morgen of Land, but desisting therefrom, for the use as aforesaid, from now forever. Promising further to keep this present grant firm, staunch, inviolable and irrevocable, and to observe and execute it,— all under obligation as provided by law.

In Witness whereof these presents are signed by us, and confirmed with our seal in red wax appendant hereto.

Done in the Fort of New Amsterdam. (The aforesaid persons are promised, if in future they should want more land, than hereabove mentioned, it will be granted them, provided they build on the land houses for dwellings, and that, if they quit, they shall then be deprived of this grant.)

(Signed) Willem Kieft.

Underneath stood:

By order of the Hon. Director General and Councilors of New Netherland,

Cornelis van Tienhoven,
Secretary. 1646.

No. 2.

(3)
Petrus Stuyvesant, in the name of the Honorable High and Mighty Lords the States General of the United Netherlands and the Honorable Lords Directors of the Privileged West India Company, Director General of the New Netherland, Curacoa, Boynairo, Aruba and the appendencies thereof, together with the Honorable Lords Councilors, Witness and declare that we on this day, the date hereinafter mentioned, have granted and bestowed upon Alexander Boyer, A Plantation situate on the South River of New Netherland, to the North of Fort Casamier on the corner between the first and second Valley on the South End of Frans Smith's, wide along the river side from the corner of the Valley to the land of the aforesaid Frans Smith North-east by East, rather Easterly, Sixty six Rods, further along said Smith into the Woods North North-West $\frac{1}{4}$ point more Westerly one Hundred and two Rods, further North North-West fifty Rods, further to the Valley South-West One hundred Rods, further along the Valley East South-East fifty Rods, further West sixty Rods, further East by South forty-four Rods, further to the first starting point South-East by East fifty-three Rods, and are herein measured two inlets of Valleys; amounting to about four and twenty Morgen. Upon express conditions and provisos, &c, the 30th of November, Anno 1656.

No. 3.

(4)
Petrus Stuyvesant, in the name of the Honorable High and Mighty Lords the States General of the United Netherlands and the Honorable Lords Directors of the Privileged West India Company,

Director General of New Netherland, Curacoa, Bonayro, Aruba and the appendencies thereof, together with the Honorable Lords Councilors, Witness and declare that we on this day, the date hereinafter mentioned, have granted and bestowed upon Thomas Broen, A Plantation situate on the South River of New Netherland below Fort Casamier, adjoining on the East side Cornelis Teunisse, wide on the South side towards East eighteen Rods, on the East side alongside Simon Leem about North North-West one hundred and thirty-two Rods and alongside Cornelis Teunissen's about South South-East long one hundred and thirty two Rods; amounting together to 2046 Rods. Upon the express conditions and provisos, &c. Done at Amsterdam in New Netherland on the 12th of April, Anno 1656.

No. 4.

(5)
Peter Stuyvesant in the name of the High and Mighty Lords the States General of the United Netherlands and the Honorable gentlemen the Directors of the privileged West India Company, Director General of New Netherland, Curacoa, Bonayro, Aruba and their Dependencies, together with Honourable Gentlemen of the Council Witness and declare that we on the Day of the Date underwritten have given and granted to Andries Hudden one Lot for a house and garden situate on the South River of New Netherland near Fort Casamier being in number the Fifteenth and landed to the Northward of the lot of Jan Andriessen and to the Southward of the Lot of Sander Fenix, is in Breadth on the Street Sixty two Feet Rynland Measure, & on both sides Three hundred Feet, and in the Rear fifty six Feet, with express conditions & Provisos &c. Done Amsterdam in New Netherland the 30th November Anno 1656.

No. 5.

(6)
Peter Stuyvesant in behalf of the High and Mighty Lords, the States General of the United Netherlands and the Honourable Gentlemen the Directors of the Privileged West India Company, Director General of New Netherland, Curacoa, Bonayro, Aruba and its Appendencies together with the Honourable the Genelemen of the Council Witness and declare that we on the Day of the Date hereunder written have given and granted to Jacob de Hinst two Lots situate on the South River at Fort Casamier, the one being in the first Row in No. the Eighteenth is wide in Front two and sixty Feet in the Rear six and fifty Feet, and in Length on both sides Three hundred Feet; the other in the second Row being in No. the sixty-seventh is wide in Front six and Fifty Feet, and in the Rear six and fifty Feet, long on both sides three hundred Feet with express conditions & Provisoes &c. Done at Amsterdam in New Netherland the 25th August Anno 1656.

No. 6.

(7)

Peter Stuyvesant in behalf of the High and Mighty Lords the States General of the United Netherlands and the Honourable Gentlemen the Directors of the privileged West India Company, Director General of New Netherland, Curacoa, Bonayro, Aruba and their Dependencies, together with the Honourable Gentlemen of the Council, Witness and Declare, that we on the Day of the Date underwritten, have given and granted, to Jan Piecolet a small tract of land situate on the South River of New Netherland, to the Southward of Fort Casamier, at the Brick Maker's Corner, between the plantations of Philip Jans & Jacob Crabbe, and stretches from the Land of the said Philip Jans, West along the Shore to the Land of Jacob Crabbe, Eight and twenty Rods, along the Land of the said Crabbe North-West six and sixty Rods to the High Way, along the High Way to the Land of Philip Jans West thirty Rods, farther to the Place of Beginning South-East Southerly sixty-four Rods, amounting in the whole to three Morgen & Eighty five Rods. With express Conditions and Provisoes &c. Done Amsterdam in New Netherland the first September Anno 1656.

N. B. An obliteration in the translation of No. 6 in the eleventh line between the words Crabbe and Eight. (The words obliterated being: "Aforesaid northwest."

No. 7.

(8)

Peter Stuyvesant in behalf of the High & Mighty Lords the States General of the United Netherland and the Honourable Gentlemen the Directors of the privileged West India Company, Director General of New Netherland, Curacoa, Bonayro, Aruba and their Dependencies, together with the Honourable Gentlemen of the Council Witness and Declare that we on the Day of the Date underwritten have given and granted to Philip Jansen Ringo one Lot for a House and Garden situate on the South River below Fort Casamier above the Brick Maker's Corner to the Southward on Cornelis Mourits is wide in Front on the Street two hundred and eighty six Feet Wood Measure, in Length along the Land of Cornelius Mourits aforesaid five hundred and seventy five Feet Wood Measure also, in Weadth back by the Plantation along the High Way two hundred and Eighty four Feet, long on the South Side six hundred and fifty Feet with express Conditions and Provisoes &c. Done Amsterdam in New Netherland the 12th September Anno 1656.

No. 8.

(9)

Peter Stuyvesant in Behalf of the High and Mighty Lords the States General of the United Netherland and the honourable gentlemen the Directors of the privileged West India Company Director General of New Netherland, Curacoa, Bonayro, Aruba, and their Dependencies, together with the honourable gentlemen of the Council Witness and Declare that we on the Day of the Date underwritten have given and granted to Constantinus Groenenburgh a Lot for a House and Garden situate on the South River below Fort Casamier being the Twentieth in number and landed to the Southward of the Lot of Cornelius Mourits and to the Northward of the Lot of Reynier Dominicus, is in Weadth in the Front on the Water Side sixty two Feet Wood Measure, in Weadth in the Rear on the High Way fifty six Feet, in Length on both Sides three hundred and eight Feet with express Conditions & Provisoes &c. Done Amsterdam in New Netherland the 30th September Anno 1656.

No. 9.

(10)
Peter Stuyvesant in Behalf of the High and Mighty Lords of the States General of the United Netherlands and the Honourable Gentlemen the Directors of the privileged West India Company, Director General of New Netherland, Curacoa, Bonayro, Aruba and their Dependencies together with the honourable gentlemen of the Council Witness and Declare that we on the Day of the Date underwritten have given and granted to Hans Albertsen van Bronswyck one Lott for a House and Garden situate on the South River of New Netherland at Fort Casamier in the second Row, directly behind Claes the Smith, on the East by Stephen Acker, on the West by Roeloff De Haes's Lot In the rear of the North Side of the plantation of Roeloff De Haes in weadth fifty six Feet, in Length on both Sides three hundred Feet with express Conditions & Provisos &c. Done Amsterdam in New Netherland the 13 September Anno 1656.

No. 10.

(11)
Petrus Stuyvesant, in the name of the Honorable High and Mighty Lords the States General of the United Netherlands and the Honorable Lords Directors of the Privileged West India Company, Director General of New Netherland, Curacoa, Bonayro, Aruba and the Appendencies thereof, together with the Honorable Lords Councilors, Witness and declare that we on this day the date hereinafter mentioned, have granted and bestowed upon Jan Hendricksen van Struckhousen, A Lot for a House and Garden, situate on the South River near Fort Casamier, being No. 35 in the second Row, adjoining North the Lot of Gerrit Jansen, South the lot of Sander Boyer, being wide in front and rear fifty six Rhineland feet (wood measure), and on both sides long three hundred feet.

Upon express conditions and provisos, &c.
Done at Fort Amsterdam in New Netherland on the 22nd of September, Anno 1656.

No. 11.

(12)
Peter Stuyvesant in Behalf of the High and Mighty Lords the States General of the United Netherlands and the Honourable Gentlemen the Directors of the Privileged West India Company, Director General of New Netherland, Curacoa, Bonayro, Aruba and their Dependencies together with the Honourable Gentlemen of the Council Witness and Declare that we on the Day of the Date underwritten have given and granted to the Widow of Roeloff De Haas one plantation situate on the South River at Fort Casamier to the Northward of the high Road behind the Lot of Jan Gerritsen is wide to the Northward Seven Rods, long on both sides one and thirty Rods, wide in the Rear Seven and an half Rod, with express Conditions and Provisoes &c. Done Fort Amsterdam in New Netherland the 20th October Anno 1656.

No. 12.

(13)
Petrus Stuyvesant, in the name of the Honourable High and Mighty Lords the States General of the United Netherlands and the Honourable Lords Directors of the Privileged West India Company, Director General of New Netherland, Curacoa, Bonayro, Aruba and the Appendencies thereof, together with the Honourable Lords Councilors, Witness and declare that we on this day, the date hereinafter mentioned, have granted and bestowed upon the widow of Roeloff de Haes, A Lot for a House and Garden, situate on the South River of New Netherlands near Fort Casamier, being the first Row on the North of the Common Road and adjoining S (outh) Claes Pietersen, and is wide in front on the Shore side sixty two feet and in the rear sixty two feet, long on both sides three hundred feet.
Upon the express conditions and provisos, &.
Done at Amsterdam in New Netherland on the 28th day of October, Anno 1656.

No. 13.

(14)
Peter Stuyvesant in Behalf of the High and Mighty Lords the States General of the United Netherlands and the Honourable Gentlemen the Directors of the privileged West India Company, Director General of New Netherland, Curacoa, Bonayro, Aruba and their Dependencies together with the Honourable Gentlemen of the Council Witness and Declare that we on the Day of the Date underwritten have given and granted to Luke Dircksen one Lot for a House and Garden situate on the South River at Fort Casamier in the first Row laying between the Lots of Ryer Moe and Claes Pietersen Smith, is Wide towards the Street sixty two Feet Wood Measure, long on both Sides three hundred like Feet; wide in the Rear Seventy Feet, with express Conditions and Provisoes &c. Done Fort Amsterdam in New Netherland the Tenth of February Anno 1657.

No. 14.

(15)
Peter Stuyvesant in Behalf of the High and Mighty Lords the States General of the United Netherlands and the Honourable Gentlemen the Directors of the privileged West India Company, Director General of New Netherland, Curacoa, Bonayro, Aruba and their Dependencies together with the Honourable Gentlemen of the Council Witness and Declare that we on the Day of the Date underwritten have given and granted to Ryer Lammersen Moe one Lot for a House and Garden situate at Fort Casamier on the South River of New Netherland between the Lots of Jan Eckhoff and Pieter Lowrussen, is wide sixty-four Feet, and long on both sides three hundred Feet with express Conditions and Provisoes &c. Done Amsterdam in New Netherland the 20th February Anno 1657.

No. 15.

(16)
Peter Stuyvesant in Behalf of the High and Mighty Lords the States General of the United Netherlands and the Honourable Gentlemen the Directors of the Privileged West India Company, Director General of New Netherland, Curacoa, Bonairo, Aruba and their Dependencies, together with the Honourable gentlemen of the Council Witness and Declare that we on the Day of the Date underwritten have given and granted to Claes Pietersen one Lot for a house and Garden situate at Fort Casamier on the South River of New Netherland in the Front on the Street between the Lots of Roeloff de Haes and Jan Schut is wide in front as well as Rear sixty two Feet and long on both Sides three hundred Feet. Note the aforesaid Lot was by order on the sixth Day of December 1652 laid out and surveyed for the said Claes Pietersen or for those who should hereafter obtain his Right with express Conditions and Provisoes &c. Done Fort Amsterdam the 11th April Anno 1657 in New Netherland.

No. 16.

(17)
Petrus Stuyvesant, in the name of the Honorable High and Mighty Lords the States General of the United Netherlands and the Honorable Lords Directors of the Privileged West India Company, Director General of New Netherland, Curacao, Bonnairo and the Appendencies thereof, together with the Honorable Lords Councilors, Witness and Declare that we on the date hereinafter written have granted and bestowed upon Barent Jansen van Swoll, A Lot for a House and Garden situate near Fort Casamier on the South River of New Netherland, behind the first row of lots, between Elias Emmens and Marten Rosemont, being wide in front as also in the Rear fifty four Feet, long on both sides three hundred feet. Upon Express Conditions and provisos, &c. Done at Amsterdam in New Netherland this 20th of February, Anno 1657.

No. 17.

(18)
Petrus Stuyvesant, in the name of the Honorable High and Mighty Lords the States General of the United Netherlands and the Honorable Lords Directors of the Privileged West India Company, Director General of New Netherland, Curacao, Bonairo, Aruba and the Appendencies thereof, together with the Lords Councilors, Witness that we on the date hereinafter written have granted and bestowed upon Pieter Hermens, A Plantation situate below Fort Casamier on the South River of New Netherland, on the East Side of Pieter Lourence and on the West side of Rosier Schot, being wide in front on the South side eighteen Rods, long on the East side 101 Rods, wide on the North side 13 Rods and long on the West side one hundred and thirty Rods, amounting together to two thousand and twenty three Rods. Upon express conditions and provisos &c. Done at Amsterdam in New Netherland this day February 29, Anno 1657.

No. 18.

(19)
Peter Stuyvesant in Behalf of the High and Mighty Lords the States General of the United Netherlands and the Honourable Gentlemen the Directors of the privileged West India Company, Director General of New Netherland, Curacoa, Bonnairo, Aruba and their Dependencies together with the Honourable Gentlemen of the Council Witness that we on the Day of the Date underwritten have given and granted to Pieter Harmense one Lot for a House and Garden situate at Fort Casamier on the South River of New Netherland between Harmer Janssen and Rynier Dominicus, is wide in Front sixty two Feet, in the Rear fifty four Feet, and long on both Sides three hundred Feet with express Conditions and Provisoes &c. Done Amsterdam in New Netherland the 29th February Anno 1657.

No. 19.

(20)
Petrus Stuyvesant, in the name of the Honorable High and Mighty Lords the States General of the United Netherlands and the Honorable Lords Directors of the Privileged West India Company, Director General of New Netherland, Curacoa Bonairo, Aruba and the Appendencies thereof, together with the Honourable Lords Councilors, Witness that we on the date hereinafter written have granted and bestowed upon Pieter Laurense, A Plantation situate near Fort Casamier on the South River of New Netherland, being wide on the South side eighteen Rods, long on the East side next to Cornelis Theunisse one hundred and thirty two Rods, long on the West side next to Pieter Harmense one hundred and thirty one Rods, amounting together to two thousand and thirty eight Rods. Upon express conditions and provisos, &c.

Done at Amsterdam in New Netherland this day February 28, 1657.

No. 20.

(21)
Peter Stuyvesant in Behalf of the High and Mighty Lords the States General of the United Netherlands and the Honourable Gentlemen the Directors of the Privileged West India Company Director General of New Netherland, Curacoa, Bonnairo, Aruba and their Dependencies together with the Honourable Gentlemen of the Council Witness and Declare that we on the Date underwritten have given and granted to Rynier Dominicus one Lott for a House and Garden situate on the South River of New Netherland by Fort Casamier between Claes Jansen and Peter Hermens is wide in Front sixty four Feet, in the Rear fifty eight Feet, long on both Sides three hundred Feet with express Conditions & Provisoes &c. Done Amsterdam in New Netherland the 30th Feb'y 1657.

No. 21.

(22)
Peter Stuyvesant in Behalf of the High and Mighty Lords the States General of the United Netherlands and the Honourable Gentlemen the Directors of the Privileged West India Company, Director General of New Netherland, Curacoa, Bonnairo, Aruba, and their Dependencies together with the honourable gentlemen of the Council witness and Declare that we on the Day of the Date underwritten have given & granted to Pieter Ebel one Plantation situate on the South River of New Netherland at Fort Casamier bounded on the North by Jan Eckhoff and to the Southward by said Fort is large four Morgen with express Conditions &c. Done Amsterdam in New Netherland the 30th February Anno 1657.

No. 22.

(23)
Petrus Stuyvesant, in the name of the Honorable High and Mighty Lords the States General of the United Netherlands and the Honorable Lords Directors of the Privileged West India Company, Director General of New Netherland, Curacao, Bonnairo, Aruba and the appendencies thereof, together with the Honorable Lords Councilors, Witnesses that we on this day, the date hereinafter written, have granted and bestowed upon Cornelis Steenwyck, A Lot for a House and Garden situate on the South River of New Netherland near Fort Casamier between the Lots of Adriaen Jacobs and Harmen Pietersen and Company and Reynier Moe, being wide in front at the Street sixty two Feet (Wood Measure), in the rear wide likewise sixty-two feet, long on both sides equally three hundred feet. Upon express conditions and provisos, &c. Done at Amsterdam in New Netherland, this 30 February, 1657.

No. 23.

(24)
Peter Stuyvesant in Behalf of the High and Mighty Lords the States General of the United Netherlands and the Honourable Gentlemen the Directors of the Privileged West India Company, Director General of New Netherland, Curacoa, Bonnairo, Aruba and their Dependencies, together with the Honourable Gentlemen of the Council Witness and Declare that we on the Date underwritten have given and granted to John Gerritsen one Lot for a House and Garden situate on the South River of New Netherland at Fort Casamier in the second Row bounded on the North by the High Way behind the Lot of Roelof De Haes is wide in Front and Rear sixty two Feet, long on both sides three hundred Feet with express Conditions and Provisos &c. Done Amsterdam in New Netherland the 30th February 1657.

No. 24.

(25)
Petrus Stuyvesant, in the name of the Honorable High and Mighty Lords the States General of the United Netherlands and the Honorable Lords Directors of the General Privileged West India Company, Director General of New Netherland, Curacoa, Bonnairo, Aruba and the appendencies thereof, together with the Honorable Lords Councilors, Witness and declare hereby, that we on this day, the date hereinafter written, have granted and bestowed upon Jacob Crabbe, A Plantation situate on the South River of New Netherland below Fort Casamier, between the first Valley and the land of Jan Picolet, extending from this Picolet's land along the shore as far as the remotest corner called "Steenbackers (Brick maker's) Corner", from which corner to a corner of the Valley, extending from each other nearly North-West and South-East by South, the valley therebetween is comprised, laid out along this and measures four morgen and one hundred and thirty Rods, West by South ½ point Southward seventy five Rods, further along the Valley North-East fifty Rods, North North-East ten Rods, North North-West fifty Rods, West North-West Ten Rods, South-West by South twenty five Rods, North-West ½ point West fifteen Rods, North by West fifteen Rods, further in the Woods North-West by West seventy five Rods as far as the Plantation of Ritsert Schot, back in the Woods North East by East seventy Rods, along the Plantation South-East by South one hundred and ten Rods, further along the land of the said Picolet as far as the first starting point, amounting together to twelve Morgen, one hundred and twenty Rods firm land, and the valley as above four Morgen and one hundred and thirty Rods, making in valley and firm land a total of sixteen Morgen and two hundred and fifty Rods. Upon express conditions and provisos, &c. Done at Amsterdam in New Netherland February 30, 1657.

No. 25.

(27) Petrus Stuyvesant in Behalf of the High and Mighty Lords the States General of the United Netherlands and the Honourable Gentlemen the Directors of the privileged West India Company, Director General of New Netherland, Curocoa, Bonnairo, Aruba and their Dependencies together with the Honourable Gentlemen of the Council Witness that we on the Date underwritten have given and granted to Sander Leendersen one Lot for a House and Garden situate on the South River of New Netherland at Fort Casamier between William De Hit and John Andriessen is wide in Front and Rear fifty six Feet, long on both sides three hundred Feet with express Conditions and Provisoes &c. Done Amsterdam in New Netherland the 1st March 1657.

No. 26.

(28) Petrus Stuyvesant, in the name of the Honorable High and Mighty Lords the States General of the United Netherlands and the Honorable Lords Directors of the Privileged West India Company, Director General of New Netherland, Curacoa, Bonairo, Aruba and the appendencies thereof, together with the Honorable Lords Councilors, Witness that we on the date hereinafter written have granted and bestowed upon Willem Tailler A Lot for a House and Garden, situate on the South River of New Netherland near Fort Casamier in the first Row at the front of the shore between Thomas Broen and Sander Leendersen, being wide in front and rear sixty five feet and long on both sides thirty feet. Upon the express conditions and provisos, &c. Done at Amsterdam in New Netherland March 1, Anno 1657.

No. 27.

(29) Petrus Stuyvesant, in the name of the Honorable High and Mighty Lords the States General of the United Netherlands and the Honorable Directors of the Privileged West India Company, Director General of New Netherland, Curacoa, Bonnayro, Aruba and the appdendencies thereof, together with the Honorable Lords Councilors, Witness and declare that we on this day, the date hereinafter written, have granted and bestowed upon Jan Eeckhoff, A Lot for a House and Garden situate on the South River of New Netherland near Fort Casamier in the Second Row No. 36, behind the Lot of Jan Andriessen, being wide in front and rear fifty six feet, long on both side three hundred feet; upon express conditions and provisos, &c. Done at Amsterdam in New Netherland June 17, Anno 1657.

No. 28.

(31) Peter Stuyvesant in Behalf of the High and Mighty Lords the States General of the United Netherlands and the honourable gentle-

men the Directors of the Privileged West India Company Director General of New Netherland, Curacoa, Bonayro, Aruba and their Dependencies, together with the honourable gentlemen of the Council Witness and Declare that we on the Day of the Date underwritten have given and granted to John St. Gaggen a Tract of Land situate on the South River of New Netherland at the First Corner above Fort Casamier, stretches on the North-East side from the Land formerly possessed by Sander Boyer along the Strand North-East Easterly sixty Rods to the Valley, further along the Side of the Valley, as follows, North-West by North Forty Rods, North North West sixty five Rods, North East Easterly twenty five Rods, North-West twenty six Rods, East North-East thirty Rods, North thirty five Rods, North-West forty-six Rods, West by North Northerly one hundred and twenty eight Rods, further from the side of the Valley into the Woods South South West Southerly one hundred and fourteen Rods, further through the Woods to the Place of Beginning, amounting in the whole to about forty one Morgen with express Conditions & Provisoes &c. Done in New Amsterdam the 20th June 1657.

No. 29.

(32)

Petrus Stuyvesant, in the name of the Honorable High and Mighty Lords the States General of the United Netherlands and the Honorable Lords Directors of the Privileged West India Company, Director General of New Netherland, Curacoa, Bonnairo, Aruba and the appendencies thereof, together with the Honorable Lords Councilors, Witness and Declare that we on this day, the date hereinafter written, have granted and bestowed upon Pieter Lourensen, A Lot situate on the South River of New Netherland near Fort Casamier, now called New Amstel, contiguous North East to the Common Road, being the fourth in No. from the Fort, commencing on the shore side, wide in front and rear sixty two feet, long on both sides three hundred feet.

(Note.—The aforesaid Lot was granted the said Pieter Lourensen in the year 1652, but whereas at that time no deed thereof was given him these presents are now issued.)

Upon express conditions and provisos, &c. Done at Amsterdam in New Netherland, on the 2d of September 1657.

No. 30.

(33)

Peter Stuyvesant, in the name of the High and Mighty Lords the States General of the United Netherlands and the Honorable Lords Directors of the Privileged West India Company with headquarters in Amsterdam, Director General of New Netherland, Curocoa, &c., together with the Honorable Councilors, Witness and declare that we on this day, the date hereinafter written, have granted Jacob Van der Veer, A Lot for a House and Garden situate on the South River of New Netherland near Fort Altenae, wide on the street or East side

sixty feet, long on the South side adjoining the Square of said Fort one hundred feet, on the West adjoining a valley wide sixty feet long on the North side next to Thomas Bruyn one hundred feet. Upon the express conditions and provisos, &c. Done at Fort Amsterdam in New Netherland, April 8, A. 1662.
New York 6th.

(34)
Grant to the Duke of York, Dated 12th March Ao. 16, Car. 2d, 1664.

(Book of Patents, No. 1,
1664 to 1667, 139.)

CHARLES THE SECOND by the Grace of God King of England Scotland France & Ireland Defender of the Faith &c To all to whom these presents shall come Greeting, Know yee that wee for divers good Causes and Consideracons us thereunto moving, Have of our especiall Grace certaine knowledge and Meere motion given and Granted And by these presents for us our heirs and Successors Do give and Grant unto our Dearest Brother James Duke of Yorke, his Heires and Assignes, All that part of the Maine Land of New England, beginning at a Certaine place called or knowne by the Name of St. Croix next adjoining to New Scotland in America, and from thence extending along the Sea Coast, unto a certaine place called Petuaguine, or Pemaquid, and so up the River thereof, to the furthest head of ye same as it tendeth Northwards, and extending from thence, to the River of Kinebegui, and so upwards by the shortest Course to the River Canada Northward, And also all that Island or Islands commonly called by the severall name or names of Matonacks or Long Island, situate lying and being towards the West of Cape Codd, and ye narrow Higansetts, Abutting upon the Maine Land between the two Rivers there called or knowne by the severall names of Conecticutt and Hudsons River, together also with the said River called Hudsons River, and all the Land from the west side of Conecticutt, to ye east side of Delaware Bay And also those severall Islands called or knowne by the Names of Martins Vinyard and Nantukes, otherwise Nantukett, Together with all ye Lands, Islands, Soyles, Rivers, Harbours, Mines, Minerals, Quarryes, Woods, Marshes, Waters, Lakes, Fishings, Hawking, Hunting and Fowling, and all other Royalltyes, Proffits Commodityes, and hereditam'ts to the said severall Islands, Lands and premisses belonging & appertaining, with theire and every of theire appurtenances, And all our Estate Right, Title, Interest, benefit, advantage, (35) Claime and demand, of in or to the said Lands and premisses, or any part or parcell thereof, And the Revercon and Revercons, remainder and Remainders, together with the Yearly, and other ye Rents Revenues and proffits, of all and Singular the said premisses and of every part and parcell thereof, To have and to hold all and singular the said Lands, Islands, hereditam'ts and premisses, with their and every of their appurtenances, hereby given and Granted, or herein before

mentioned to be given and granted, unto our Dearest Brother James
Duke of Yorke his heirs and Assignes for ever. To the onely proper
use and behoofe of the said James Duke of York his heirs and Assigns
for ever, To be holden of us, our heires and Successors as of our mannor of East Greenwich in our County of Kent in free and Common
Soccage, and not in Capite, nor by Knight Service, Yielding and rendering, And the said James Duke of Yorke doth for himself, his Heirs
and Assignes, Covenant and promise to Yield and render, unto us our
Heirs and Successors of and for the same, yearly and every year forty
Beaver Skins, when they shall be demanded, or within ninety days
after, And we do further of our speciall Grace, certaine knowledge,
and meere motion for us our heires and Successors Give and Grant
unto our said Dearest Brother James Duke of Yorke his Heires, Deputyes, Agents, Commissioners and Assignes by these presents, full and
absolute power and Authority to Correct, punish, pardon governe and
Rule all such the Subjects of us our heires and Successors &c from
time to time adventure themselves into any the parts or places aforesaid, or that shall or doe at any time hereafter Inhabite with in the
same, according to such Lawes, Orders, Ordinances, Directions and
Instruments, as by our said Dearest Brother or his Assignes, shall be
Established, And in Defect thereof in Cases of Necessity, according to
the good discrecons of his Deputyes, Commissioners, officers or Assignes respectively, as wee in all Causes and matters Capitall and
Criminall, as Civill, both Marine and others, soe alwayes, as the said
Statutes, Ordinances and proceedings be not Contrary to, but as neare
as conveniently may be agreeable to the Lawes Statutes and Government of this our Realme of England, And saving and reserving (36) to
us Our heires and Successors ye receiving hearing and determining of
the Appeale and Appeales of all or any persons or persons, of, in, or
belonging to ye Territoryes or Islands aforesaid, in or touching any
Judgment or Sentence to be there made or given, And further that it
shall and may be Lawful to and for our said Dearest Brother, his
Heires and Assignes by these Presents from time to time to nominate
make Constitute Ordaine and Confirme by such name or names Stile
or Stiles as to him or them shall seeme good, and likewise to revoke
discharge, Change and alter, as well all and Singular Governors Officers & Ministers which hereafter shall be by him or them thought fitt
and needfull to be made or used within the aforesaid parts & Islands,
And also to make Ordaine and Establish all manner of Orders, Lawes,
directions, Instructions formes and Ceremonyes of Government and
Magistracy fitt and Necessary for and concerning the Government of
the Territoryes and Islands aforesaid so alwayes as the same be not
Contrary to the Lawes and Statutes of this our Realme of England, but
as near as may be agreeable thereunto, and the same at all times hereafter to put in Execution, or abrogate, revoke or Change not only
within the precincts of the said Territoryes or Islands, but also upon
the Seas in going and coming to and from the same, as hee or they
in their good discrecons, shall thinke to be fittest for the good of the

Adventurers, and Inhabitants there, And wee do further of our speciall Grace, certaine knowledge and meere motion, Grant Ordaine and declare That such Governors Officers and Ministers as from time to time shall be authorized, and appointed in manner and forme aforesaid, shall and may have full power and authority to use and Exercise Marshall Law, in Cases of Rebellion, Insurrection, and Mutinie, in as large and ample manner as our Lieutenants in our Countyes within our Realmes of England, have or ought to have by force of their Commission of Lieutenancy, or any Law or Statute of this our Realme, And we do further by these presents, for us our Heirs and Successors Grant unto our said Dearest Brother, James Duke of Yorke, his Heires and Assignes, that it shall and may be Lawfull to and for the said James Duke of (37) Yorke his heires and Assignes, in his or theire discretions from time to time, to admit such, and so many person and Persons to Trade and Traffique unto and within the Territoryes and Islands, aforesaid, and into every or any part & parcell thereof, and to have possess and Enjoy, any Lands, or hereditaments, in ye parts and places aforesaid, as they shall thinke fitt according to the Lawes, Orders, Constitutions and Ordinances, by our said Brother, his Heires Deputyes Commissioners and Assignes, from time to time to be made and established, by vertue of, and according to the true intent and meaning of these presents and under such Condicons, Reservacons, and agreements, as our dr. Brother, his Heirs or Assignes shall set downe, Order, direct and appoint and not otherwise, as aforesaid, and wee do further of our especiall grace certaine knowledge and meere motion, for us our Heires and Successors give and Grant, to our said Deare Brother his Heires and Assignes by these presents. That it shall and may be lawfull to and for him them, or any of them, at all and every time and times hereafter, out of any our Realmes or Dominions whatsoever, to take, leade, Carry, and Transport in and into their Voyages, and for and towards the Plantacon of our said Territoryes and Islands, all such and so many of our Loveing subjects, or any other Strangers, being not prohibited or under restraint, that will become our Loving Subjects and live under our Allegiance, as shall willingly accompany them in the said Voyages together with all such Cloathing, Implements, furniture, and other things, usually transported and not prohibited, as shall be Necessary for the Inhabitants of the said Islands and Territories, and for theire use and defence thereof, and manageing and carrying on the Trade with the People there and in passing and returning to and fro. Yielding and paying to us our heirs and Successors the Customes and Dutyes therefore due and payable, according to the Lawes and Customes of this our Realme, And we do also for us our Heires and Successors Grant to our said Dearest Brother, James Duke of Yorke, his Heires and Assignes, and to all and every such Governor or Governors or other (38) Officers or Ministers, as by our said Brother his Heirs or Assignes shall be appointed to have power and Authority of Government and Command in and over the Inhabitants of the said Territoryes or Islands that they and every of them shall and lawfully may from time to time, and at all times hereafter forever, for theire severall defence and safety Encounter, expulse, repell, and resist by force of arms as well by sea, as by Land, and all ways and means whatsoever, all such Person and Persons as without the speciall Licence of our said Deare Brother his Heirs or Assignes, shall attempt to Inhabit within the severall precincts and Limits of our said Territoryes, and Islands, And also all and every such person and persons whatsoever, as shall enterprize or attempt at any time hereafter, the destruccon, invasion, detriment or annoyance to ye parts, places or Islands, aforesaid, or any parte thereof, And lastly our Will and pleasure is, and wee do hereby declare and grant, that these our Letters Patents, or the Inrollment thereof shall be good and effectuall in the Law, to all Intents and purposes whatsoever, Notwithstanding the not reciting or menconing of the premisses or any part thereof, or the meets or Bounds thereof, or of any former, or other L'1es Patents or Grants heretofore made or Granted of the Premisses or of any part thereof by us, or of any of our Progenitors, unto any other person or persons, whatsoever, Bodyes Politique or Corporate, or any Act, Law, or other restraint, incertainty or imperfection whatsoever, to the Contrary in any wise notwithstanding, although express mention, of the true yearly value, or certainty of the Premisses, or any of them, or of any other guifts or Grants by us, or by any of our Progenitors or Predecessors heretofore made to the said James Duke of Yorke, in these Presents, is not made, or any Statute, Act, Ordinance, provision, Proclamation, or restriction, heretofore had, made, Enacted Ordained or provided, or any other matter, cause or thing whatsoever to the Contrary thereof in any wise Notwithstanding. In Witnesse whereof (39) Wee have caused these our Letters to be made Patents, Witnesse ourselfe at Westminster the twelfth day of March in the Sixteenth Yeare of our Raigne.

By the King,
Howard.

Folio 145.

  JAMES DUKE OF YORKE & ALBANY, Earle of Ulster Lord high admiral of England and Ireland &c Constable of Dover Castle, Lord Warden of the Cinque Ports and Governour of Portsmouth &c. Whereas it hath pleased the Kings most Excellent Majestie my Soveraigne Lord and Brother, by his Majesties Letters Pattents, bearing date at Westminster, the 12th day of March, in ye sixteenth yeare of his Majesties Raigne to give and Grant unto me, and to my heires and Assignes all that part of the Maine Land of New England, beginning at a certaine place called or known by the name of St. Croix, next adjoining to New Scotland in America, and from thence Extending along ye Sea Coast, unto a Certaine place called Petuaguine or Pemaquid, and so up the River thereof to the furthest head of the same, as it tendeth Northwards, and extending from thence to the River of Kenebequi and so upwards by the shortest

Course, to the River Canada Northwards, and also all that Island or Islands Commonly called by the severall name or names of Matonacks or Long Island, situate lying and being towards the West of Cape Codd and the Narrow Higansetts, abutting upon ye Maine Land between the two Rivers there called or knowne by the severall names of Connecticutt and Hudsons River, together also with the said River called Hudsons River, and all the Land from the West Side of Connecticutt River, to the East Side of Delaware Bay, and also all those severall Islands called or knowne by the Name or Martin Vinyards & Nantukes, otherwise Nantuckett, Together with all the Lands, Islands, Soyles, Rivers, (40) Harbours, Mines, Mineralls, Quarryes, Woods, Marshes, Waters, Lakes Fishings Hawking Hunting and Fowling and all other Royalltyes, proffits, Commodityes, and Hereditaments to the said several Islands Lands and premisses belonging and appertaining with their and every of their appurtenances, To hold the same to my own proper use and behoofe, with Power to Correct punish, pardon Governe and Rule ye Inhabitants thereof by myselfe or such Deputyes, Commissioners or Officers as I shall think fitt to appointe, as by his majesties said L'res Pattents, may more fully appeare; And whereas I have conceived a good opinion of the Integrity, prudence, Ability and fittness of Richard Nicholls Esq. to be Employed as my Deputy there. I have therefore thought fitt to Constitute and appointe and I do hereby Constitute and appointe him the said Richard Nicolls Esq. to be my Deputy Governour within the Lands Islands and places aforesaid to performe and Execute all the Lands Islands and places aforesaid to performe and Execute all and every the Powers which are by the said Letters Patents granted unto me to bee Executed by my Deputy Agent, or Assigne To have and to hold, the said place of Deputy Governour, unto the said Richard Nicolls Esquire during my will and pleasure onely, Hereby willing and requiring all and every the Inhabitants of the said Lands Islands and places to give Obedience to him the said Richard Nicolls Esq. in all things according to the Tenor of his Majesties said Letters Pattents; And the said Richard Nicolls Esq. to Observe follow and Execute such Orders and Instructions, as hee shall from time to time receive from myselfe. Given under my hand and Seale at Whitehall this second day of Aprill, in the Sixteenth Yeare of the Raigne of our Soveraigne Lorde Charles the second, by the Grace of God King of England Scotland France and Ireland &c. Anno Domini 1664.

                 James.

By Command of his Royal Highnesse,
        W. Coventry.

(41)
Book of Entries &c.
No. 1 A—1664,
Sept. 3d.
Fo. 34

A Copie of Robert Carrs Commission to goe to Delaware Bay.

Whereas wee are enformed that the Dutch have seated themselves at Delaware Bay on his Majestie of Great Brittaines territoryes, without his knowledge and Consent, and that they have fortifyed themselves there and drawne a great trade thither, and being assured, that if they bee permitted to goe on, the gaininge of this place will be of small advantage to his Majesty, Wee his Majesties Commissioners, by vertue of his Majestics Commission and Instructions to us given, have advised and determined to endeavor to bring that place, and all strangers thereabout in Obedience to his Majesty, And by these do Order and appoint that his Majesties Frygotts the Guinney and the William & Nicholas and all the Souldyers which are not in the Fort, shall with what speed they conveniently can goe thither, under the Command of Sir Robert Carr to reduce the same, willing and commanding all Officers at Sea and Land and all Souldyers to obey the said Sir Robert Carr during this Expedition; Given under our hands and Seales at the Fort in New Yorke upon the Isle of Manhatans the 3rd day of September, 1664.

             R. Nicolls
       S. Meverick
             G. Cartwright.

Fo. 50

Instructions to Sir Robert Carr for the Reducing of Delaware Bay, and settling the People there under his Majesties Obedience.

When you are Come neare unto ye Fort which is possessed by the Dutch you shall send your Boate on shoare, to Summon the Governor and Inhabitants to yield Obedience to his Majestie as the Rightfull Soveraigne of that Tract of Land; and lett him and them know, that his Majestie is graciously plaesed that all the Planters shall Enjoy their Farmes Houses Lands Goods and Chattels with the same priviledges and upon the same Termes, which they do now possesse them, onely that they change their Masters, whether they be the West India Company or the City of Amsterdam. To the Swedes you shall remonstrate their happy returne, under (42) a Monarchicall Government and his Majesties good inclinacon to that Nation, and to all men who shall Comply with his Majesties Rights and Title in Delaware, without forces of Armes. That all the Cannon Armes and ammunison which belongs to the Government shall remaine to his Majestie.

That the Acts of Parliament shall be the Rules of future Trading.

That all People may Enjoy Liberty of Conscience.

That for six Monethes next ensuing, the same Magistrates shall continue in theire Offices, onely that they and all others in authority must take the Oath of Allegiance to his Majestie and all Publique Acts be made in his Majesties Name.

If you find you cannot reduce the place by force nor upon these Conditions, you may add such as you find necessary upon the place, but if those, nor force will prevaile, Then you are to dispatch a messenger to the Governor of Maryland with this L're to him and Request his assistance and of all other English who live near the Dutch Plantacons.

Fo. 59

Your first care (after the reducing of the place) is to protect the Inhabitants from Injuryes, as well as violence of the Sould'rs; which will be Easily effected if you settle a Course for Weekly or daily Provisions, by agreement with the Inhabitants which shall be satisfied to them, either out of the proffitts Customes or Rents belonging to their present Master, or in case of Necessity from hence.

The Lawes for the present cannot be altered, as to the administration of right and Justice betweene Partyes.

To my Lord Baltimores Sonn you shall declare and to all the English concerned in Maryland, that his Majestie hath at his great expence, sent his shipps and Soudiers to reduce all forraigners in those parts to his Majesties Obedience, and to that purpose onely, you are Employed, but the reduction of the place being at his Majesties Expence, you have Commands to keepe possession thereof for his Majesties owne behoofe and Right, and that you are ready to Joyne with the Governor of Maryland upon (43) his Majesties Interest in all occasions, and that if my Lord Baltimore, doth pretend Right thereunto by his Patent (which is a doubtful Case) you are to say that you onely keep possession till his Majestie is informed and satisfied otherwise, In other things I must leave you to your discretion and the best advice you can get upon the place.

Fo. 60

Articles of Agreement between the Honorable Sir Robert Carr Knight, on the behalfe of his Majestie of Great Brittaine, and the Burgomasters on the behalfe of themselves and all the Dutch and Swedes Inhabiting in Delaware Bay, & Delaware River.

(1) That all the Burgers and Planters will submit themselves to his Majesties Authority without making any Resistance.

(2) That Whoever of what Nation soever doth sumbit to his Majesties Authority, shall be protected in their Estates reall and personall whatsoever, by his Majesties Lawes and Justice.

(3) That the present Magistrates shall be continued in their Offices, and Jurisdiccons to Exercise their Civill Power as formerly.

(4) That if any Dutchman or other person shall desire to depart from this River, that it shall be Lawfull for him so to doe, with his Goods within six Months after the date of these articles.

(5) That the magistrates and all the Inhabitants (who are included in these articles) shall take the Oaths of Allegiance to his Majestie and of Fidelity to the present Government.

(6) That all the People shall Enjoy the Liberty of theire Conscience, in Church Discipline as formerly.

(7) That whoever shall take the Oathes is from that time a free Denizen, and shall Enjoy all the privileges of Trading into any of his Majesty's Dominions as freely as any Englishman, and may require a Certificate for so doing.

(44) (8) That the Scout, the Burgomasters Sheriffe and other Inferior Magistrates, shall use and Exercize their Customary Power in administration of Justice, within theire precincts, for six monthes or untill his Majesties pleasure is further knowne.

The Oath:

I do Sweare by the Almighty God, that I will beare faith and Allegiance to his Majestie of Great Britaine, and that I will obey all such Commands, as I shall receive from ye Governor Deputy Governor or other Officers appointed by his Majesties Authority so long as I live within these or any other his Majesties Territoryes.

Given under our hands & Seales in the behalfe of ourselves and ye rest of ye Inhabitants ye 1st day of October in the yeare of our Lord God 1664.

Given under my hand and Seale this 1st day of October, in the yeare of our Lord God 1664.

Robert Carr.

    Fob Put Gout
    Henry Johnson
    Gerrett Saunders Vantiell
    Hans Block
    Lucas Peterson
    Henry Casturier.

Book of Records,
No. 100 Relating
to the several
Courts of Assizes.

    An Order for Olle Olleson Niels Nielsen &c. to Enjoye ye benefitt of what is granted to them in their Patent.

Upon ye Petition of Olle Olleson Niels Nielsen Senr. & ye rest concerned in yet Patent graunted by my Predecessor Coll. Richard Nicolls for each of them to have a Plantation with proportion of meadow ground for Hay for their Cattle on Verdrietiges or Trinity Hook at Delaware, for ye which they had a graunt before those parts were reduced to his Majesties Obedience, who Complayne that Mr. William Tom having by misinformation obteyned a Patent for all that Marsh or Meadow ground whereon they had their proportion, hath by Order of ye Court at Delaware forbad them to cut Hay or to make bridges for their Cattle to goe into that Marsh without his leave ye which without reliefe will prove much to (45) their prejudice, having taken ye same into Consideration I doe thinke fitt to Order that ye said Olle Olloson Niels Nielsen & ye rest in ye said Patent Exprest shall Injoy ye benefit of what is granted them in their said Patent any Patent graunt or Order of Court made in favour of Mr. Tom to be Contrary notwithstanding. Given under my Hand at Fort James in New Yorke this 16th day of May 1670.

Fo. 280.

An Order for James Mills to purchase a Neck of Land for a plantation at ye whorekill.

Whereas James Mills hath made Request unto me that he may have my Lycence to purchase a Certaine point or Neck of Land for a Plantation lyeing to the Southward of ye Towne at ye whorekill in Delaware Bay, The which as he alleadges was Consented unto by ye Commissioners there, & ordered by them to be certifyed & recomended unto me but was omitted by their Clarke, I have thought fitt to graunt his Request if it be as is alleadged, but Expect that the Commissioners do make certificate thereof and likewise of ye Extent & Quality of the said Lands whereupon he shall have further Assurance by Patent for the same. Given under my Hand & Seale at Fort James in New Yorke this 12th day of January in ye 22nd yeare of his Majesties Raigne Anno Domini 1670.

Book Patents.
No. 1. Pa. 114.

A Patent graunted unto Captain John Carr, for his Enjoyment of the Estate of Gerrett Van Swerring.

Richard Nicolls Esq. Principall Commissioner from his Majestie into New England, Governor General under his Royal Highnesse James Duke of York and Albany &c of all his Territoryes in America, and Commander in Chiefe over all the Forces Employed by his Majesty, to reduce the Dutch Nation, and all their usurped Lands and Plantations, under his Majesties Obedience, makes knowne unto all men by these presents, That in consideration of the Good Service performed by Captain John Carr in Storming and reducing (46) the Fort at Delaware, I have thought fitt to give and Grant, and by these presents do give Ratify, Confirme and Graunt, unto the said Capt. John Carr his heires and Assignes, all the Lands Houses and Estate, reall or personall, which is, or shall be found, to have beene really and truly in the possession of or appertaining unto Gerrett Van Swerring, at the time when the said Fort was reduc't by Force, to his Majesty's Obedience it being sufficiently knowne that the said Gerrett Van Swerring then Schout was in Hostility against his Majesty, for which reason all his Estate stands Confiscated, And for the reasons aforesaid is given and Graunted unto the said Capt. John Carr, with all and singular the Appurtenances. To have and to hold, the said Lands Houses, Estate and Premisses, unto the said Capt. John Carr his Heires and Assignes, unto the proper use and behoofe of the said Capt. John Carr, his heirs and Assignes for ever Yielding and paying yearly and every yeare, unto his Majesties use, for and in Consideration of the said Lands Houses and Estate, Eight Bushells of Wheate, as a Quitt Rent, when it shall bee demanded, by those Persons in Authority, which his Majesty shall please hereafter to Empower and Establish in Delaware River, and the parts and Plantations adjacent, In Confirmation and Testimony whereof I have hereunto sett my Hand and Seale at Fort James in New Yorke the 20th day of June, in the 17th yeare of his Majesties Reigne. Anno Domini 1665.

Rich'd Nicolls.

Fo. 116

A Patent graunted unto Mr. William Tom, for an Island at Delaware.

Richard Nicolls Esq. Principall Commissioner from his Majesty into New England, Governor Generall, under his Royall Highnesse, James Duke of Yorke and Albany &c of all his Territoryes in America, and Commander in Chiefe, over all the (47) Forces employed by his Majesty to reduce the Dutch Nation, and all their usurped Lands and Plantations, under his Majesties Obedience, makes knowne unto all Men by these presents, that in Consideration of the Good Service performed by Mr. William Tom at Delaware, I have thought fitt to give and Graunt, and by these presents do give Ratify, Confirme and Graunt, unto the said William Tom a certain Island with the Plantation thereupon, heretofore belonging unto Peter Alrichs, lying about seven miles below New Castle towards the Mouth of ye River, the said Island standing confiscated upon the Accompt of the said Peter Alrichs, who was in Hostility against his Majesty at ye reducing of the Fort at Delaware, And I do likewise hereby give and graunt unto the said William Tom, a certaine piece of Meadow Ground or Valley, lying at the Mouth of the said River at Delaware, between Christine Creeke or Kill and Verdrechts Hooke, being bounded on the back side with a Creeke commonly called Brandywine Kill Conteining by Estimacion five hundred Acres, bee they more or less; As also a small Parcell of Land lying within the Towne, containing, about halfe an Acre of Ground Bounded on the South with the Mill, on the North by the High Way on the East the Strand, and on the West the Mart. To have and to hold, the said Island Piece of Meadow and small Parcell of Land and premisses, unto the said Willm Tom, his Heires and Assignes, unto the proper use and behoofe of the said William Tom, his heires and Assignes forever. Yielding and Paying yearly and every Yeare, unto his Majesties use, for and in Consideration of the said Island and premises, Eight Bushells of Wheate, as a Quitt Rent, when it shall be demanded, by those Persons in Authority, which his Majesty shall please hereafter to Empower, and Establish in Delaware River, and the parts and Plantations adjacent: In Confirmation and testimony whereof, I have hereunto sett my Hand and Seale, at Fort James in New Yorke, the 20th day of June, in the 17th yeare of his Majesties Reigne, Anno Domini 1665.

R. Nicolls.

(48)
Book—Minutes of Council,
1668-1678, fo. 64.
At a Council held in ye Fort ye 21st June, 1671.
Book—
Minutes of Council 1668 1678 fo. 64.
   Present
      The Governor
      Mr. Steenwyck
      The Secretary.
   The Matter first under Consideration, is the Busynesse of Delaware, about granting Patents there.
   Capt Carr declares that Governor Nicolls gave ye Officers Order to make Grants of Land to those that would plant there, which being remitted to ye Governor, he was pleased to give Patents for them.
   The signing of Patents for those Parts concluded on.
   An Order also relating the Grant to Mr. Mills the which is to extend only to ye Whore kill Lands, though mentioned Parts adjacent, on ye South side of the Whorekills.

Fo. 91-94
   At a Councell held in Fort James May ye 17th 1672.
   Present
      The Governor
      Capt. Delavall
      Mr. Steenwyck
      Capt. Willett
      The Secretary.
Maryland and the Whore kill.
   Upon Consideration had of a Certificate brought by Capt. Jno. Carr from New Castle in Delaware River about ye pretences from Maryland to the whore kill and their sending Surveyors to lay out Lands without the Consent or approbation of the Officers thereunder ye Protection of his Royall Highness, who withstood their Proceedings therein, it is Ordered that ye Magistrates there be vindicated in what they have done, to whom a Letter of Thanks is to be sent & it is likewise expected that they continue in their Observance of such Orders & Directions as they shall receive from this his R. Highness Government & none other, untill his Majesties or his (49) Royall Highness Pleasure be signified to the Contrary.
                                             By Order &c.

Book Records
Foreign & Domestick
1674 1677 fo. 1.
   His Majesties Letters Patents to his Royall Highnesse, Recorded November 4th, 1674.
   Charles the second by the Grace of God, King of England Scotland France and Ireland, Defender of the Faith &c. To all to whom these Presents shall come Greeting: Know Yee, that Wee for divers

good Causes and Considerations, Have of our Espetial Grace certaine knowledge and meere motion, Given and granted, and by these presents for us our Heirs and Successors; Do give and Grant unto our Dearest Brother, James Duke of Yorke, his Heirs and Assignes, All that part of the Maine Land of New England, beginning at a Certaine place called or knowne by the Name of St. Croix, next adjoining to New Scotland in America; and from thence extending along the seacoast unto a Certaine place called Petuaguine or Pemaquid, and so up the River thereof, to the furthest head of the same, as it tendeth Northwards, and extending from the River of Kinebeque, and so upwards by the shortest Course to the River Canada Northwards; And all that Island or Islands commonly called by the severall name or names of Matonacks or Long Island, situate and being towards the West of Cape Codd and the narrow Higansetts, abutting upon the Maine Land, between the two Rivers there, called or knowne by the severall names of Connecticut and Hudsons River, together also with the said River called the Hudsons River, and all the land from the West side of Connecticut River, to the East side of Delaware Bay; And also all those severall Islands called or known by the Names of Martin Vineyards and Nantukes, otherwise Nantuckett; Together with all the Lands, Islands, Soiles, Rivers, Harbors, Mines Mineralls, Quarryes, Woods, (50) Marshes, Waters, Lakes, Fishings, Hawking, Hunting and Fowling; and all other Royalties, proffits, Commodoties, and Hereditaments, to the said severall Islands, Lands and premisses, belonging and appertaining with their and every of their appurtenences, and all our Estate, Right, Title and Interest, benefit and advantage Claime and demand, of, in or to the said Lands or premisses, or any part or parcell thereof, and the Revercon and Revercons, remainder & remainders together with the yearly and other Rents, Revenues and Proffits of the premisses and of every part and parcell thereof; To have and to hold all any singular the said Lands and primesses, with their and every of their appurtenances hereby given and graunted, or herein before mentioned to bee given and graunted, unto our said Dearest Brother, James Duke of Yorke his Heirs and Assignes forever; To be holden of us our Heirs and Successors as of our Mannor of East Greenwich, in our County of Kent, in free and Common Soccage and not in Capite or by Knight service. Yielding and rendering, And the said James Duke of York for himselfe his Heirs and Assignes doth Covenant and promise to yield and render unto us our Heirs and Successors of and for the same yearly and every yeare, Forty Beaver Skins, when they shall be demanded, or within ninety dayes after such demand made; And wee do further of our special Grace certaine knowledge and meere Motion, for us our Heirs and Successors, Give and Graunt unto our said Dearest Brother James Duke of Yorke, his Heirs Deputyes, Agents, Commissioners and Assignes by these Presents, full and absolute Power and authority, to Correct, punish, pardon, Govern and Rule, all such the Subjects of us our Heirs and Successors, or any other Person or Persons as shall from time to time ad-

venture themselves into any the parts or places aforesaid, or that shall
or do at any time hereafter (51) Inhabit within the same, according to
such Lawes, Orders, Ordinances, directions and Instructions as by our
said Dearest Brother, or his Assignes, shall bee Established; And in
defect thereof in cases of Necessity, according to the good Discretions
of his Deputyes Commisioners, Officers or Agents respectively, as
well in all Cases and matters Capitall and Criminall, as Civill Marine
and others, so alwayes as the said Statutes Ordinances and proceedings, bee not Contrary to, but as neare as may bee agreeable to the
Lawes Statutes and Government of this our Realm of England; and
saving and reserving to us, our Heirs and Successors the receiving,
hearing and determining of the Appeal and Appeals of all or any Person or Persons, of, in or belonging to the Territoryes or Islands aforesaid, or, touching any Judgment or Sentence to bee there made or
Given, and further, that it shall and may be lawfull, to and for our said
Dearest Brother, his Heirs and Assignes by these presents, from time
to time to Nominate make Constitute, Ordaine and Confirme, such
Lawes as aforesaid, by such Name or Names, Stile or Stiles as to
him or them shall seem good. And likewise to revoke discharge,
change and alter, as well all and singular Governors Officers and Ministers which hereafter shall bee by him or them thought fit and needful
to be made or used within the aforesaid Islands and parts; And also
to make Ordaine and Establish all manner of Lawes, Orders, Directions, Instructions, formes and Ceremonyes of Government and Magistracy, fit and necessary, for and concerning the Government of the
Territoryes & Islands aforesaid, so alwayes as the same bee not Contrary to the Lawes and Statutes of this our Realme of England, but as
near as may be agreeable thereunto, and the same at all times hereafter, to put in Execution or Abrogate, revoke or change, not onely
within the precencts of the said Territoryes or Islands, but also upon
the Seas in going and coming to and from the same as (52) hee or
they in their good discretions shall think fittest for the good of the adventurers and Inhabitants. And wee do further of our Especiall grace,
certaine knowledge and meere motion., Grant Ordaine and Declare,
That such Governors, Deputyes Officers and Ministers, as from time
to time shall be authorized and appointed, in manner and forme aforesaid, shall and may have full power and authority within ye Territoryes aforesaid, to use and exercise Marshall Law, in cases of Rebellion,
Insurrection and Mutiny in as large and ample manner, as our Lieutenants in our Countyes, within our Realme of England, have or ought
to have by force of their Commission of Lieutenancy, or any Law or
Statute of this our Realme, And Wee do further by these presents,
for us our Heirs and Successors, grant unto our said Dearest Brother,
James Duke of York his Heirs & Assignes That it shall and may bee
lawfull, to and for the said James Duke of Yorke his Heirs and Assignes, in his or their discretion, from time to time, to admit such and
so many person and persons, to Trade and Trafficke into and within ye
Territoryes and Islands aforesaid, (and into every or any the Territor-

yes and Islands aforesaid) & into every, or any part and parcell thereof; And to have, possesse and Enjoy any Lands & Hereditaments, in the P'tes and places aforesaid, as they shall think fitt, according to the Lawes, Orders, constitutions and ordinances, by our said Brother, his Heires Deputyes Commissioners and Assignes from time to time to bee made & established, by Vertue of, and according to the true Intent and meaning of these presents and under such Conditions, reservations and Agreements as our said Dearest Brother his Heirs and Assignes shall set downe Order, direct and appoint, and not otherwise as aforesaid, and wee do further of our especiall Grace, certaine knowledge & meere motion for us our Heirs and Successors, give and (53) Graunt unto our said Dearest Brother his Heires and Assignes by these presents that it shall and may be lawfull to and for him them or any of them, at all and every time and times hereafter out of any of our Realmes or Dominions whatsoever to take lead carry and transport in and into their Voyages, for and towards the Plantation of our said Territoryes and Islands aforesaid, all such and so many of our Loving subjects, or any other Strangers, being not prohibited, or under restraint, that will become our Loving subjects and live under our Allegiance and shall willingly accompany them in the said Voyages together with all such Cloathing, Implements, Furniture and other things usually transported, and not prohibited, as shall be necessary for the Inhabitants of the said Islands and Territoryes, and for their use and defence thereof, and manageing and carrying on the Trade with the People there, and in passing and returning to and fro. Yielding and Paying to us our Heirs and Successors, the Customes and Dutyes therefore due and payable, according to the Lawes and Customes of this our Realme, And Wee do also for us our Heirs and Successors, graunt to our said Dearest Brother James Duke of Yorke his Heirs and Assignes and to all and every such Governor or Governors or Deputies, their Officers or Ministers, as by our said Brother, his Heirs or Assignes, shall bee appointed to have power and Authority of Government, or Command, in or over the Inhabitants of the said Territoryes or Islands, that they, or every of them, shall, and lawfully may from time to time, and at all times forever hereafter, for their Severall defence & Safety, encounter, repulse and expell and resist by force of Armes (as well by Sea as by Land) and all wayes and meanes whatsoever, all such Person and Persons, as without the speciall Licence of our Dearest Brother, his Heirs and Assignes shall attempt to Inhabit within the Severall precincts and Limits of our said Territoryes and Islands. And also all and every such Person and Persons whatsoever, as shall enterprize and attempt at any time hereafter, the Distruction invasion, detriment or annoyances to the parts, places or Islands (54) aforesaid, or any part thereof; And Lastly, our will and pleasure is, And wee do hereby declare and graunt, That these our L'res Patents, or ye enrollment thereof shall bee good and effectuall in the Law to all intents and purposes whatsoever, Notwithstanding the not well and true reciting or mentioning of the premisses, or any part thereof, or the Limits or Bounds thereof, or of any former or other L'res patents or graunts whatsoever, made or graunted or of any part thereof, by us or any of our progenitors, unto any Person or Persons whatsoever, Bodyes politick or Corporate, or any Law or other restraint, incertainty or imperfection whatsoever to the contrary in any wise notwithstanding; Although expresse mention of the true yearly value or certainty of the premisses, or of any of them, or of any other guifts or Graunts by us or by any of our progenitors, heretofore made to the said James Duke of Yorke in these presents is not made, or any Statute, Act Ordinance, provision, proclamation or restriction heretofore had made enacted or provided, or any other matter cause or thing whatsoever, to the contrary thereof, in any wise notwithstanding. In Witness whereof wee have caused these our L'res to bee made patents, Witnesse ourselfe at Westm. the 29th Day of June, in the 26th yeare of our Reigne.

Pigott.

Fo. 4

His Royall Highnesse Commission to Governour Edmund Andros.

James Duke of Yorke and Albany, Earle of Ulster &c.

Whereas it hath pleased the Kings most excellent Majesty, my Soveraigne Lord and Brother, by his L'res Patents to give and graunt unto mee and to my Heirs and Assignes, (55) All that part of the Maine Land of New England, beginning at a certaine place called or knowne by the name of St. Croix, next adjoining to New Scotland in America, and from thence extending along the Sea Coast, unto a certaine place called Petnaquine or Peniaquid, and so up the River thereof to the furthest head of the same as it tendeth Northwards, and extending from thence to the River of Kinebequi and so upwards to the shortest Course, to the River Canada Northwards, And also all that Island or Islands, commonly called by the severall Name or Names of Matonacks or Long Island, situate lying and being towards the West of Cape Cod, and the narrow Higansetts, abutting upon the maine Land, between the two Rivers there, called or knowne by the severall names of Connecticutt and Hudsons River, together also with the said River called Hudsons River, and all the Land from the West side of Connecticutt River, to the East side of Delaware Bay; and also all those severall Islands called or knowne by the name of Martins Vineyards, and Nantukes, otherwise Nantuckett, together with all the Lands Islands Soiles Rivers Harbours, Mines, Mineralls, Quarryes, Woods, Marshes, Waters, Lakes, Fishings, Hawking Hunting and Fowling, and all other Royalties and Proffits, Commodities and Hereditaments, to the said severall Islands Lands and Premisses belonging and appertaining, with their and every of their appurtenances. To hold the same to my owne proper use and behoofe, with power to Correct punish Pardon Governe and Rule the Inhabitants thereof by myselfe or such Deputyes, Commissioners or Officers as I shall think fitt to appoint, as by his Majesties said L'res patents may more fully appeare. And whereas I have (56) conceived a good Opinion of the integrity prudence, ability, and fitnes, of Major Edmund Andros, to bee employed as my Lieutenant there. I have therefore thought fit to Constitute and appoint him the said Major Edmund Andros, to be my Lieutenant and Governor within the Lands Islands & places aforesaid to perform and execute all and every the powers, which are by the said Letters Patents graunted unto me to be executed by mee, my Deputy Agent or Assignes. To have and to hold the said place of Lieutenant and Governor unto him the said Edmund Andros Esq. but during my Will and pleasure onely; Hereby willing and requiring all and every the Inhabitants of the said Lands, Islands and places, to give Obedience unto him the said Edmund Andros Esq. in all things according to the Tenour of his Majesties Letters Patents & the sd. Edmund Andros Esq. to observe, follow and execute such Orders and Directions, as hee shall from time to time receive from myselfe, Given under my hand and Seale at Windsor this 1st day of July 1674.

By command of his Royall Highnesse.   James.
Jo. Werden.

  Copies from the Originals on File.

By vertue of a Warrant from the Co't of New Castle of a Resurvay of the Land lately to Mr. William Toms Deceased with an addition thereunto to Mr. John Williams.

Laid out for Mr. John Williams a Certen Island heretofore belonging to Mr. William Tom situated lying and being on ye West side of Delaware River & about sevean Myles below ye Towne of New Castle in ye byte of ye said River ye said Island being in Length 200 pearches & in breath 40 pearches and Containing in Acres 60 & also for ye said Williams Laid out at ye back of ye said Island a peace of new Land begening at a Corner marked wt oake standing upon a point & by ye edge of a Marsh (57) & by a Creeke Commonly called Mr. Toms Creeke which Devides this Land from Mr. Peter Alrichs Land & runing into ye Woods a Longe ye said Creeke North West & by West 282 pearches to a Corner marked black oake standing by ye highway which Leads to apogenimy & Maryland then South with a Line of marked Trees to a Corner marked hicory 340 pearches, then West and by North to a Corner marked wt oake standing at the side of a banke and by a small branch of ye Read Lyon Creeke 170 pearches then from ye said marked oake a Longe ye said Branch South West & by West 26 pearches then a Longe ye Swamp of Read Lyon Creeke East and by South 294 pearches to a Corner marked wt. oak standing upon a Point by a Marsh side at ye backe of Island then from ye Oak North East & by East to ye first mentioned marked oake 460 pearches laid out boath Island & Woodland for 507¼ Acres of Dry Land & 50 Acres of Marsh or fly being laid out ye 6 Day of March 1679-80.

                                       by Ed Cantwell.

Jan'ry ye 19 Day 1679.
By vertue of a Warrant from ye Co't of New Castle bearing Date ye 3 Day of June last past Laid out for Benjamin Gumly one peace of Land situated on ye South side of blacke birds Creeke towards ye head thereof begening at a Corner marked Spanish Oak standing upon ye side of a banke at the side of blacke birds Creeke & at ye mouth of a brance which parts & Devides this Land from Joseph holdens Land South East alonge ye said brance to a Corner marked white oake standing in a forke at ye Deviding of ye said brance 100 pearches then South west by a Line of marked Trees to a Corner Spanish oake standing at ye Eadge of a pann of water in ye woods 320 poles or pearches then North by a Line of marked Trees to a Corner marked Chesnut standing upon ye side of a high banke by a Swampe side at ye head of blacke birds Creeke 180 pearches then from ye said Chesnut ye severall Courses of ye Creeke to the first mentioned Corner Spanish oake 320 pearches Containg & laid out for 280 Acres of Land Laid out by me.
                Ed Cantwell.
 Recd. Feb. 26 1679-80.

(58)
 Jan'ry ye 19 Day 1679-80
By vertue of a warrant from ye Co't of New Castle bearing date the 1 Day of July last past Laid out for Thomas Snelling one peace of Land situated on ye North side of Black Birds Creeke & begening at a marked wt. oak standing upon a point by black birds Creeke side and from ye said Oake ye severall Courses of ye Creek South-West & by West 230 pearches to a Marke Oak standing by a brance of black birds Creeke which brance Devides this Land from Persifell Wostendell & Companys Land & from ye said oake a Long ye said Brance into the Woods North West and by North 240 pearches to a marked poplar standing by a small pann of Water & from ye said poplar by a Line of marked threes ye same Course 80 pearches to a Corner Marked Spanish Oake & from ye said Oak a Crose ye Woods by a Line of Marked Threes Northeast & by North 230 pearches to a Corner marked White Oak standing by a brance of black birds Creeke Commonly called ye Beaver Dam brance which said brance partes & Devids this Land from ye Land of John and Henry hartop & a Longe ye said brance South East and by South 320 pearches to ye first mentioned Corner white Oak being laid out for 460 Acres of Land & Six Acres of Sonkon Marsh Laid out by me.
                Ed Cantwell.
 Recd. Feb. 26 1679-80.

Aprill the 22th 1676.
 Surveyed for Abraham Enloes a parcell of Land called Abrahams Delight, scituate and being on the West side of Delaware River, & on the North side of St. Augustines Creeke next adjoining to ye Land of Mr. Peter Alricks. Beginning at a Corner marked white oak Standing on a Point in ye first fork of ye sayd Creek and from ye sayd oak

Runing North East, sixty eight perches, North sixty four perches North Westerly 58 degrees two hundred twenty and three perches (bounding on ye Northern branch) to a Corner marked white oak standing on a small point between the two head (59) branches of ye sayd Northern Branch from thence South by West by a line of marked Trees, sixty and two perches to a Corner marked white oak standing at ye East side of ye head of a Swamp which proceedeth out of ye maine branch of St. Augustines Creek and from thence downe the severall Courses of ye sayd Swamp & Creek to the first mentioned white oak, Conteining and now layd out for One hundred and Seaventy Acres of Land.

          by me Walter Wharton.
  By order and appointment of Capt. Edmond Cantwell Surveyor Generall.

  Surveyed the 23rd Day of July 1675 for Thomas Jacobson Olie Paulson & Arent Johnson, Two hundred forty & Eight Acres of Land, Called Red Clayes point, scituate on the Westward side of Delaware River, and on the North & Northwest side of Broad & Cheese Island, & is more than halfe Compassed with a branch of Christiana Creek, Called Red Clayes Creek; Begining at a Corner marked White Oak standing at ye mout small Branch of Red Clayes Creek Called hevin nch devideth this from the Land of Jacob   & from the sayd oak Runing North-Easterly seven degrees up the said branch or Rivolets One hundred and Sixty perches, then from the sayd Rivolet North by a Line of marked Trees one hundred and Sixty perches to a Corner marked white oak standing on a Levell, from thence West by a Line of marked Trees one hundred perches to a Corner marked white oake standing under a high bank by a small Swamp, nigh unto the side of Red Clayes Creek; and from thence runing downe the severall Courses of the said Creeke to the first mentioned white oak at the mouth of Herrang branch (Viz) one hundred Acres part hereof being formerly granted unto the said Thomas (60) Jacobson, Olie Paulson & Thomas Snelling by Patent bearing date the first day of October 1669 (since which time Arent Johnson is Invested in the Right of Thomas Snelling) And one hundred & forty eight Acres the other part hereof being new Land.

          by me   Walter Wharton
          by order of Capt. Ed Cantwell
          Surveyor Generall.

      May ye 16th 1676.
  Surveyed for Maurice Daniel, a parcel of Land Called Drummers Neck Situate and being on the West side of Delaware River, & on the North west side of Appquenemink Creek; Begining at a Corner marked white oak standing on a Point by the sayd Creek at the upper side of a branch, which at ye Mouth thereof divideth this from the Land of Bernard Hendrickson: And from ye sayd oak Runing up ye branch North North-West, forty perches and then NorthWest, by ye

sayd Bernards Line of marked trees, four hundred and Eighty perches to a Corner marked hickry from thence South West by a line of marked Trees sixty perches to a Corner marked Red oak, being the upper Corner Tree of a parcell of Land formerly granted to Jacob Hiden: from thence South East by ye sayd Jacobs Line of marked Trees four hundred perches into a Swamp: and then downe the Swamp South-South East, sixty perches to ye aforesaid Creek: and finally downe along the Creek to the first mentioned white Oak Conteining one hundred and Ninety Acres of Land: which was formerly granted unto John Bradbourn, by Patent bearing date ye 17th day of June 1671 and by him deserted.

        by me   Walter Wharton.
   By Order & appointment of Capt. Edmond Cantwell Surveyor Generall.
17th June 1671. Survey of Land for Morris Daniel.

(61) Track of La side of Delaware Bay & on ye North anch of A creek Called Duck Creik Bay Begining at a White Oak being a track of Land called Whitehall Creik 500 pearches to another Bounded side from thence North by a Line of Bounded White Oak standing in ye ence East by a line marked Trees to a bounded White by a great Criple 500 pearches from thence South by a Line of marked Threes to the first bounded Tree—Containing one thousand Acres By me.
Examined By me Walter Wm. Taylor by Appointment of Mr.
Wharton Surveyor. Walter Wharton G. Surveyor.

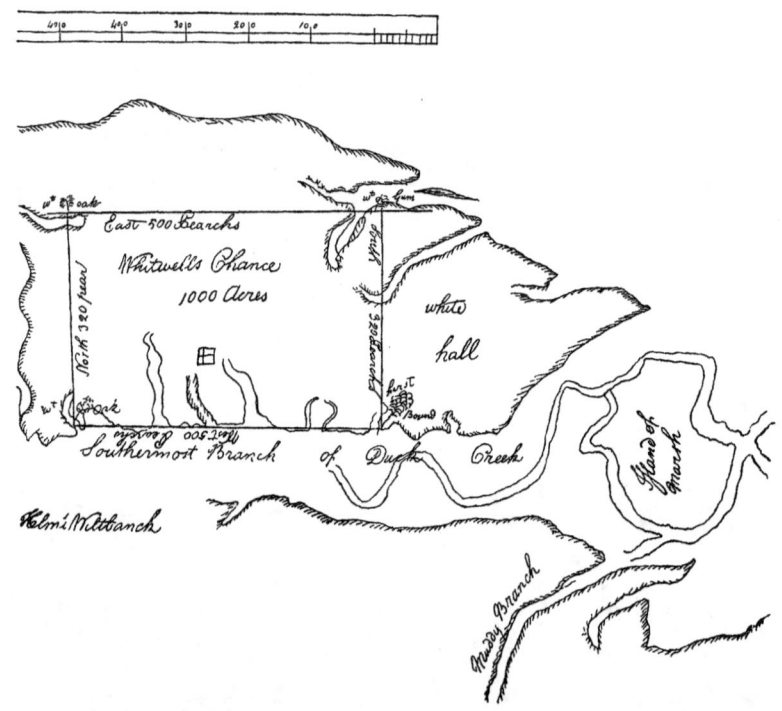

(62)

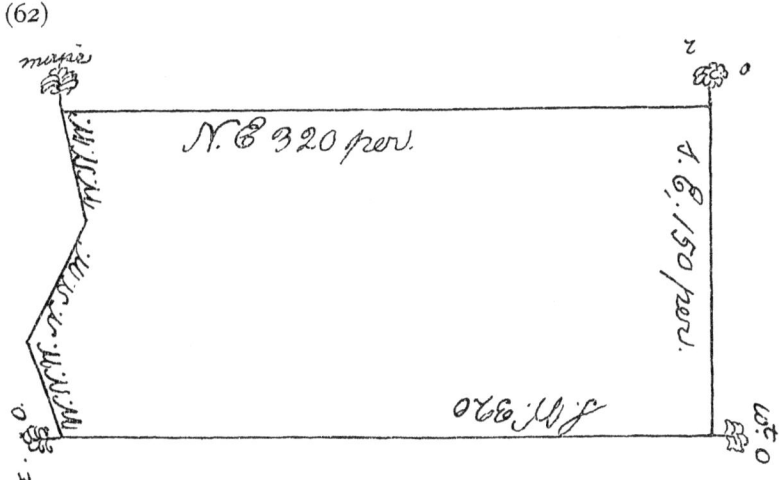

By Vertue of a warrant from the Whore kill Co't Bearing date ye 14th Day of Febru. Ao. 1679-80 Layd out for Thomas Garvess a parcell of Land Called Garvess his Likeing situated on the West side of Delaware Bay & on the North side of a Creeke Called St. Jones Creeke Beginning at Marked Red Oake being the Bounded Tree of the Land of John Brinekloe standing on the said Creekes side & Running from thence West NorthWest fifty perches binding on the said Creeke, then North-North West one hundred perches binding on the said Creeke, and then West North West on the said Creek fifty perches to a marked beach Tree standing by a Little branch by the side of the said Creeke and from thence North East with a Line of Marked Trees three hundred & twenty perches, to a marked Red Oake standing in the Woods by a Meadow & from thence South East with a Line of marked Trees to a Bounded white oake of John Brinkloe & from thence Southwest parallell with the Line of marked Trees of said John Brinkloe three hundred and Twenty perches to the first bounded Red oake Containing & Laid out for three hundred Acres of Land February ye 18th Ao. 1679-80 by
                             Cornelis Verhoofe Surveyor.

At a Co't held for the Whore kill
Sept. the 2th A 1680: Certified the above named is not Seated.
    Luke Wattson.

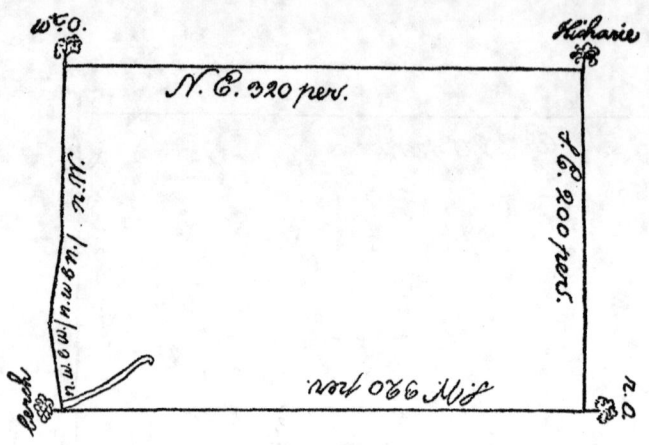

(63)

By Vertue of a Warrant from the Whore kill Cort, bearing Date ye 14th of Febru. Ao. 1679-80

Laid out for Thomas Clifford a parcell of Land called Clifford his purchase scituated on the West side of Delaware Bay and on the North side of a Creeke called St. Jones his Creeke Beginning at a marked beach Tree being the Bounded tree of Thomas Garvess standing by a Little Branch on the sd Creeks side & running from thence North West by West fifty perches binding on the said Creek then North West by North fifty perches binding on the said Creeke & then North West one hundred perches binding on the said Creeke to a marked white oake standing on the said Creekes side and from thence North East with a Line of marked Trees three hundred and twenty perches to a marked Hickarie standing in the Woods and from thence South East with a Line of marked Trees two hundred perches to the Bounded Red Oake of Thomas Garress and from thence parallel with the marked Line of Trees of said Garress three hundred and Twenty perches to the first bounded Beach Tree Conteining and Laid out for fowr hundred acres of Land.

by Cornelis Verhoofe Surveyor.

February ye 20th, Ao. 1679-80
 At a Co't held for the Whore kill
  Sept. ye 2th Anno 1680. Certified the above named is not seated.
  Luke Wattson.

THE DUKE OF YORK RECORD.

At a Calld Court for the Whore Kill the 5th Day of July Ao. 1679.

Comr.
Capt. John Avery
Mr. Alex Molestine
Mr. Luke Wattson
Mr. John Roades
Mr. James Wells
present.

Barnard Hodges petitioner.

Whereas the Petitioner hath made appeare that hee hath been setled upon the Land he now Dwells not knowing but the said Land being Clear and free of any Clayme & haveing built Cleared manured & Dwelt there upon the said Land about Eighteen Monthes & haveing Imployed William Taylor thereunto to Survey the same which Survey not being returned to the Office for a Patent the petitioner being Doubtfull that any other person or persons might proceed and Clayme the Petitioners J'st Right thereof, The Court (64) hath Allowed the Petitioner to proceed when he please to Cause the Surveyor to Survey the said Land

Vera Copia.
Test Cornelis Verhoofe C. & Cu'. Whore Kill

> By Vertue of an order of Court from the Justices of the Whorekill bearing date the 5th Day of July A. D. 1679.

Laid out for Barnard Hodges a parcell of Land Called Hodges Deserts & now called James his Valley was also formerly called ye Mullberry Swamp being situated on the West side of Delaware bay and on the North side of a Creeke called St. Jones Creeke, being a parcell of Land by Information formerly laid out for one Thomas Merrett, now Deceased Beginning at a Bounded Red oake being the first Bounded tree of Richard Levrick & Gabrie Jones their Land Running from the said Oake Nort East with a Line of marked Trees binding upon the said Land of said Levrick & Jones three hundred and twenty perches to a Bounded Hickarie being said Levrick & Jones their uppermost bounded Tree & from thence South East by a Line of marked Trees two hundred perches to the uppermost bounded wt. oake of Walter Wharton Deceased his Land now belonging unto Walter Dickison (65) by purchases Then Downe the said Line with marked Trees South West three hundred & Twenty perches to a Marked Blacke oake standing by a marsh near the said Creeke, then North West two hundred tches binding on the said St. Jones Creeke to first bounded Red Oake Containing & laid out for four hundred Acres of Land

ly 15th Ao. 1679   by Cornelis Verhoofe
                                Surveyor.

Examined and Certified that the Land is allready seated by the above named   John Avery.

At a Calld Court held
July 25th 1679:

Entratt In the Booke S V: the Records of Surveyor Test Corn. Verhoofe Cler. & Surveyor.
Lib. 24 & 25.

                                Surveyor.
Walter Dickinson hath a Patent for the same & Copies hereof sent.

A Scale of English pertches

20 50 80 100

John Kipshaven & peter Hanson their plott of 413 acres of Land

W.N.W. 320 per.

March 8th Ao. 1676-7

Laid out for John Kipshaven & Peter Hanson Jointly one Tract of Land called Hopewell situated on the Westward side of Delaware Bay & on the North side of a Creeke Called Murther Creeke Beginning at a Red Oake standing by a marsh side proceeding from a Branch seperating the Land of Jonathan Hopkins and Running from ye said Red Oake North by West one hundred & five pertches unto a Point near unto the aforesaid Murther Creeke and from the said point Running North-West by North one hundred and five pertches unto a Marked white oake, And from thence West North West into the Woods three hundred and twenty pertches unto a marked white oaked standing by a Meadow. And from thence South South East two hundred pertches unto (66) a marked popular, And from thence East North East three hundred & twenty perches unto the first Bounded Red Oake Containing four hundred & thirteen Acres of Land. By order & appointment of   by Cornelis Verhoofe
Capt. Ed Cantwell Surveyor.   Deputy Surveyor.
                Vera Copia
From the Booke S V the Record of Survey Lib. ii
    Test. Cornelis Verhoofe Cler. & Surv'r.
Mr. Peter Groenendyk hath the same Land granted him by Order of Court dated Sept 10th 1679. Certified to bee l'd out 13 Nov. 1679.

Copia from
a: Copia.

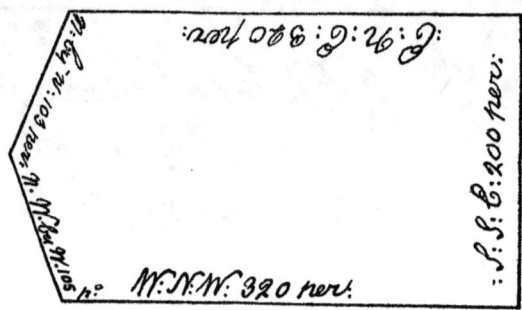

By Vertue of a Warrant from ye Whore Kill Court Bearing Date ye 10th of September Ao. 1679.
Layd out for Peter Groenendyck a parcell of Land Called new Seavenhoven scituated on the West side of Delaware Bay and on the North side of a Creeke called   Murther Creeke beginning at a Red Oake standing by a Marsh side proceeding from a Branch separating the Land of Jonathan Hopkins & Running from the said Red Oake North by West One hundred & five perches unto a point neare unto the aforesaid Murther Creeke & from ye said point Running North-West by North One hundred and five perches unto a marked white oake & from thence West North West into ye woods three hundred and twenty perches unto a White oake standing
            addon & from thence South South East two hundred perches unto a marked poplar & from   East three hundred and twenty perches unto ye first Bounded Red Oake Containing & laid out for fower (67) hundred & thirteen Acres of Land which said Land being formerly Laid out for John Kipsha   and peter Hanson.
November ye 13th   by Cornelis Verhoofe Surveyor
Ao. 1679.   was signed,
Test. Corn. Verhoofe   John Avery.
    Cler. & Surveyor.
A New Survey for Mr. Peter Groenendyck of the Land that was afore laid out for John Kippshoven & Peter Hansen, Nov. 13th, 1679.

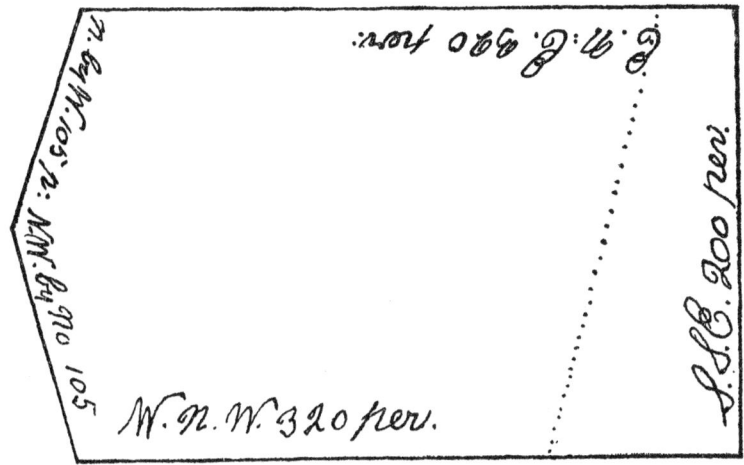

March 8th A. D. 1676-7

Laid out for John Kipshaven & Peter Hanson Joyntly one Tract of Land called Hopewell scituated on the Westward side of Delaware Bay and on the North side of a Creeke called Murther Creeke Beegining at a Red Oake standing by a marsh side proceeding from a Branch Seperating the Land of Johnathan Hopkins and runing from the said Red oake North by West One hundred and five pertches unto a point neare unto the aforesaid Murther Creeke & from the said point Runing North West by North one hundred and five pertches unto a marked white oake and from thence West North West into the Woods three hundred and twenty Pertches unto a White oake standing by a Meadow & from thence South South East two hundred pertches unto a Marked popular & from thence East North East three hundred and twenty pertches, unto the first Bounded Red Oake Containing fowr hundred & thirteen Acres of Land.   by Cornelis Verhoofe
By Order and Appointment of Capt   Deputy Surveyor.
   Edm'd Cantwell Surveyor.
                Vera Copia
        Test. Cornelis Verhoofe Cler.

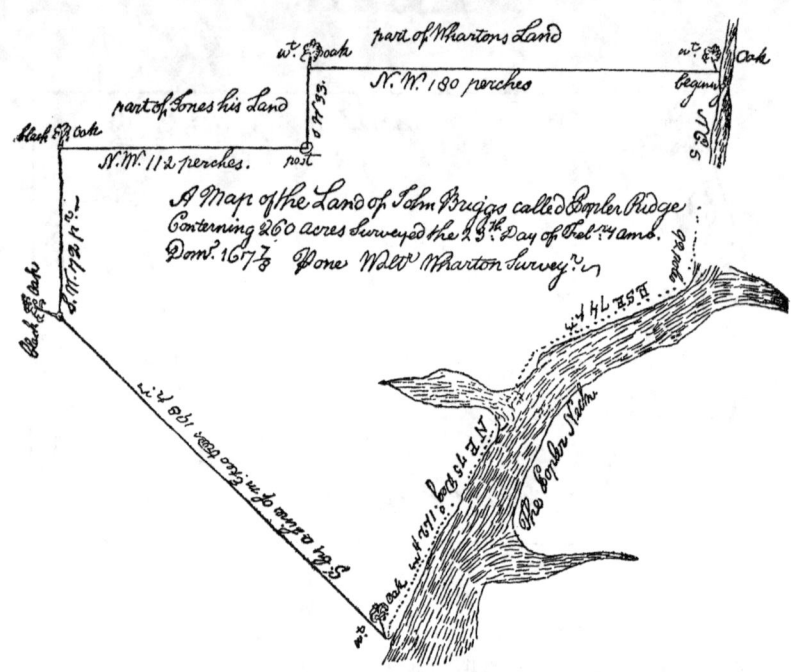

See the Patent
Page 256

By Vertue of a Warrant from the Court at the Whore Kill Dated ye 10th of Jan'ry 1677-8.

Layd out for John Briggs a parcell of Land Called Popler Ridge scituate & being on the West side of Delaware Bay about two miles above St. Jones Creeke (Being bounded as followeth) Beginning at a Corner marked white Oak standing at the South East side of a Swamp which divideth this from a piece of Land Called Popler neck: And from the sayd oak Runing Downe ye sayd Swampe, North Easterly 55 Degrees, ninety & two perches, East South-East, Seventy & four perches, and North-Easterly 75 Degrees; one hundred, forty and two perches to another Corner marked white oak standing on a Point at the South East side of the sayd Swamp: from thence South by a Line of marked Trees one hundred ninety & Eight perches to a Corner marked black oak, standing on a Barren Levell, from thence South West by a Line of marked Trees (69) Seventy and two Perches, to a Corner Marked Black oak standing in the head Line of the Land of Robert Jones from

thence North West (along the sayd Jones his Line of marked Trees) one hundred and twelve perches to the upper Corner of the said Jones his Land being marked with a post in the Ground: from thence South West thirty & three perches to a Corner marked white oake of the Land of Walter Wha   and from thence, by his Line of marked Trees, North West one hundred & Eighty perches to the first mentioned white oake Containing two hundred and sixty Acres of Land.
Feb'ry ye 23rd   By me Walter Wharton Surveyor
   1677-8   Helm. Wiltbanck.

(70)

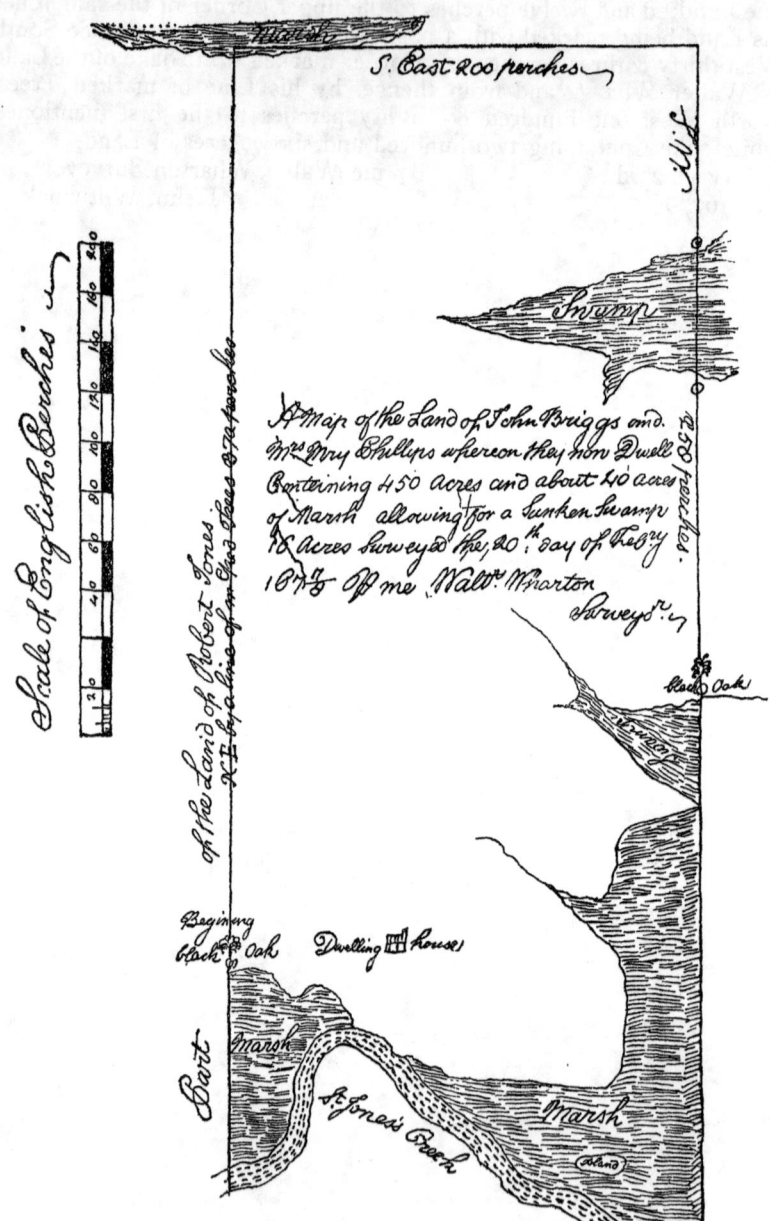

See Patent,
Page 257.
 by Vertue of a Warrant from the Court at the Whore Kill dated the 12th day of March 1677-8.
Layd out for John Briggs and Mary Philips a Tract of Land called Kingston upon Hull situate and being on the West side of Delaware Bay, and on the North-East side of St. Jones's Creek being the Land and plantation whereon they now Dwell and is bounded as followeth (Vizt.) Begining at a Corner marked black Oake standing by the side of the (71) Marsh which Lyeth between the Land and the Creek nigh unto the upper side of the Cleered grownd And from the said Oak Runing North East by a Line of marked Trees, dividing this from the Land of Robert Jones three hundred and Seventy perches to the side of a Marsh which proceedeth from the maine Bay and from thence South East two hundred perches and then South West by a Line of marked Trees dividing this from the Land belonging to the Towne point, two hundred fifty and Eight perches to a Corner marked Black Oak standing at the Head of a Great Marsh branch, which divideth this from the Towne Point. And from thence following the severall Courses of the Marsh, and Creek to the first mentioned Corner black oak: Conteining four   and fifty Acres of Land, and about forty a   Marsh lying between this Land and the aforesaid Creek; as by a Map of the same hereto annexed may more plainly appear four George Wale by Pattent bearing date in June 1671 and fifty Acres the Residue being new Land.
By me   Walter Wharton Surveyor.

Helm. Wiltbanck.
The survey being made before the Warrant was granted, Returne was made to the Court the same Day. by W. W.

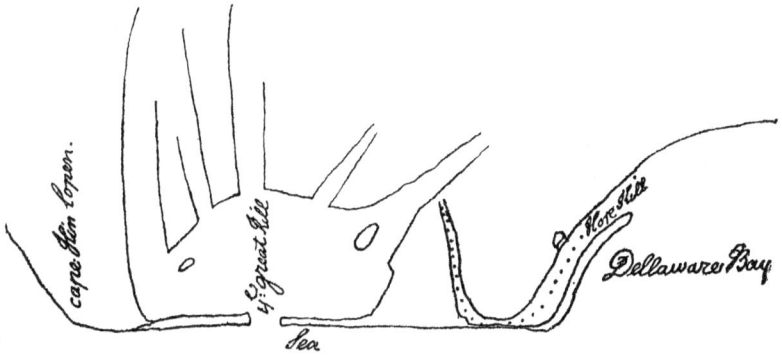

To the Right Honorable Francis Lovelace Esquire Governor General of his Royall Highness Dominions in Armeryca.
The humble Petition of James Mills presenteth
That the Comitioners at the Hore Kill, consented your Peti-

tion'r should have a poynt or neck of Land lying to the Southward of the Towne and ordered the Clarke to certifie your Honor thereof,, according to your Honor Instructions, The Clarke also promised to certifie your Honor (72) thereof, in his Letter, but hath not dunn it,
Therefore your Petitioner humbly Requests your Honor will be pleased to grant him Liscence to purchas of the Indians the said Neck of Land and Your Pettioner shall pray.

January 15th Anno 76-7

Whore Kill

Laid out a parcell of Land for Cornelis Johnson called Johnsons Delight situated on the West side of Delaware Bay and on the North side of a Creeke called Kimbels Creeke beginning at a bounded popular of the Land formerly Surveyed for Helmanus Wiltbanck and running from thence North West three hundred and twenty pertches to a Marked Red Oake and from thence South West two hundred pertches to a marked popular and then North West One hundred and fifty pertches to a Red Oake and from the said Redd Oake North East one hundred and seventy pertches to a white Oake, and from thence East North East two hundred Eighty four fertches unto a point binding upon the marsh, and from the said point South by East four hundred and twelve pertches binding upon the said Marsh unto a marked popular and from the said Popular South West Seaventy pertches unto the first bounded popular Conteining six hundred and twenty-two Acres of Land.

By a grant of Court.   by Cornelis Verhoofe
        Helm. Wiltbanck.   John Avery.
Edward Southrin,
Paul Marsh.

January 15th Anno 1676-7

Whore Kill

Laid out for Richard Peaty a parcell of Land Called Maiden heads ticked situated on the West Side of Delaware Bay and on the South side of a Creeke called the great Creeke beginning at a marked oake standing upon a point Running from thence by severall Courses up the said Creeke South W   by a Marsh near to a Little Creek said Great Creeke and from thence   hundred and Sixty pertches Intersecting with the   of Henry Herman and from thence paralell with said Line one hundred and Eighty pertches and then by severall Courses travissing North unto the first bounded oake, Containing four hundred and twenty one Acres of Land

By a grant of Court.   by Cornelis Verhoofe
        John Avery   Helm's. Wiltbanck.

(73)

January 15th Anno 1676-7

Whore Kill

Laid out a parcell of Land for Henry harmen Called Harmans Choice situated on the West side of Delaware Bay Beginning at a marked hickarie standing by a Marsh called Kimbels Neck and from thence travessing by severall Courses about a point unto a marked white oake and from the said white oake South South West Eighty pertches then South West two hundred and Sixty pertches unto a Market Red Oake then North West One hundred and fifty pertches to a marked hickarie and from thence North East paralell with the Line of Cornelius Johnson unto the first bounded hickarie three hundred fifty five pertches Containing four hundred Acres of Land. By a Grant of Court May.

Cornelis Verhoofe.
Helm Wiltbanck
John Avery

Jun the fiftenth 1676.

A Survey mad of a parsill of Land for Edward bodell Called by the name of Edwards Choys Lien in the Woods South South East from the horkill town distants three mills ner unto A branch called the gren branch beginen At A markid ock from thens Runin South West three hundred and twenty five perches to a Markid heckry from thens Ronin North West one hundred and fifty perches to a markid oake and from thens Ronin North Est three hundred and twenty five perches with a line dran parilell to the furst bounded tree South Est on hundred and fifty perches Contained and laid out for three hundred Ackers by Order and Apointment of Captain Edmond Cantwell to me Given As Witness my Hand this Day and yer Above writen.

John Avery.

Whore Kill ss Samuel Stiles and Robert Trale

March 12th 1676-7

Laid out for a parsell of Land called Andersons Delight situated on the Westward side of Delaware Bay and on the North side of a Creeke Called Misspann Creeke beginning at a marked White Oake standing by the edg of a Mash proceeding from the aforesaid Bay and by a pann in the said Mash and runing from thence West by South two hundred and thirty pertches up the sd. Misspann Creeke and from (74) thence North West two hundred and forty pertches then North East one hundred and eighty five pertches then South East two hundred and fourty five pertches, then North East one hundred and fifty pertches then North West One hundred and Seaventy pertches and from thence South East two hundred and fifty pertches unto the aforesaid mash and from thence South West by several Courses unto the aforesaid bounded White Oake three hundred and fifty eight pertches Containing Seaven hundred and fourty four Acres of Land.

by Cornelis Verhoofe.

(Note) These was done by Capt. Ed. Cantwell in the present of mee Cornelius Verhoofe.

Cornelis Verhoofe.
Whore Kill ss.—Robert hart Jun'r
March 11th Anno 1676-7

Laid out a pesell of Land for................Called prittcheds adventure situated on the West side of Delaware Bay and on the North side by a Creeke called Misspann Creeke begining at a Marked White Oake standing by the Edg of a Mash neare a Litel Creek and Running West by North six hundred and two pertches binding upon the sd. Litle Creeke Beaver dam and up a Branch and from thence North by East one hundred and sixty pertches and from thence East by South six hundred and twenty perches unto the said Maine Misspann Creeke deviding and separating with the Land of John be   and from thence up the said Misspann Creeke South South West unto the first bounded White Oake Containing Six hundred Ackers of Land.

by Cornelis Verhoofe.

(Note) These was done by Capt. Cantwell in the present of me Cornelius Verhoofe.

Whore kill ss.

Laid out a Tract of Land for Otto Wolgast situated upon the Black Wallnut Neck near unto Rehoba Called the Vineyard Beginning and Binding upon George Young at a Marked White Oake standing by a Branch side and running from the said White oake South along the Sea side four hundred pertches Binding upon John Roades his point and from thence West one hundred and ninety five pertches untill it intersect with the Line of the said George Young and from thence paralell with the said Line four hundred and fifty pertches unto the aforesaid bounded white oake Containing two (75) hundred and fourty Acres of Land.

by Cornelis Verhoofe.

(Note) These was not Excepted by Capt. Ed Cantwell but returned to dispose of to others by me Cornelius Verhoofe.

Whore Kill ss.   Ed Cantwell, Henry Streetcher, Abraham Clement.
March 16th Anno. 1676-7.

Laid out a parcell of Land Joyntly for Thomas Welburne, John Welburne, William Welburne, Jonathan Walterland, and Robert Beverly called Welburnes Wildernes situated on the West side of Delaware Bay begining at a point which being bounded on the North with a Creeke called the Great Creeke and on the East with another Creeke proceeding from the said Great Creeke and extending itselves West South West up the said Great Creeke Nine hundred pertches and from thence South South East nine hundred pertches and from thence North by West Downe the Creeke unto the aforesaid bounded point containing two thousand five hundred and thirty one Acres of Land.

by Cornelis Verhoofe.

(Note) These was done by Capt. Ed Cantwell in the present of me Cornelius Verhoofe.

THE DUKE OF YORK RECORD. 51

March 11th Anno 1676-7

Whore Kill ss. Cornelis Verhoofe
Laid out a parcell of Land for* Called the Orphans Lott situated on the West side of Delaware Bay and on the North side of a Creeke called Mispann Creeke Begining at the said Creeke at a marked White Oake standing by a Little Creeke and Runing up the said Little Creeke West North West Six hundred and fourty Pertches, and from thence South South West One hundred and Sixty Pertches, and from thence East South East paralell with the Land of Peter Pritched and the maine Mispann Creeke aforesaid six hundred and fourty Pertches unto the binding and Separating of the said Pritched his Land and from thence with a Line North North East binding upon the aforesaid Mispann Creeke unto the first bounded White Oak Containing six hundred Acres of Land. Cornelis Verhoofe.

(Note) These was done by Order of Capt. Cantwell by me Cornelis Verhoofe.

These p   tifficates was produced in Coart and Sworne to by Curnel Verhoofe that what he hath annexed and subscribed unto is (76) the trueth and nothing but the trueth, this 12th Sept. 1678.
       Helm. Wiltbanck
       Hen Smith
       Ed Southrin
       John Roades.

 Henry Stretcher sweareth in Court that the Certificate altered by Capt. Cantwell from Will Andrus unto Samuel Stiles and Robert traile, as aloe the Satifficate of Mr. Welback & others altered unto Capt. Cantwell. Abra. Dlement & myself was done by the said Cantwell in my sight: 12 Sept. 1678.
       Henry Stretcher.

Sworne this 12th Sept. 1678 before us
 Helm. Wiltbanck
 Hen. Smith
 Ed Southrin
 John Roades.

 December the Ayte date 1676, A Survay made of a Parsill of Land for James Loten situated Lien and beein in a creeke called Sedar Creeke Called by the name of Harts Delight beginin at a White Oake by the Creeke sid from thens Runin North by West too hundred pertches too a Line oke and from thens Runin West by South three hundred and twenty pertches to a marked hickery and from thens Runin South and by Est too hundred perches to a marked Red Oake And from thence Runin Est and by North three hundred and twenty perches to the first bounded Tree Containen and laid out for fouer hundred Ackers by Order and appointment of Captain Edward Cantwell.
 by me by Order of the Court. John Avery
 Luke Wattson
 Helm. Wiltbanck

---
*The name of John Betts is here crossed out.

Whore Kill   March 11th Ao. 167

Laid out for Cornelis Verhoofe a parcell of Land called New seven haven, Lying on the North side of a Creeke called Mispann Creeke beginning at a marked white oake, standing by a Little Creeke Called Indyan bridge Creeke, and running from thence South, South West, three hundred Perches binding upon the aforesaid Mespann Creeke, unto a White Oake standing by a little Creeke called Beaver Creeke, & Runing from thence West (77) North West, binding upon the said Beaver dam Creeke Beaver dam and Branch six hundred and fifty perches and from thence North North East three hundred Perches unto a Branch proceeding from the aforesaid Indyan Bridge Creeke, and from thence binding with a Course East South East upon the said Indyan Bridge Creeke six hundred and fifty five Perches unto the first bounded White Oake Containing twelve hundred and Eighteen Acres of Land   John Avery.   Helm. Wiltbanck.
By a grant from the Court.

Surveyed by Cornelis Verhoofe & allowed by the Court in Capt. Ed Cantwell. Test.

Helm. Wiltbanck.

The Quantity too great unlesse for one or more that would settle presently, having hands sufficient.

M. N.

March 11th Anno. 1676-7.
Whore Kill ss.

Laid out a parcell of Land for Cornelis Verhoofe called new Sevenhaven Situated on the West side of Delaware Bay and on the North side of a Creeke called Mispann Creeke begining at a marked white oake standing by a Little Creeke called Indian Bridge Creeke and Runing from thence South South West three hundred pertches Binding upon the aforesaid Mispann Creeke unto a White Oake standing by a Little Creeke Called Beaverdam Creeke and Runing from thence West North West binding upon the said Beaver dam Creeke, Beaver dam and Branch six hundred and fifty five pertches and from thence North North East three hundred pertches unto a Branch proceeding from the aforesaid Indian Bridge Creeke and from thence binding with a Course East South East upon the said Indian Bridge Creeke Six hundred and fifty five pertches unto the first bounded White Oake Containing and Laid out for twelve hundred and Eighteen Acres of Land.   Ed Cantwell Survayor.
By order of Court
          Helm Wiltbanck
                    Entred.

July the 7th day Anno 1675.

Surveyed for Alexander Molestady a Tracke of Land lying and being upon the Whore Kill neere unto the Mouth of the Kill begining at (78) a bounded Cedar runing up the Kill for breadth South East   bounded read oake, standing by the kill

and from thence South West binding upon Wm. Tom three hundred entie peartches to a bounded read oake standing by paganes Creeke and from thence North West down the said Creeke fourty pertches to a Bounded White Oake standing by the Creeke, from thence North East binding upon the Woods three hundred and Twentie pertches to the first bounded Ceader standing by the the Whore kill. Containing eightie Acres.
By Order of the Survayer generall
 Capt. Cantwell Survayed by mee
  William Taylor.

         July the 7th Day Anno 1675.
 Survayed for har Woolbanck a Tract of Land lying and being upon the Whore K ll begining at a bounded red oake stretching by the side, runing South East up the Kill, for Breadth Sixtie seven pearches to a bounded White Oake post stretching by the Kill or Creeke, And from thence South West three hundred and Twentie Pearches to a bounded Hickery standing upon Paganes Creeke, from thence North West down the said Creeke Sixtie seven pearches to a bounded White Oake, and from thence North East to the first bounded Read Oake standing by the Kill, Three hundred and Twentie peartches Containing One hundred Thertie and foure Acres.
By Order of the Survayer Generall
 Capt. Cantwell surveyed by me
  William Taylor.

         Jully the 7th Day Anno 1675.
 Survayed for Mr. Wm. Tom a Track of Land lying and being upon the which was formerly begining at a bounded White Oake standi the Kill side And from thence South East runi bounding upon the Kill, sixtie six peartches to bounded hickery standing by the said Kill, from thence by a Line of marked Trees South West to a Bounded Red Oake standing by the side of paganes creeke Three hundred and Twentie peartches, bounded upon harmanus Woolbanck, from thence downe the said Creeke North West sixtie six peartches to another bounded read oake, And from thence North East by a Line of marked Trees down to the first bounded White Oake standing upon the Whore kill, (79) Three hundred and twenty peartches bounded upon Alexander Molestedy land, Conteining one hundred Thirty Two Acres.
By Order of Capt. Cantwell Survayer
generall Survayed by me
  William Taylor.

Whore Kill ss. Whereas By Capt. Edm. Cantwell was lately send sum Certaine Certificates of Land to this Court whose Names quantitie & Quantities may be Certified as followeth Vizt:

		Acres.	
Imprs,	Thomas Goward	600	Already seated.
	Francis Meggs & John Crolley	600	Intended to seate next Winter
	Paul Marsh	600	Already seated.
	James Leten	400	Already seated.
	Anthony Eenloss	150	Allready seated.
	Simon Paling	300	Allready seated.
	John Oakey	400	Intended to seate next Winter
	Cornelis Verhoofe	1218	Intended to seate next Winter
	Robert Highnet & John Crius	900	Allready seated.
	Cornelis Johnson	622	Intended to seate next Winter

Hendrick Molestine		Already seated & the Certificate
John Kipshaven Jun'r	800	Left in Custody of M. John
Cornelis Verhoofe		Kipshaven who is bound for
Harmon Cornelis		New Yorke and to procure a Patten for the same.

Jeffrey Sumerford	300	Intended to seate next Winter
Richard Peaty	421	Intended to seate next Winter
Henry Harman	400	being part seated.
Capt. John Avery	800	The land taken from him & Referr to another Conveniency.
Alex. Molestine & John Brigs	800	Intended to seate next Winter
Andries Dupre	400	Being part seated.
Capt. Hans Morinson		Being out of this pairts & unaquainted with it.
Thomas Merritts		Wee Know neither his Person nor the Land whether seated or not untill further Inquiry.

These aforementioned Certificates Examined in Court and the which persons as yet not seated Wee know nothing to the Contrary but are all here in place and intended to seat their Lands the next Winter Insueing. Examined in Court May 13th A. D. 1679 & Humbly Certified by the Court.

Test. Cornelis Verhoofe Cler.

THE DUKE OF YORK RECORD. 55

(80)
SURVEYS RETURNED BY CAPT. EDM. CANTWELL
Nov. 18th, 1678.
N. Y.

Date of Survey — Acres

(1) Aug. 15, 1676. Thomas Howard & Knights Howard, Land at the Whore kill signed by Helm. Wiltbanck & John Avery 600
(2) Aug. 29-76 Francis Meges & John Crolley land near the Whorekill—signed by John Avery & Helm. Wiltbanck. 600
(3) Aug. 17-76 Paul Marsh, land at the Whorekill, signed by Helm. Wiltbanck & John Avery. 600
(4) S. 8—76. James Loten, Land at the Whorekill; signed John Avery, Helm. Wiltbanck. 400
(6) Aug. 15—76. Simon Pollin, Land at ye Whore kill, signed Helm Wiltbanck, John Avery. 300
(5) Aug. 11—76. Anthony Inles Land at the Whorekill signed John Avery, Helm Wiltbanck. 150
(7) 11-76 John Okey, Land at the Whore kill, signed John Avery, Helm. Wiltbanck. 400
(8) Exception—Mar. 11 76-7 Cornelys Verhoofe, Land at the Whore kill, signed Helm. Wiltbanck. 1200
(9) Aug. 21-76 Rob't Hignat & John Crue Land at the Whorekill signed Helm. Wiltbanck, John Avery. 900
(10) Jan. 15, 76-7 Cornelys Johnson land at the Whore kill, signed Helm. Wiltbanck, Edward Southrin, Paul Marsh &c. 622
(11) Mar. 8—76-7 Hendr. Molesteyn, John Kipshaven jun'r Cor. Verhoofe & Herm. Cornelys, signed Helm. Wiltbanck Cor. Verhoofe as Surveyor. 800
(12) July 19, 76 Jeffrey Sumerford, Land at the Whorekill, signed Helm. Wiltbanck, John Avery. 300
(13) Jan. 15, 76-7 Rich'd Peaty land at the Whore kill, signed Helm. Wiltbanck. &c. 421
(14) Jan. 15, 76-7 Henry Harman, land at the Whorekill signed Helm. Wiltbanck. 400
(15) Dec. 4, 76 Alex. Moleston & John Briggs land at the Whore kill signed Helm. Wiltbanck &c. 800
(16) Dec. 16, 76. John Avery land at the Whorekill, signed Helm. Wiltbanck. 800
(17) Jan. 20, 77 Andries du Pree Land at the Whorekill, signed Helm. Wiltbanck, John Avery. 400
(18) Sept. 20, 75 Capt. Hans Mounson Land at the Schuylkill. Surveyed by Walter Wharton long in his Possession. 1100

The foregoing Surveys to bee certified as allowed now, the parties being in possession, or ready to goe upon the Land.

By order & Direction of the Go.
W. N. Secr.

(81)

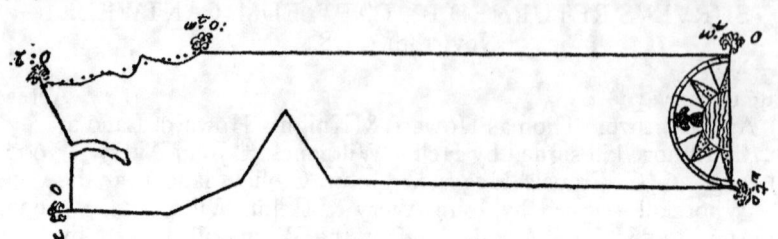

By Vertue of a Warrant from ye Whorekill Court bearing date ye 10th of May Ao. 1680.

Laid out for William Sharrett a parcel of Land Called Sharretts Choyse scituated on the West side of Delaware Bay and on the South side of a creeke called Duck Creeke Beginning at a marked Red oake standing by the said Creekes side and Running from thence South fourty six perches binding on the said Creeke to a bite of Marsh then South South East fourty perches, then South East by East fourty perches binding on a Cruple of the said Marsch to a small branch & then South West by West fourty perches to a marked white oake standing near by the said Cruple And from thence South with a Line of marked Trees two hundred perches to a marked white oak standing by the side of a Great Swampe and from thence East binding on the said Swampe Sixty perches to a marked white oake and from thence North with a Line of marked Trees two hundred Sixty and three perches to a marked white oake standing by a Creuple of the said Duck Creeke and from thence North by West Eighty perches binding on the said Creuple to a marked Red oake standing on a point by the marsches of ye said Creeke, then South West by South thirty two perches binding on the said Marsch to a small branch & from thence West twenty and Eight perches to the first bounded Red Oake Containing and laid out for one hundred & Sixteen Acres of Land.

            Cornelis Verhoofe Surveyor.

May ye 26th Ao. 1680.
 At a Court held for ye Whore kill.
 Sept. ye 2nd Ao. 1680: Certified ye above named is seated.
  Luke Wattson.

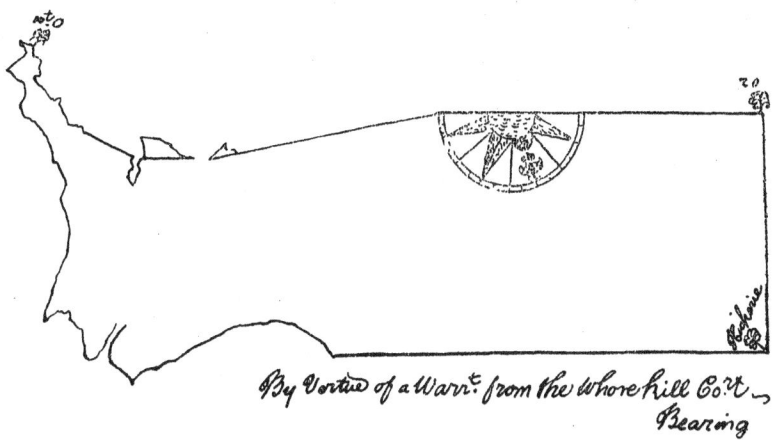

(82)

By Vertue of a Warrant from the Whore kill Court Bearing date ye 10th Day of May Ao. 1680.

Laid out for John Dawson a parcell of Land called Woodstock bower Scituated on the West side of Delaware Bay and on the North side of a Branch dividing this and the Land of George Martine Beginning at a White Oake standing on a Point by the Marsches by the Mouth of the said Branch & Running from thence North thirty perches on the said branch then North by West thirty perches, then North North West twenty and two perches, then North West fourty & Eight perches binding on the said branch, then West North West fifty Perches and then West by North one hundred ninety and fouer perches binding on the said Branch, & then Running still up the said Branch West North West two hundred & Sixty perches to a marked Red Oake, & from thence North North East with a Line of marked Trees one hundred and Seaventy perches to a marked Hickarie & from thence East South East with a Line of marked Trees three hundred fourty & Eight perches to the marsches from ijdons Creeke, then binding on the said marsches by severall Courses biting Southerly in this Land to a point bearing Dito Course & Distance one hundred and Sixty perches, & from thence binding by severall Courses on the said Marsches to ye first bounded White Oake Containing and laid out for six hundred Acres of Land.

By Cornelis Verhoofe Surveyor.

May 27th Ao. 1680.

At a Court held for the Whore kill Sept. ye 2th 1680. Certified ye above named is Seated.

Luke Wattson.

(83)

By Vertue of a Warrant from ye Whore Kill Court,
bearing date ye 11th of February Ao. 1679-80.
    Laid out for John Roades a parcell of Land scituated on ye West side of ye Sea near Delaware Bay Beginning at a point on ye Beatch of ye sd. Sea and Running from ye said point West bounding on Rehobah bay & Marshes two hundred ninety and fouer perches to a point near a small Creeke dividing this from ye Land of Capt. John Avery his Land and from the said Point North East binding on ye said Marshes of ye said Creeke one hundred and fifty two perches to ye Branch of ye said Little Creeke & then North West by North binding on ye said Branch one hundred & twenty perches to a marked white oake, standing by ye said Branch and from ye said White Oake North East with a Line of marked Trees fourty & Eight perches to a bounded hickarie of James Wells his Land standing in ye Woods near a Branch proceeding from a pann Lyeing in this said John Roades his Land and from ye said Hickarie Dito North East with a Line of marked Trees binding upon Dito Wells his Land two hundred thirty & six perches to a salsafrick tree standing in ye said Line & then North East by East binding on ye Branch dividing this from ye Land of ye said Wells Eightie perches to a point on ye Sea Beach & mouth of ye said Branch And from ye said point South binding on ye said Sea Beatch to ye first bounded point fower hundred ninety & Six perches Containing & Laid out for five hundred and fifty Acres of Land.
                                    By Cornelis Verhoofe Surveyor
                                        John Avery.
Aprill ye 5th Ao. 1680.
    (Examined and compared July 6, 1767. by Thos. M. Kean)

(84)

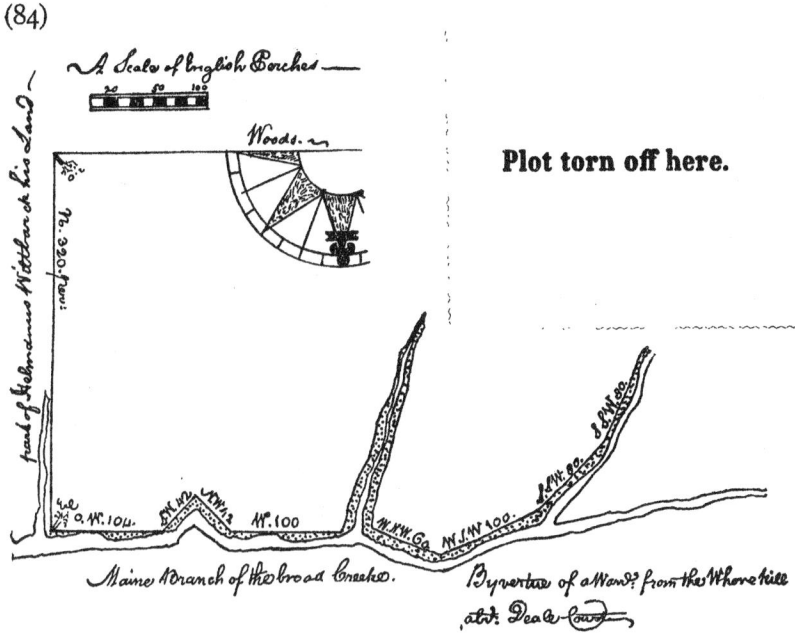

By vertue of a Warr. from the Whorekill alias Deale Court.
    Laid out for Richard Dawson a parcell of Land called Dawsons Lott Situated on the west side of Delaware Bay and on the South side of the maine Branch of a Creek called the broad alias great Creek Beginning at a Marked white Oake standing by a little branch called Dawsons branch and running from the said Marked oake by the several Courses fower hundred fourty & Eight perches binding on the Cypress Swamp of the said maine branch to the mouth of another Branch and from thence by the several Courses Binding on the said Branch three hundred and twenty perches to a Marked white oake standing on the said Branch and from thence South with a line of Marked trees Sixty and two perches to a Marked white oake standing in the Woods and from thence East with a line of marked trees Six hundred and fourteen perches to a Bounded Red oake and from thence North with a line of Marked trees three hundred and twenty perches to the first bounded white oak Containing and laid out for One thousand Acres of Land. primo March Ao. 1680-1   Cornelis Verhoofe Surveyor.
    At a Court held at Deale by the Kings Authority the 14th February 1681, the above Survey is Certified by the Court not to be as yet Seated.

                                                              Luke Wattson.

(85)

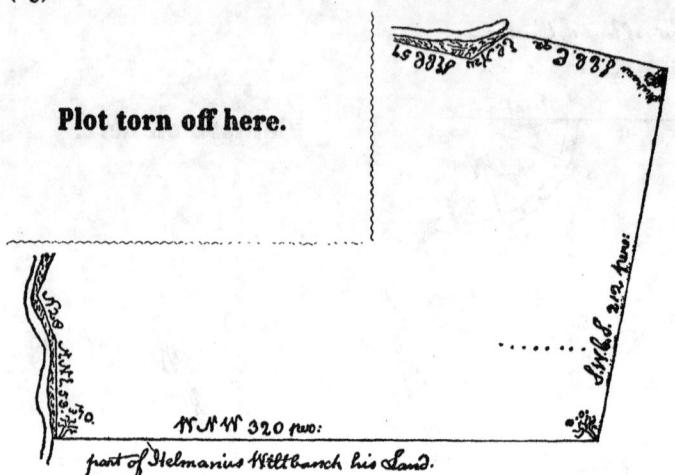

By Vertue of a Warr. from the Whorekill alias Deale Court.

Laid out for Bryand Rowles a parcell of Land Called Swampoint Situated on the West side of Delaware Bay and on the North side of a Creek called the broad alias Great Creek Beginning at a Marked white oake Standing by a slade of Marsh on the said Creek being the Bounded tree of Helmanus Wiltbanck and Running from thence West North West with a line of Marked trees binding on the said Land of Helmanus Wiltbanck three hundred and twenty perches to a Marked Corner Red oake standing in the Woods and from thence South West by South with a line of Marked trees two hundred and twelve perches to a Corner Bounded Hickarie standing in the Woods and from South East by East with a line of Marked trees ninety and two perches to a Marked Hickarie standing on the Cypress Swampe of the maine Branch of the said broad Creeke then binding with the several Courses two hundred Sixty and six perches on the said Cypress Swamp to the head of the said Creek and from thence by severall Courses One hundred Sixty and One perches binding on the said Creek and Marshes thereof to the first bounded white oake Containing and laid out for four hundred acres of Land.

by Cornelis Verhoofe Surveyor.

March 2nd A. 1680-1

At a Court at Deale by the Kings Authority the 14th Feb. 1681 the above Survey is Certified by the Court to be already seated.

Luke Wattson.

(86)

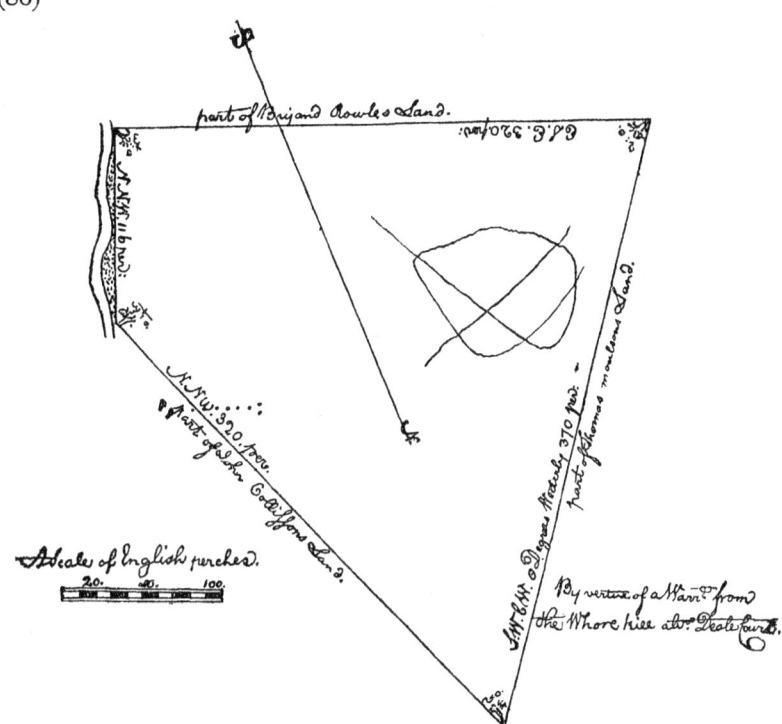

By Vertue of a Warr. from the Whorekill alias Deale Court.

Laid out for Helmanus Wiltbanck a parcell of Land Called Hopewell and situated on the West side of Delaware Bay and on the North side of a Creek Called the broad alias the Great Creek Beginning at a Marked white oake Standing by a Sladge of Marsh on the said Creekes side and running from thence North North East One hundred and sixteen perches Binding on the said Creek to a white oake Bounded tree of John Cleisson standing on the said Creekes side and from thence North North West with a line of Marked trees three hundred and twenty perches to a marked corner red oake standing in the woods by a little Valley and from thence South West by South Eight Degrees westerly with a line of marked trees three hundred and seventy perches to a marked Corner red oake standing in the woods and from thence East South East with a line of marked trees three hundred and twenty to the first Bounded white oake Containing and laid out for four hundred sixty and nine acres of land.

March ye 3 A 1680-1   by Cornelis Verhoofe Surveyor.

At a Court held at Deale by the Kings Authority the 14th Feb. 1681 the above Survey is Certified by the Court to be in part Seated.

Helmanus Wiltbanck   Luke Wattson.

(87)

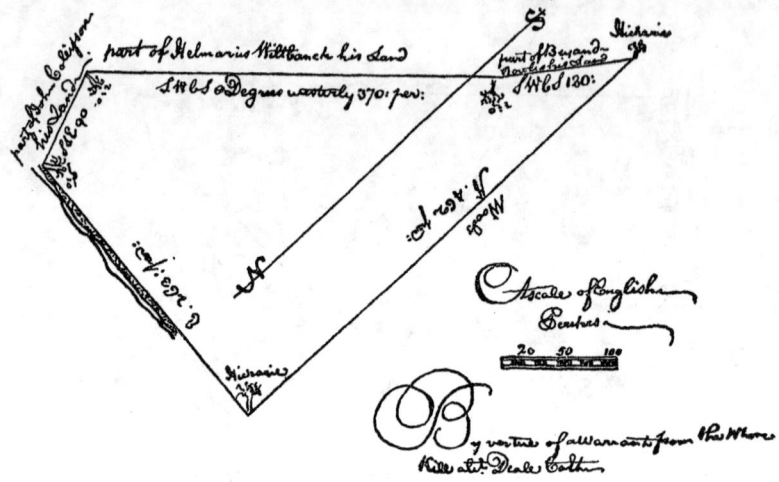

By Vertue of a Warrant from the Whore kill alias Deale Court.

Laid out for Thomas Morilson a parcell of Land called Fortune Situated on the West side of Delaware Bay and on the South side of a branch and Beaver dam which Seperating, this from a neck Commonly called Daniel Haste his neck on the South side of Priume hooke Creek Beginning at a marked corner white oake Standing on the said Branch and running from thence South South East with a line of marked trees ninety and six perches to a red oake Corner Bound of Helmanus Wiltbanck and from thence South West by South Eight Degrees westerly binding on the line of Marked trees of the said Helmanus his Land three hundred and seventy perches to a marked Corner Red oake of the said Helmanus and Bryand Rowles their Land and from thence South West by South One hundred and thirty perches binding on the line of marked Trees of the said Bryand Rowles to a Corner marked Hickarie and from thence North with a line of marked trees four hundred Sixty and two perches to a Corner Marked Hickarie standing in the woods and from thence East with a line of marked trees and part binding on the aforesaid Branch two hundred sixty and three perches to the first Bounded white oake. Containing and laid out for five hundred Acres of Land.

March ye 4th A. 1680-1   Cornelis Verhoofe Surveyor.

At a Court held at Deale by the Kings Authority the 14th February 1681: the above Survey is Certified by the Court to be in part Seated.   Luke Wattson.

(88)

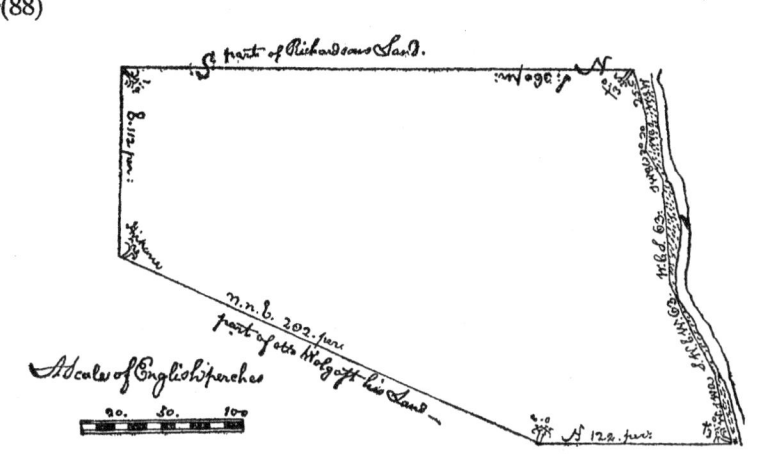

By vertue of a Warr. from the Whore kill alias Deale Court.

Laid out for Helmanus Wiltbanck a parcell of Land Called Sieck By Change Situated on the West side of Delaware Bay and on the South side of a Creeke called the broad alias great Creeke Beginning at a Marked white oake standing by the mouth of a branch called Dawsons Branch and on the South side of the said Creeke and running from thence South with a line of Marked trees binding on the said Richard Dawson his Land to a marked Corner red oake standing in the woods three hundred sixty and eight perches and from thence East with a line of marked trees One hundred and twelve perches to a Marked Corner Hickarie standing in the woods and from thence North North East with a line of Marked trees two hundred Eighty and two perches to a Marked red oake then North with a line of Marked trees One hundred twenty and two perches to a Marked white oake standing on the Marshes of the said Creeke and from thence with the several Courses two hundred thirty and two perches Binding on the Marshes of the said Creeke to the first bounded white oake Containing and laid out for four hundred twenty and five acres of Land.

March ye 5th A. 1680-1   by Cornelis Verhoofe Surveyor.

At a Court held at Deale by the Kings Authority the 14th day of Feb. 1681; the above Survey is Certified to be already seated.

                                            Luke Wattson.

(89)

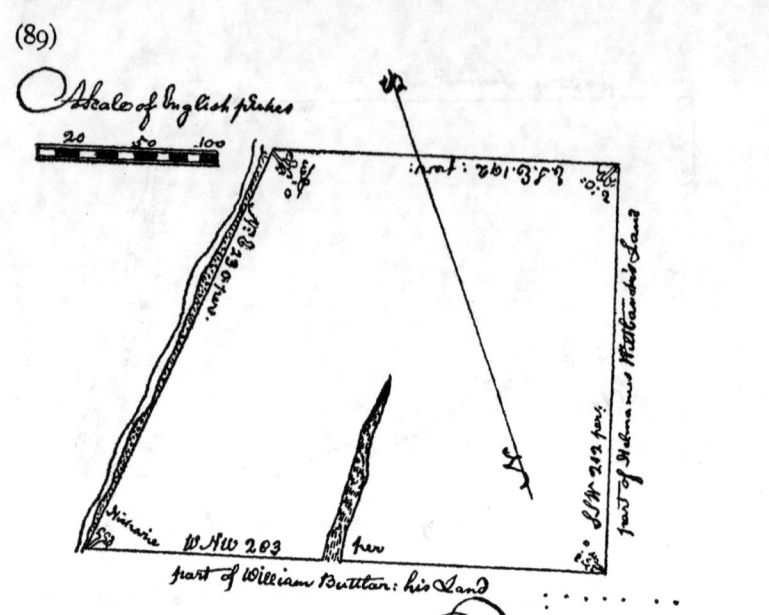

By vertue of a Warr. from the Whorekill alias Deale Court.

Laid out for Otto Wolgast a parcell of Land called the Orphant Lott situated on the West side of Delaware Bay and on the North West side of a Creek proceeding from ye broad Creeke and called mill Creeke Beginning at a marked Hickarie standing on the side of the said mill Creeke and Running from thence West North West with a line of Marked trees two hundred eighty and three perches Intersecting with the line of Helmanus Wiltbanck his land to a Marked Corner Red oake of this and then binding on the said Line South South West two hundred and twelve perches to a marked Corner red oake of this and from thence East South East with a line of Marked trees One hundred ninety and two perches to a marked white oake standing on the said Creeke side and from thence North East two hundred and thirty perches binding on the said Creeke to the first bounded Hickarie Containing and laid out for three hundred acres of Land.

March ye 6th A. 1680-1   Cornelis Verhoofe Surveyor.

At a Court held at Deale by the Kings Authority the 14th Feb. 1681 the above Survey is Certified by the Court to be already Seated.

                                   Luke Wattson.

(90)

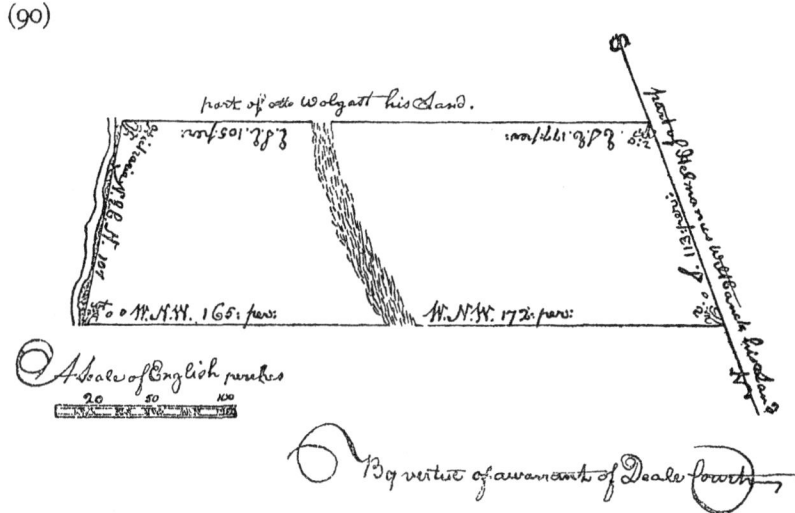

By vertue of a warrant of Deale Court.
    Laid out for William Butlar a parcell of Land called the Adventure situated on the West side of Delaware Bay and on the North West side of a Creek proceeding from the broad Creek and called Mill Creek Beginning at a marked Hickarie Bound of Otto Wolgast his Land and running from thence North East by North One hundred and seven perches Binding on the said Creek to a marked white oake standing on the Marshes of the said Creek and from thence West North West with a line of marked trees three hundred thirty and seven perches to a red oake bounded tree Intersecting with the line of Halmanus Wiltbanck his land and then binding on the said line South One hundred and thirteen perches to a red oake bounded tree of Otto Wolgast his Land and then East South East binding on Dito Line of Dito Wolgast his Land two hundred Eighty and three perches to the first bounded Hickarie Containing and laid out for two hundred acres of Land.
March the 6th Ao. 1680-1   Cornelis Verhoofe Surveyor.
    At a Court held at Deale by the Kings Authority the 14th Feb. 1681 the above Survey is certified by the Court to be not as yet seated.
Luke Wattson.

    This Survey being inlarged by vertue of a Warrant, which shall return with ye next therefore need no pattent.
        Cornelis Verhoofe.

(91)

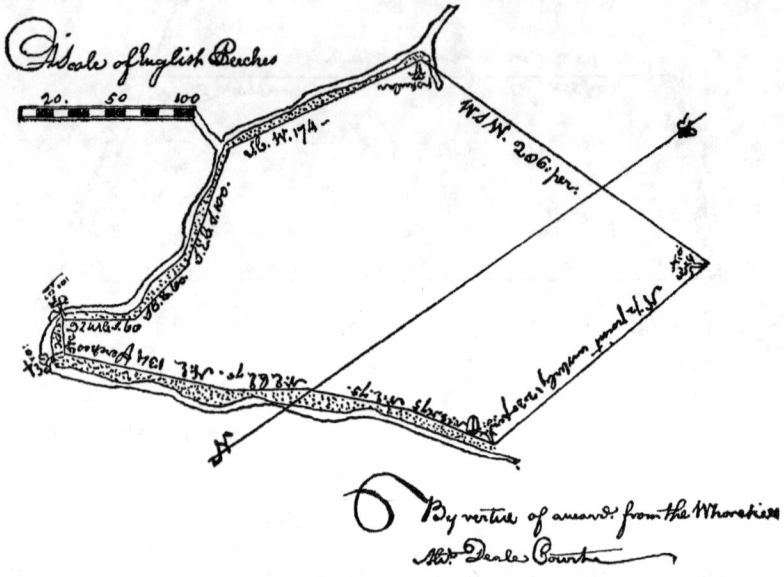

      By vertue of a warr. from the Whorekill alias Deale Court.
      Laid out for Capt. Paull Marsh a parcell of Land called the Good Hope situated on the west side of Delaware Bay and on the South side of a Creeke called Marshes Creeke Beginning at a marked white oake standing on a point by the said Creeke and running from thence South East by East Thirty perches binding on the Marshes of another branch to a marked white oake and from thence with ye severall Courses three hundred ninety and four perches Binding on the marshes of the said branch and part on a Beaver dam to a marked Popular standing on the branch above the said Beaver dam and from thence West South West with a line of marked trees two hundred eighty and six perches to a Corner marked white oake standing in the woods and from thence north a half point westerly with a line of marked trees two hundred and thirty perches to a marked white oake standing on the Marshes of the said Marshes Creeke and from thence with the several Courses three hundred fifty and nine perches binding on the marshes of the said Creeke to the first bounded white oake Containing & laid out for six hundred acres of Land.
March ye 8th A 1680-1.   Cornelis Verhoofe Surveyor.
      At a Court held at Deale by the Kings Authority the 14th day of Feb. 1681; the above Survey is Certified by the Court to be seated already.   Luke Wattson.

(92)

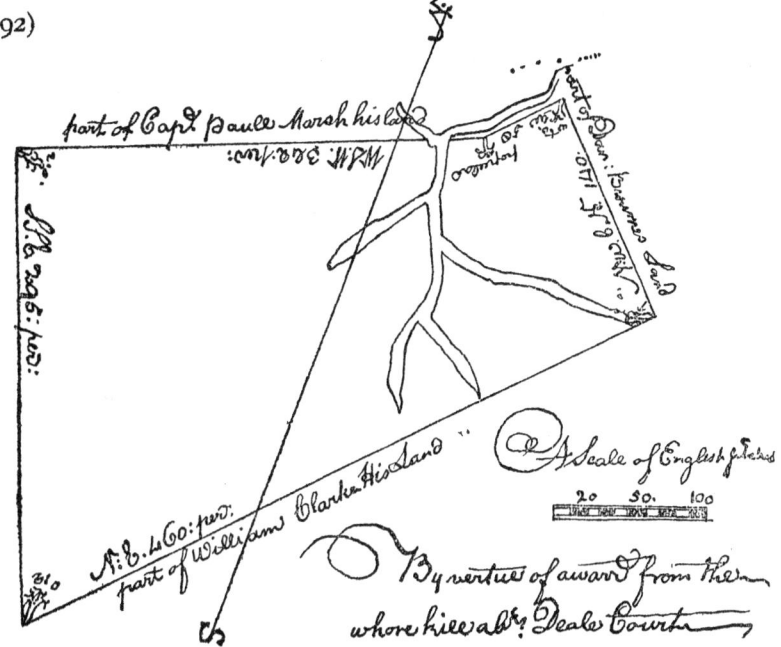

By vertue of a Warr. from the Whorekill alias Deale Court.

Laid out for Michael Chambers a parcell of Land called Orkny Scituated on the west side of Delaware Bay and about two miles westward from Deale town in the woods beginning at a white oake post standing by a Dead marked Hickarie head bound stump of Edward Southrin and Daniell Browne and running from thence North west by North binding on the head line of the said Daniell Browne One hundred and forty perches to a marked white oake standing by the Beaver dam of the said Browne and Capt Marsh theire Land and from thence South west binding on and over the said Beaver dam fifty and eight perches to a bounded popular........of the said Marsh and from thence West South West binding part on the line of said marsh his Land and part with marked trees three hundred fourty and two perches to a marked Corner red oake standing in the woods and from thence South South East with a line of marked trees two hundred ninety and five perches to a marked Corner read oake standing in the woods and from thence North East with a line of marked trees fower hundred and sixty perches intersecting the head line of Edward Southrin and then North West by North eight perches binding on the said head line to the first bounded white oake post Containing and laid out for five hundred acres of Land.

March ye 9thA 1680-1   Cornelis Verhoofe Surveyor.

At a Court held at Deale by the Kings Authority the 14th Feb. 1681 the above Survey is Certified by the Court to be already Seated.

                                                       Luke Wattson.

(93)

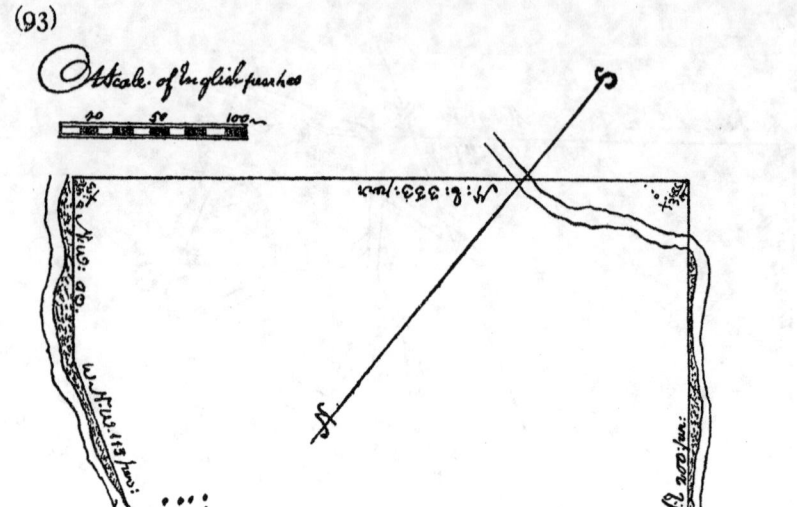

By vertue of a warr. from Deale alias Whorekill Court.

 Laid out for William Ematt a parcell of Land called Tanners Hall Scituated on the West side of Delaware Bay and on the South West side of a Creek Called Middle Creek which proceeding out of Rehobah Bay Beginning at a marked white oak standing on the said Creeke by a slayde of a small branch and running from thence South West with a line of marked trees two hundred ninety and three perches to a Corner Bounded white oak near a branch and standing by the Usefull Indian Path and from thence South East Two hundred perches binding most part on the said branch or beaver dam to a marked Corner white oak standing over the said beaver dam and from thence North East with a line of marked trees three hundred thirty and three perches to a marked white oake standing on the said Creeke and from thence North west ninety and three perches binding on the said Creek and then West North West Binding on the said Creek One hundred and fifteen perches to the first bounded white oak Containing and laid out for fower hundred acres of Land.
March ye 27th A 1681.   Cornelis Vorhoofe Surveyor.
 At a Court held at Deale by the Kings Authority the 14th Feb. 1681 the above Survey is Certified by the Court not to be as yet seated.
                  Luke Wattson.

(94)

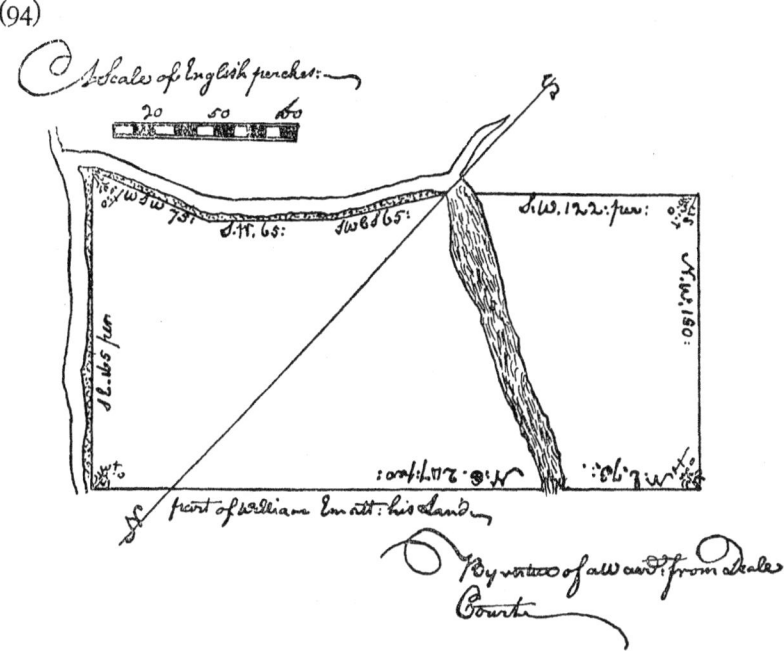

By virtue of a Warr. from Deale Court.

Laid out for Capt. John Avery a parcell of Land called Goulden quartere, Scituated on the West side of the Delaware Bay and on the South West side of a Creeke called middle Creeke which proceeding out of Rehobah Bay Beginning at a marked white oak standing on a point at the mouth of a little Creek Called Harring Creeke and Running up the said Creeke with ye several Courses three hundred twenty and three perches to a Corner marked white oake standing in the woods by a Valley and from thence North West with a line of marked One hundred and fifty perches to a head bounded white oake of William Ematt his Land and from thence North East binding on the said line three hundred thirty and three perches to the white oake bounded tree of the said William Ematt standing on the said middle Creeke side and from thence South East One hundred Sixty and five perches Binding of the said William Ematt standing on the said middle Creeke side and out for three hundred acres of Land.

March ye 28th A 1681.   Cornelis Verhoofe Surveyor.

At a Court held at Deale by the Kings Authority the 14th day of Feb. 1681: the above Survey is Certified by the Court to be as yet unseated.   Luke Wattson.

(95)

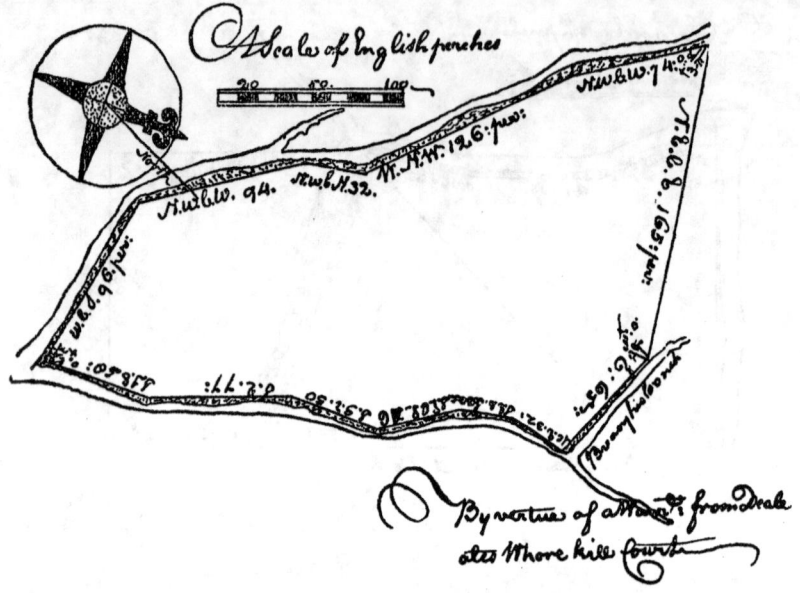

By vertue of a Warr. from Deale alias Whorekill Court.
    Laid out for Robert Richardson a parcell of Land called Robert his Choyse scituated on the West side of Delaware Bay and on the North side of a Creek called middle Creek proceeding out of Rehobah Bay Beginning at a marked white oak standing on a point by the said Creekes side and Running from thence with the several Courses fower hundred twenty and two perches binding on the said Creeke and maine branch to a Corner marked white oak standing on the said branch and from thence North East by East with a line of marked trees one hundred sixty and five perches to a marked Corner white oake standing on a branch of the said Creeke Called Breaoy his branch and from thence with the several Courses three hundred and sixty perches binding on the said branch to the first bounded white oake Containing and laid out for two hundred ninety and two acres of Land.
March ye 29th A. 1681.   Cornelis Verhoofe Surveyor.
    At a Court held at Deale by the Kings Authority the 14th Feb. 1681, the above Survey is Certified by the Court to be already Seated.
                                           Luke Wattson.
    This Survey being inlarged by vertue of a Warr. which shall return per next therefore need no patten.
                             Cornelis Verhoofe Surveyor.

(96)

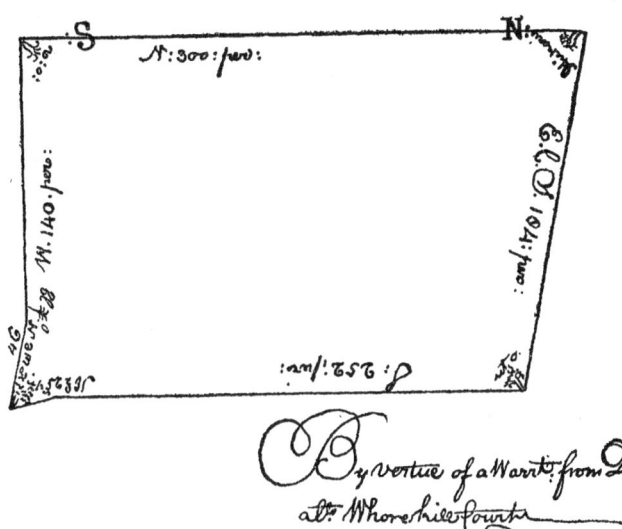

By vertue of a Warr. from Deale alias Whore Kill Court.

Laid out for Robert Breacy a parcell of Land called Purchase Lott scituated on the West side of Delaware Bay near at Rehobah Beginning at a marked Hickarie standing in the woods near the marked head bound of his now Dwelling Soate of land and running from thence West by North with a line of marked trees fourty and six perches to a black oake Corner head bound of the said Robert Breacy his Dwelling land and from thence West with a line of marked trees One hundred and fourty perches to a marked corner red oake standing in the Woods and from thence North with a line of marked trees three hundred perches to a marked Corner Hickarie standing in the woods near a white oake marked bound of Nathaniell Broadford his Land and from thence East by South with a line of marked trees One hundred Eighty & fower perches to a marked corner white oake standing in the woods and from thence south with a line of marked trees two hundred fifty and two perches. Then South by East with a line of marked trees twenty and five perches to the first bounded Hickarie Containing and laid out for three hundred twenty and two acres of Land.

March ye 30th, A. 1681.   Cornelis Voorhoofe Surveyor.

At a Court held at Deale by the Kings Authority the 14th Feb. 1681, the above Survey is Certified to be as yett not seated.

                   Luke Wattson.

(97)

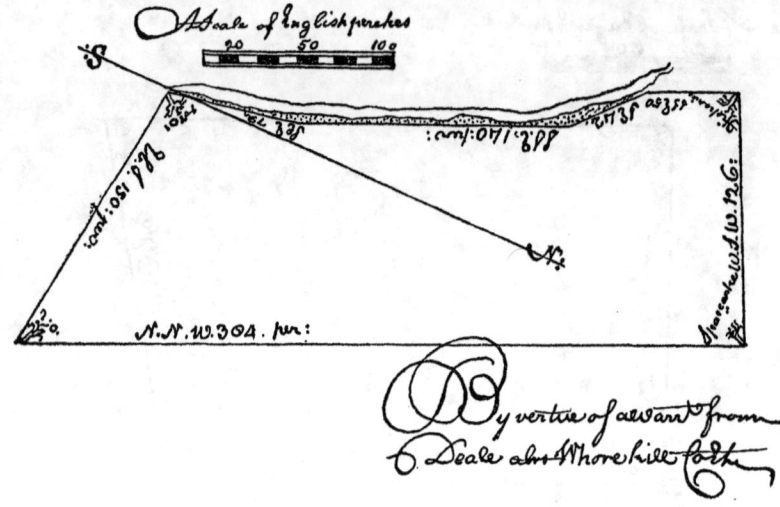

By vertue of a Warr't. from Deale alias Whorekill Court.

Laid out for Richard Showlster a p'cell of said Land called Showlsters Inheritance scituated on the west side of Delaware Bay near Rehobah about one mile distance Southwestwards from Loues Creeke beginning at a bounded white oake being the bounded tree of Francis Meggs his land and running from thence East by South with a line of marked trees One hundred and fifty perches binding on the said meggs his land to a Corner marked red oake standing in the woods and from thence north north west with a line of marked trees three hundred eighty and fower perches to a Corner marked Spanish oake standing in a Swampe woods and from thence west South west with a line of marked trees One hundred twenty and six perches to, a Corner marked Hickarie standing the woods and from thence South South East with a line of marked trees fifety perches to a marked black oake Standing in the branch of Robert Breacy his Land and then with the severall Courses two hundred fifety and fower perches binding in the said branch which Dividing this from the said Land of the said Robert Breacy to the first bounded white oake Containing and laid out for two hundred fifety and five acres of Land.

April ye 1 A. 1681.   Cornelis Verhoofe Surveyor.

At a Court held at Deale by the Kings Authority the 14th Feb. 1681. the above Survey is Certified by the Court to be not as yet seated.
                                                          Luke Wattsone.

This Survey being inlarged by vertue of a Warr. which shall returne with the next therefore need no patten.
                                       Cornelis Verhoofe Surveyor.

(98)

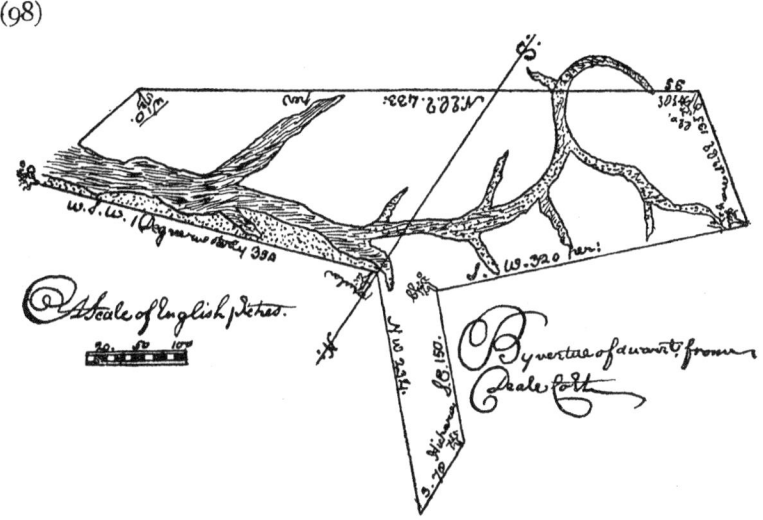

By vertue of a warr. from Deale Court.

Laid out for Stephen Whitman a parcell of Land called Whitmans Choise scituated on the West side of Delaware Bay and on the South side of a Creeke called Deale Creeke Beginning at a marked white oake being the bounded tree of Anthony Eenloss standing on a point of woods and a branch on the Marshes of the said Deale Creeke and running from thence west South west One Degree westerly three hundred fifety and fower perches binding on the land of Anthony Eenloss to a bounded popular of the said Anthony Eenloss and John Kipshaven and from thence Northwest two hundred thirty and fower perches binding on the head line of the said John Kipshaven his Land to Patricks Creeke and from thence South Seaventy and eight perches to a bounded Hickarie of the Land the said Stephen Whitman purchased from John Siming and from thence South East binding on the said Land One hundred and fifety perches to a marked black oake & from thence Southwest binding on the said Land to a marked Corner Hickarie—Standing in the woods and from thence South East by East with a line of marked trees One hundred thirty and five perches to a Corner marked black oake standing in the woods and from thence with a line of marked trees North East by East thirty and five perches to a branch and then by several Courses binding on part of the said branch One hundred and twenty perches to the Course aforesaid and from thence Dito, North East by East fower hundred and thirteen perches with a line of marked trees and part binding on a branch to a marked white oake standing on a point of woods and on the marshes of the said Deale Creeke and then North North East to the first bounded white oake Containing and laid out for five hundred acres of Land.

June ye 6th A. 1681.   Cornelis Verhoofe Surveyor.

At a Court held at Deale by the Kings Authority the 14th Feb.

1681 the above Survey is Certified by the Court to be already seated, but hath taken away John Kipavens privilege of going to the Marsh which is not allowed of by the Court.

Luke Wattson.

(99)

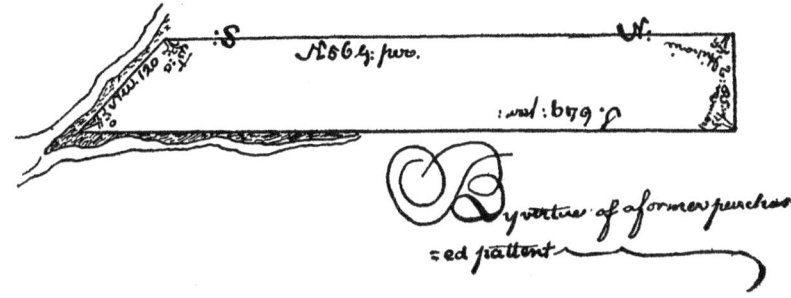

By vertue of a former purchased pattent.

Laid out for William Fritcher a parcell of land called Fritchers purchase scituated on the West side of Delaware Bay at Rehobah Beginning at a marked red oake standing at a point on the North side of Rehobah Creeke now called Loues Creeke and Running from thence Northwest One hundred and twenty perches binding on the said Creeke to a marked white oake standing on the Marshes of the said Creeke near a branch and from thence North with a line of marked trees five hundred sixty and fower perches to a Corner marked Hickarie standing in ye woods and from thence East with a line of marked trees Eighty and five perches to a Corner marked popular Standing in the woods and from thence South with a line of marked trees Six hundred fourty and nine perches to the first bounded red oake Containing and laid out according to former patten for three hundred twenty and two acres of Land.

June the 9th A. 1681.   Cornelis Verhoofe, Surveyor.

At a Court held at Deale by the Kings Authority the 14th day of Feb. 1681 the above Survey is Certified by the Court to be in part Seated.   Luke Wattson.

This Survey being part thereof Cast for Law and afterwards by vertue of a warr. altered in proportion which shall return per next therefore nee   no patten.

Cornelis Verhoofe Surveyor.

(100)

By vertue of a patten.

Laid out for Capt. Nathaniell Walker a parcell of Land called Walkers purchase Scituated on the West side of Delaware Bay and on the North side of a Creeke called the Broad alias Great Creeke Beginning at marked red oake standing on the edge of the Clear Ground of the plantation on the marshes of the lower and Eastermost part of the neck and running from thence West South West fower hundred and ninety perches binding on the Marshes of the said Creeke Intersecting with the Land of Simon Paling to a marked white oake standing near the marshes of the said Creeke and from thence North North West with a line of marked trees two hundred and sixty perches binding on the said Land to a Corner Bounded Hickarie of the said Simon paling and from thence West South West One hundred and fifty perches to a red oake Corner head bound of the said Paling his land intersecting with the land of Anthony Heaverla then North North West Sixty perches binding on the said Land to a marked Hickarie and from thence East North East with a line of marked trees six hundred and fourty perches a little distance in the Marsh which doth adjoyn to the Land and from thence South South East three hundred and twenty perches binding on the said Marsh to the first bounded red oake and the Islands extending Eastwards from the Lands in the Marsh being in quantity of sixty and fower acres thereunto Included Containing and laid out to Gather for Eleven hundred Acres of Land.

June ye 16th A. 1681. Cornelis Verhoofe, Surveyor.

At a Court held at Deale by the Kings Authority the 14th Feb. 1681, the above Survey is Certified by the Court to be great part thereof Seated and pattoned by Thomas and night Howard and have been for five or six years last past, which the Court alloweth not of.

Luke Wattson.

(101)

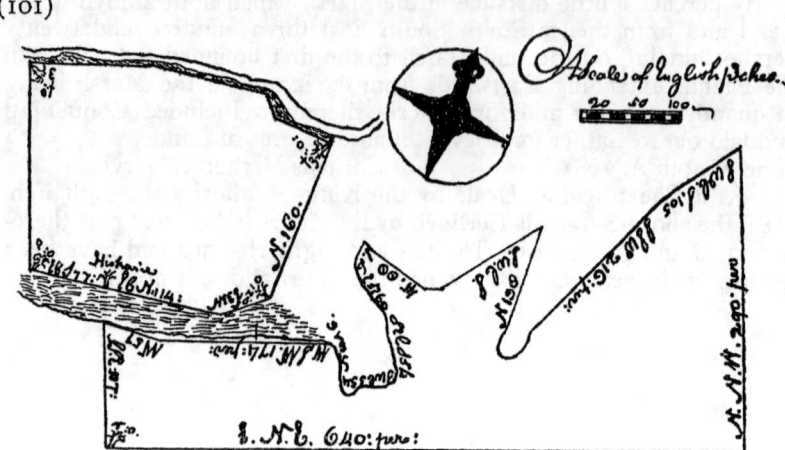

By vertue of a warr. from the Whorekill alias Deale Court.

    Laid out for Capt. Nathaniel Walker a parcell of land called Walkers Choyse situated on the west side of Delaware Bay and on the South side of a Creeke called priume hooke Creeke part upon a neck Comanly called winders neck and part upon another neck Comanly called Daniell Hust his neck beginning at a Corner marked red oake standing in the line of Antoney Heaverla his land and running from thence East North East Six hundred and fourty perches with a line of marked trees binding on the land of Capt. Nathaniell Walker which he purchased from Capt. John Winder into the edge of the Bay Marshes at the same bounded place of the said purchased land and from thence North North west two hundred and ninety perches binding on the said marshes to a point near Priume hooke Creeke and from thence with the several Courses binding part on the said priume hooke Creekes marshes and part on another little Creekes marshes One thousand Sixty and three perches to an opposite Hickarie Standing on the North side of a beaverdam, and from thence East by North One hundred and fourteen perches binding on the said Beaverdam then North East by East fifty perches binding Dito to a marked red oake standing on a point by the marshes of the said little Creeke and from thence North One hundred and sixty perches binding on the said marshes to a marked white oake standing on a point by the marshes of Priume hooke Creeke and from thence with the several Courses binding on the said Creeke and marshes to a marked white oake Standing on the marshes side near a branch and from thence South South East with a line of marked trees two hundred perches to a marked red oake standing on the aforesaid Beaverdam and from thence East by North Seaventy and seaven perches binding on the said beaverdam to the aforesaid marked Hickarie and from thence opposite South South East with a line of marked trees binding on the said land of Antoney

Heaverla One hundred and seaventeen perches to the first bounded red oake Containing and laid out for One thousand acres of Land. June 17th A. 1681. Cornelis Verhoofe Surveyor.

At a Court held at Deale the 14th Feb. 1681, by the Kings Authority the above Survey is Certified to be in part Seated.

Luke Wattson.

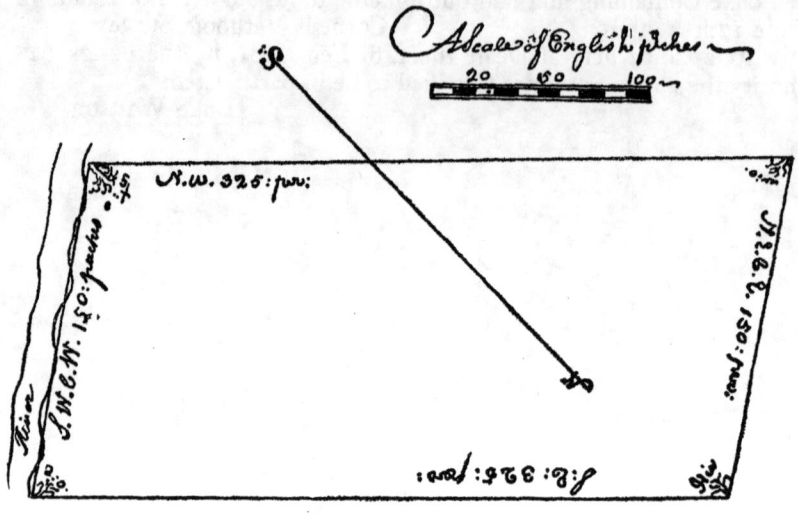

By Vertue of a Warr. from Deale alias Whore kill Court

Laid out for William Caning Junior a parcell of Land called   and Situated on the west side of Delaware Bay & on the North side of the South River formerly called the Indian River Beginning at a marked red oake standing by a point of Marsh and a Valley on the River side and running from thence South West by West One hundred and fifety perches binding on the said River to a marked white Oake standing on the Rivers side and from thence North West with a line of marked trees three hundred twenty and five perches to a marked white Oake standing in the Woods and from thence with a line of marked trees North East by East One hundred and fifety perches to a marked Hickarie standing in the woods and from thence South East with a line of marked trees three hundred twenty and five perches to the first Bounded red oake Containing and laid out for Three hundred acres of Land.

Surveyed September ye 6th A. 1681.

Cornelis Verhoofe Surveyor.

At a Court held for the Towne and County of Deale by the Kings Authority the 14th & 15th days of March 1682-81 the above Survey is Certified by the Court that the said Land is not as yet seated.

Luke Wattson.

(103)

By Vertue of a Warr. from Deale alias Whore kill Court.

Laid out for Edward Southrin a parcell of Land called Heilderness Situated on the west side of Delaware Bay and on the North side of the South River formerly called the Indian River Beginning at a Red oake bounded tree of William Caning Junior standing by a point of marsh and a Valley on the Rivers side and running from thence Northwest three hundred twenty and five perches binding on the line of marked trees of the said William Caning his Land to his head bounded Hickarie—Standing in the woods and from thence north East by East with a line of marked trees One hundred Eighty and two perches to a marked red oake standing in the woods and from thence South East with a line of marked trees two hundred and Eighty perches to the head of a branch of a Creeke called Southrins Creeke and then South East by South binding on the said Creeke two hundred and fower perches to a marked white oake standing at the mouth of the said Creeke and from thence by———severall Courses hundred fifety and fower perches binding on the South River to the first bounded red oake Containing and laid out for fower hundred acres of Land.

Surveyed September the 7th A. 1681.

Cornelis Verhoofe Surveyor.

At a Court held at Deale for the towne and County of Deale by the Kings Authority the 14th & 15th days of March 1682-81 the Survey is Certified by the Court that it is not as yet Seated.

Luke Wattson.

(104)

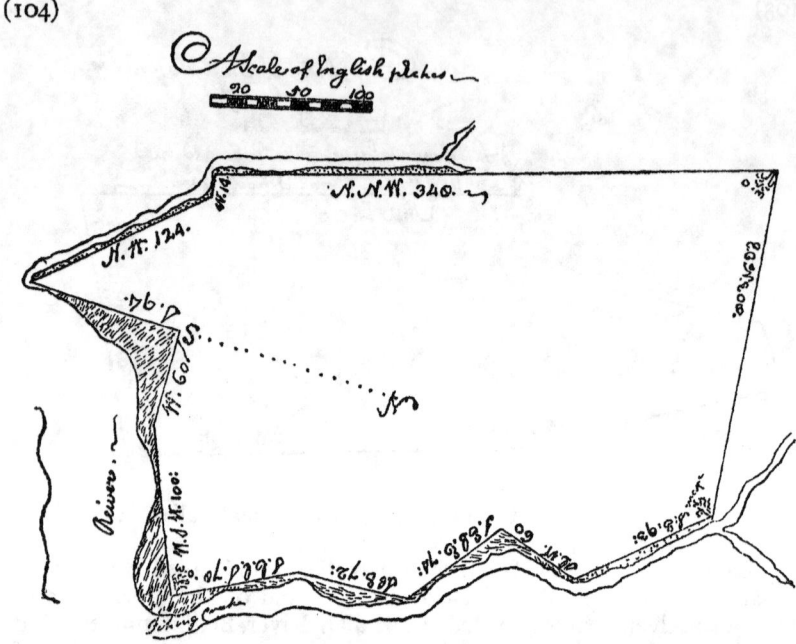

By vertue of a warr. from Deale Court.

Laid out for Richard Stephens a parcell of Land called Hopewell Situated on the west side of Delaware Bay and on the North side of a River called the South River formerly called the Indian River Beginning at a marked white oake standing at a point by the mouth of a Creeke called fishing Creeke and on the marshes of the said River and running from thence with the several Courses three hundred ninety and two perches binding on the said Marshes to a branch & from thence North North West binding on the said Branch One hundred and sixty perches to the head of the said branch then dito Course North North West with a line of marked trees One hundred Eighty and eight perches to a marked white oake standing in the Woods and from thence East by North with a line of marked trees two hundred and Eighty perches to a marked Maple tree standing on the branch of the aforesaid fishing Creeke and from thence with the Several Courses part binding on the said branch and marshes of the said Creeke three hundred Seaventy and Seaven perches to the first bounded white oake Containing and laid out for five hundred and fifty acres of Land. Surveyed Septem. ye 8th A. 1681.

Cornelis Verhoofe Surveyor.

At a Court held at Deale for the Town and County of Deale by the Kings Authority the 14th & 15th days of March 1682-81; the above Survey is Certified by the Court that it is not as yet seated.

Luke Wattson.

(105)

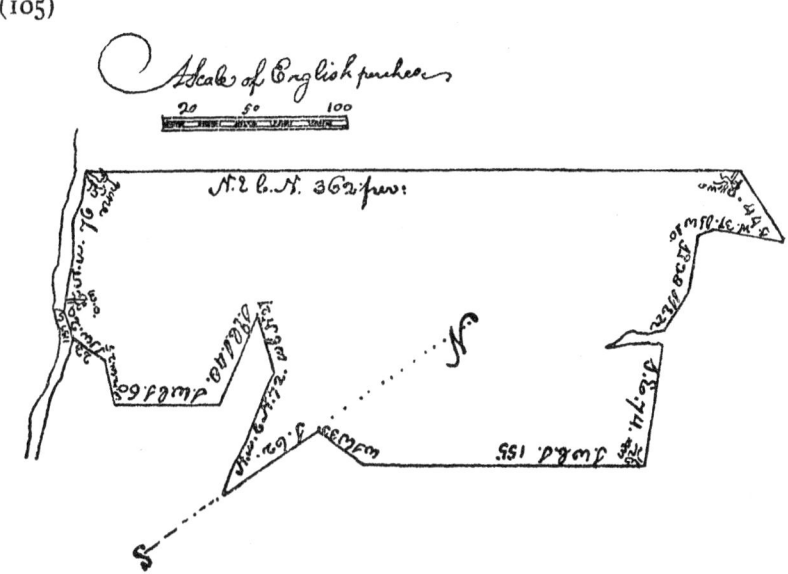

By vertue of a warr. from Deale alias Whore kill Court.

Laid out for George Young a parcell of Land called Luck by chance situated on the west side of Delaware Bay and on the North East side of a Creeke Called fishing Creeke proceeding from the South alias Indian River Beginning at a marked white oake standing on the marshes of the said Creek and running from thence Northwest Seaventy perches binding on the said Creeke to a marked pine standing by the marsh of the said Creeke and from thence North East by North three hundred Sixty and two perches with a line of marked trees to a marked white Oake standing by a Glade of Marsh proceeding from the middle Creeke of Rehobah bay and from thence with severall Courses One hundred Sixty and one perches binding on the said marsh and a branch then South East with a line of marked trees seaventy and fower perches to a marked red oake standing in the Woods and from thence South west by South with a line of marked trees One hundred fifty and five perches Intersecting with the marshes from the said River and Creeke and then with the severall Courses binding on the said Marshes three hundred sixty and nine perches to the first bounded white Oake Containing and laid out for three hundred acres of Land.

Surveyed Septem'r ye 9th A. 1681.

Cornelis Verhoofe Surveyor.

At a Court held for the Towne and County of Deale by the Kings Authority the 14th & 15th days of March 1682-01, the above Survey is Certified by the Court that the s'd Land is not as yet Seated.

Luke Wattson.

(106)

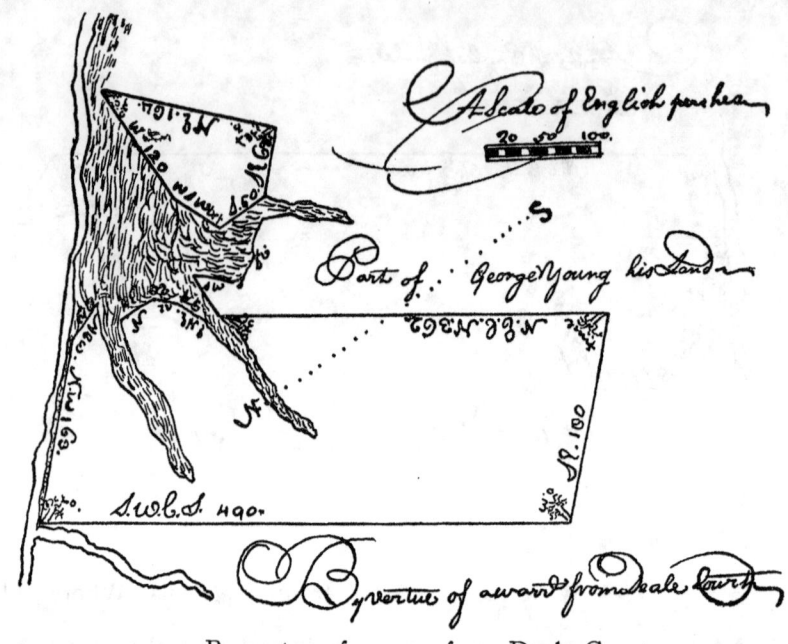

By vertue of a warr. from Deale Court.

Laid out for Thomas Golledge and John Golledge a parcell of Land Called   situated on the west side of Delaware Bay and on the South west side of a Creeke called middle Creeke Beginning at a marked white Oake standing at the mouth of a Creeke called Harring Creeke alias Gould Smiths Creeke and running from thence South west by South with a line of marked trees fower hundred and ninety perches to a marked white Oake standing by a Creekes side Called fishing Creeke and from thence South East One hundred and Eighty perches binding on the said marshes of the said Creeke to a bounded pine of George Young standing on the marshes of the said Creeke and from thence North East by North binding on the line of marked trees of the said George Young to his bounded white oake standing by the marshes which proceeding from the said middle Creeke of Rehobah Bay then from the branch South East binding part upon the marked head line of George Young to a bounded white Oake standing in the said head-line and from thence North East with a line of marked trees One hundred Sixty and fower perches to a marked white Oake standing near the said marshes and from thence with the severall Courses fower hundred ninety and seaven perches binding on the marshes of the said middle Creeke to the first bounded white Oake Containing and laid out for Six hundred acres of Land.

Surveyed the 10th of Septem'r A. 1681.

         Cornelis Verhoofe Surveyor.

At a Court held at Deale the 14th & 15th days of March 1682-81 by the Kings Authority; the above Survey is Certified by the Court that the said Land is not as yet Seated

Luke Wattson.

(107)
Edmund Andros, Esq'r Whereas there is a certain tract of land called St. Augustine lying on the West side of Delaware River on the North side of Apoquemini Creek opposite to the lower end of Reed Island. The which by Vertue of a warrant hath been laid our for Augustine Hermans the said land being bounded on the East with the said River; on the South with Apoquemini Creeke and the land of Dirck Williamson & Dirck Lawrenson & also with the land of Claes Kireton on the North with a small Ckeeke called St. Augustines Creek dividing this from a Tract or parcell of Land granted to Mr. Peter Alricks, and on the West with the main Woods Conteying & layd out for four hundred Acres of land, with the Marshes thereunto belonging, as by the returne of the Survey brought in by the Surveyor doth and may appear. Now for Confirmation &c Quitt Rent four Bushell dated the   day of   Anno Dominie 167
Examined, Q. R., 4 bushells.
Augustin Harmans.
Book of Delaware Grants
Unbound No. 1. fo. 1

Edmund Andros Esq'r Whereas there is a certain parcell or Tract of Land lying upon the Whor Kill the which by virtue of a warrant hath been layd out for Alexander Molestody beginning at a black Wallnut Post running from thence one the said Kill, for breath standing on the point of a Marsh Two hundred Perches South East and from thence with a line South west, binding upon Abraham Clemence, To a great poplar, standing upon a branch of paganes Creeke foure hundred & eighty nine perches, and from thence upon the said branch North west, to a certaine hickory, standing upon the said branch two hundred perches and from thence with a line North East down to the afores'd black Wallnutt Post, standing upon the Whore Kill four hundred and eighty nine perches Containing and layd out for six hundred and eleven acres of land as by return of the survey under the hand the Survey'r doth and may appear. Now know yee &c Quitt Rent six Bushell. dated the   day of   Anno Domini: 167
Examined Q. R. 6 bushell.
Alex. Molestody
fo 1.

Edmund Andros Esq'r Whereas there is a certain parcell or Tract of Called Tower hill lying upon pagans Creeke neare the Whor Kill, the w'ch by virtue of a Warrant hath been layd out for Daniell Browne, being bounded as followeth (viz) beginning at a bounded white Oake Standing Upon the fores'd Creeke running up the s'd Creeke for breath South east & by South, two hundred Perches

to a great poplar standing upon the s'd Creek, And from thence with a line South West and by West parting Edward Southeron and keup to a certain w't Oake Standing by a beaver dam Three hundred and twenty Perches & from thence North west and by North, down the said beaver dam (108) to a bounded red Oake Two hundred perches binding upon the Beaver dam, and from the s'd red Oake with a line of marked trees running North east and by east down to the first bounded white Oake standing upon the fores'd pagans Creeke, Three hundred and twenty perches, Containing and layd out for four hundred Acres as by the return of the Survey under the hand of Cap't Edmond Cantwell doth and may appeare   Now know yee. &c Quitt Rent: four Bushell Dated the   day of   Anno Domini 167
Examined Q. R. 4 bushell.
Daniel Brown.
Fo 2.

 Edmund Andros Esq'r Whereas there is a certaine parcelle or Tract of land on the west side of Delaware Bay and on the South west side of a Creeke called Bancom brig Creeke the which by vertue of a warrant hath been layd out for Sam'll Barbary, being bounded as followeth (viz) beginning at a bounded red Oake by the by y'e Creeke, & running up the Creeke South three hundred and twenty perches, then by a line west one hundred perches, & by a line North three hundred and twenty Perches to abounded Poplar Then by aline drawn East one hundred Perches to the first bounded Oake, Containing and layd out for two hundred Acres as by return of the Survey under the hand of the Survey doth and may   Now know yee: Quitt Rent: 2 Bushells dated the   day of   Anno Domini
Examined Q. Rent 2 bush.
Sam'll Barbary
Fo 3.

 Edmund Andros Esq'r Whereas there is a certain parcell or tract of Land called Would have more, one the west side of Delaware Bay, and on the North side of a Creeke of the said Bay Called Duck Creeke, in the middle branch of the said Creeke, the which by virtue of a warrant hath been layd out for John Woodhus, the said Land beginning at abounded Oake by the Creeke & running west up the Creeke two hundred Perches, then by a line North three hundred and twenty perches then East two Hundred Perches, and by a line South three hundred and twenty Perches to the first bounded Oake Containing and layd out for four hundred Acres of land as by returne (109) of the survey under the hand of the Survey'r doth and may appear.   Now know yee &c Quitt Rent 4 Bus. date the day of   Anno Domini 1676.
Ex'd. Q Rent 4 bush.
John Woodhus
Fo 4.

 Edmund Andros Esq'r Whereas there is a certain tract of land called Lester on the west side of Delaware bay & on the North side of a

Creeke of the said bay called Duck Creeke, in the middle branch of the said Creeke, the which by vertue of awarrant hath been layd out for Morris Lester the said land beginning att abounded Oake being the uppermost tree of John Woodhus and running west up the Creeke two hundred Perches to a bounded white Oake by the Creeke and by a marsh, then by aline North three hundred and twenty Perches, then East Two hundred Perches & by aline South three hundred and twenty perches to the first bounded Oake Containing and lay'd out for four hundred Acres more or less as by returne of the Survey doth and may appear under the of the Surveyor. Now know yee Quitt Rent four Bushell Dated the day of   Anno Domini 1676
Ex'd Q Rent 4 bush
Morris Lester
Fo 4.

Edmund Andros Esq'r Whereas there is a certaine Tract of land on the west side of Delaware bay and on the North west side of a Creeke of the said bay called Blackbird Creeke, the which by vertue of a warrant hath been layd out for Percifell Woodersell, Jno. Barker John Street, James & Edward Williams the said land beginning, at a bounded White Oake by a small branch, and running South West up the Creeke Six hundred Perches, to a bounded Oake by the Creeke, & by aline North West three hundred and twenty Perches then by line North East Six hundred Perches, then South East three & twenty Perches to the first bounded Oake, Containing and layd out for twelve hundred Acres of land as by the returne of the Survey under the Surveyor doth and may appear   Now know yee &c   Quitt Rent   12 Bushell, dated the   day of   Anno Domini 167
Ex'd Q. R. 12 bushells.
Percifell Woodersell & Company
Fo. 5.

(110)
Edmund Andros Esq'r Whereas there is a certaine tract of land Called Whitehall on the west side of Delaware bay, and on the North East side of a branch of a Creeke, up the said bay called Duck Creeke, the which by vertue of a warrant hath been layd out Francis Whittwell the s'd land beginning at a marked white Oake being the first bounded tree of the land laid out for Nicholas Bartlet Running East down the Creeke two hundred Perches, to a marked Pohickory by the Creeke side then binding by the Creeke and marsh North three hundred and twenty Perches, then West two hundred Perches to the land of the s'd Bartlett, and by his land three hundred and twenty Perches to the first bounded Oake Containing and layd out for four hundred Acres of land, as by returne of the Survey under the hand of Cap't. Edmund Cantwell doth and may appear, with all the Marsh thereunto adjoining. Now know yee &c. Quitt rent four Bushells dated the day of Anno Domini. 167
Ex'd Q. R. 4 bushell
Francis Whitney.
Fo. 6.

Edmund Andros, Esq., Whereas there is a certaine parcell of land called Palmore on the west side of Delaware Bay, and on the South side of a Creeke of the sd bay Called Duck Creeke the which by vertue of a warrant hath been layd out for Henry Palmer the sd land beginning at amarked white Oake by a branch of the sd Creeke called muddy branch running down the branch two hundred Perches, to amarked Oake, then by a line drawn South three hundred and twenty Perches, then by a line west, two hundred Perches, then by a line North three hundred and twenty perches, to the first bounded Oake Containing and layd out for four hundred Acres of land, as by returne of the Survey under the hand of Capt Enmond Cantwell the Surveyor doth and may appear. Now know yee &c. Quitt Rent four Bushells. Dated the day of   Anno Domini 167

Ex'd Q. R. 4 bushell.
Henry Palmer,
Fo. 7.

(111)
Edmund Andros Esq. Whereas there is a certaine tract of land Called Diason on the west side of Delaware bay, and on the North side of a Creek Called Drayer's Creeke the which by vertue of a warrant hath been layd out for Bryan Omella, the sd land beginning at a bounded Peckikory being the bounded tree of the land formerly laid out for Claus Cassen running north northeast three hundred and twenty Perches by the land of the said Cassen, then West North West one hundred Perches, then by a line drawn South South west three hundred and twenty Perches, to the Creek, and by the Creek, one hundred perches to the first bounded Peckikry, Containing and layd out for two hundred Acres, be it more or less, as by returne of the Survey, under the hand of Capt. Edmund Cantwell doth and may appear. Now know yee &c. Quitt rent two Bushells, dated the   day of Anno Domini 167

Ex'd Q. R. 2 bush.
Bryan Omella
Fo. 7.

Edmund Andros Esqr. Whereas there is a certain Lot of ground below the fort at Newcastle upon Delaware the which by Vertue of a warrant hath been layd out for James Wallem the boundaries being as followeth, bounded upon the South East with the river on the west with the common on the North East with a small Creeke, Containing in breadth sixty foot and length three hundred foot allowing a pathway from the Towne dike that leads into the towne the same to be excepted Bee it more or less as by returne of the Survey under the hand of the Surveyor doth and may appeare &c. Now know yee and dated the day of   Anno Domini   167.

Ex'd Q. R.
James Wallem
Fo 8.

Edmund Andros Esqr. Whereas there is a certaine Parcell of Land called Salsberry Plaine, lying on the western side of Delaware River, in St. George's Neck the which by vertue of a warrant hath been layd for Evan Salisbury, the sd land beginning at a marked wt. Oake Standing upon (112) a point of a Beaver Dam, & running North one hundred and and fifty Perches, to a marked Pokickry Standing upon a poynt by a Swamp side, and from the said tree with a line drawn West three hundred and twenty Perches, for length into the wood, and from the end of the sd line with a line drawn South one hundred and fifety Perches & from thence East Three Hundred and twenty perches to three first bounded tree, Containing and layd for three hundred Acres of land More or less, as by the returne of the Survey under the hand of Capt. Edmund Cantwell the Surveyor doth and may appear. Now know yee Quitt Rent three bushells Dated the   day of Anno Donimi 167.

Ex'd Q. R. 3 bushells
Evan Salisbury
Fo 9.

Edmund Andros Esqr. Whereas there is a certaine a tract of land called Jackson's Neck, on the west side of Delaware Bay, and on the South side of a Creeke of the sd bay called Cedar Creeke the which by vertue of a warrant hath been layd out for John Ashman and Sammuel Jackson the sd land begining at a bounded Poplar by a branch running North West one hundred and fifty Perches, to a bounded red Oake by a small branch, then by a line South west three hundred and twenty Perches, into the woods, then by a line South East, one hundred and fifty Perches, and by a line drawn North East three hundred and twenty Perches, to the first bounded Poplar Containing and layd out for three hundred Acres of Land as by returne of the Survey under the hand Capt. Edmund Cantwell the Surveyor doth and may appear. Now know yee & Quitt rent three bushells. Date the   day of Anno Domini 167.

Ex'd Q. R. 3 bushells
John Ashman
Fo 10.

Edmund Andros Esqr. Whereas there is a certaine tract of land on the west side of Delaware Bay and on the Southwest of a Creeke of the sd bay called Banksum brigs Creeke, the which by Vertue of a warrant hath been layd out for W. Troth the said land beginning at a (113) marked red Oake by the Creeke, Running down the Creeke North one hundred Perches to another bounded Oake, then by a line drawn west Three hundred & twenty Perches then South one hundred Perches, then by a line East three hundred and twenty Perches to the first bounded Oake Containing and layd out for two hundred Acres as by return of the Survey under the hand of Capt. Edmund Cantwell the

Surveyor doth and May appeare. Now know yee &c. Quitt rent two
bushells dated the   day of   Anno Domini 167.
Ex'd Q. R. 2 bushells
Willm Troth.
Fo 11.

    Edmund Andros Esqr. Whereas there is a certaine Parcell of Land called Swandall on the west side of Delaware bay & on the northwest of a Creeke of the bay called black bird Creeke the which by vertue of a warrant hath been layd out for Edward Swandall the said land begining at a red Oake by a small branch running South west by the Creeke one hundred Perches then by a line drawn North west, three hundred and twenty Perches, then by a line North East one hundred Perches, then by a line South East three hundred and twenty perches, to the first bounded Oake, Containing and layd out for two hundred Acres of land as by return of the Survey under the hand of Capt. Edmund Cantwell the Surveyor doth and may appear. Now know yee &c. Quitt rent two Bushells, dated the   day of   Anno Domini
Ex'd Q. Rent 2 bushells
Edward Swandall.
Fo 11.

    Edmund Andros Esqr. Whereas there is a certaine Tract of land called Ashmore on the west side of Delaware bay & on the South side of a Creeke called Cedar Creeke, the which by vertue of a warrant hath been laid out for John Ashman & Samll Jackson the sd land begining at a bounded Red Oake, by the river runing west North west, for breadth up the Creeke, one hundred and fifety perches, to a bounded white Oake, by a branch, then South South West for breadth one hundred one hundred and sixty Perches, then West North west one hundred Perches to a bounded white Oake by a small branch, then South South West, one hundred and Sixty perches then by a line South East Two hundred and fifety Perches, then by a line North North (114) West, three hundred and twenty Perches, to the first bounded red Oake Containing and layd out for foure hundred Acres, with the marshes thereunto belonging as by returne of the Survey under the hand of Captain Edmund Cantwell the Surveyor doth and may appear. Now know yee &c. Quitt Rent foure bushells dated the   day of Anno Domini 167
Ex'd Q. R. 4 bushells
John Ashman
Samll Jackson
Fo 12

    Edmund Andros Esq. &c. Whereas there is certaine Tract of land Called Maulbery on the west side of Delaware bay & on the South east side of a Creeke of the said bay Called black bird Creeke, the which by vertue of a warrant hath been layd out for Robt Tallant, the said land begining att a bounded Spanish Oake, att the head of a branch of the said Creeke, runing down the branch Northwest fifety Perches, to the Creeke, then North one hundred Perches, to a marked Oake then East three hundred and twenty Perches to a bounded Oake in the Woods, then South one hundred Perches, then North west two hundred and Seventy Perches to the first bounded Spanish Oake, Containing and layd out for two hundred Acres of land as by returne of the Survey under the hand of the Surveyor doth and may appear. Now know yee &c. Quitt rent 2 bushell dated the   day of   Anno Domini

Ex'd Q. R. 2 bushells
Robt Tallant
Fo 13

Edmund Andros Esqr. &c. Whereas there is a certaine parcell of land called Maidestone lying on the westerne side of Delaware River and the first divideing of St. George's Creeke, the which by vertue of a warrant hath been layd out for John Scott, the sd land begining at a marked Oake standing upon the poynt of the forke and running with the Northwest Branch Twenty five Perches to a marked pokickery tree standing upon a knowle by the branchside, and from the said tree with a line drawn up ye sd branch Four hundred & eighty Perches, west north west, to another marked Oake and binding with the sd branch and from thence runing (115) cross the neck South South west Two hundred perches to another branch of the Creek binding with the sd branch it being the South west branch of the Creeke & downe the sd branch Four hundred and eighty perches to a marked white Oake standing by the branch side & from thence binding with the branch to ye first marked red Oake Containing and layd out for four hundred acres of land as by return of the Survey under the hand of Capt. Edmund Cantwell the Surveyor doth and may appear. Now know yee &c. Quitt rent four bushells dated the   day of   Anno Domini 167

Ex'd Q. R. 4 bushells
John Scott
Fo 14.

Edmund Andros Esqr. Whereas there is a certaine Tract of Land Called the Partnership, lying on the westerne side of Delaware River, inn St. George's Neck on the North side of the Dragon Swamp, ye which by vertue of a warrant hath been layd for William Currer & William Goldsmith, the sd land begining at a marked Oake standing by the River side upon a poynt, being a bounded tree of the land of Henry Ward, and runing Southwest One hundred and sixty perches to a marked Oake of the sd Henry Ward standing by a branch of the Draggon Swamp and from thence Forty perches binding with the sd Branch, to a marked white Oake Standing by the Draggon Swamp, Then with a line drawn west and by north binding with the Draggon Swamp, for ye length of three Hundred and twenty perches to a marked red Oake Standing at the head of branch of the sd Swamp, then with a line drawn North East three and twenty Perches, to a marked white

Oake Standing at ye head of a Beaver dam, then by a line drawn South East binding with the sd beaver dam, to the first bounded tree, Containing and layd out for Six hundred Acres of land, as by return of the Survey under ye hand of ye Surveyor doth and may appeare. Now know yee &c. Quitt rent six bushells, dated the   day of   Anno Domini 167
Ex'd Q. R. 6 bushells
William Currer &
William Goldsmith
Fo 15.

(116)
  Edmund Andros Esqr. Whereas there is a certaine parcell of land called Brooksbay, lying on the west side of Delaware bay, and on the west side of the Southermost branch of a Creeke Called Duck Creeke, & in a little branch running somewhat Easterly, into a lake which makes out into severall Branches, the which by vertue of a warrant hath been layd out for Francis Whittwell the said land begining upon a long poynt, runing into the marsh pretty near the Creeke at a marked Plum tree & runing South for breadth, one hundred Perches, to a marked hickory Standing on the south side of the Poynt by the marsh then west six hundred and forty Perarches, then north one hundred Perches then east six hundred and forty Pearches to the first named tree with all the Marshes thereunto appeartaining Containing and layd out for four hundred Acres of land as by returne of the Survey under the hand of the Surveyor doth and may appear. Now know yee &c. Quitt rent four bushells dated the   day of   Anno Domini 167
Ex'd Q. R. 4 bushells
Francis Whitwell
Fo 16.

  Edmund Andros Esqr. Whereas as there is a certaine tract of land Called Petty France on the west side of Delaware bay and on the North East side of a branch of a Creek of the sd bay Called Duck Crceke the which by vertue of a warrant hath been layd out for Nicholas Bartlett the sayd land begining at a marked white Oake Runing west up the Creeke two hundred Perches to a marked Poplar on the South west with a line drawne North Three hundred and Twenty Perches, then with a line drawn East, two hundred perches to a marked red Oake then South two hundred and twenty Perches to the first bounded Oake with the Marsh thereto adjoyning, Containing and layd out for four hundred acres of land as by returne of the Survey under the hand of Capt. Edmund Cantwell the Surveyor doth (117) and may appear Now know yee &c. Quit Rent four bushells dated the   day of   Anno Domini. 167
Ex'd Q. R. 4 bushells
Nicholas Bartlett
Fo 17.

  Edmund Andros Esqr. Whereas there is a certaine tract of land lying on the Westerne side of Delaware River next adjoyning to the

land of Evan Salisbury in St. George's Neck the said land begining at a bounded Pokickery standing in the west line of the sd. Evan Salisbury, & running for breadth from the sd. tree North, two hundred & fifty Perches to a marked Oake, & from the sd. Oake by a line Drawn west Three hundred & twenty Perches, for length to another marked Oake, & from the sd. Oake with a line drawn south Two hundred and Fifety perches to another mark'd Oake then East three hundred and twenty perches to the first bounded Pokickery, containing and layd out for five hundred acres of land more or less as by returne Survey under the hand of Capt. Edmund Cantwell the Surveyor doth and may appear. Now know yee &c. Quitt rent five Bushells dated the   day of   Anno Domini
Which by vertue of a warrant
hath been layd out for John
Pitt of Maryland.
Ex'd Q. R. 5 bushells
John Pitt.
Fo 18.

Edmund Andros Esqr. &c. Whereas there is a certaine tract of land called St. Martins lying upon Paganes Creeke the which by vertue of a warrant hath been layd out for Edward Southeron the sd. land begining at a bounded Poplar Standing by the point of a small marsh running up the sd. Creeke, for breadth South East & by South Two hundred Perches, to a bounded hickory Standing upon the sd. Creek by a small Marsh from thence up the sd. Marsh South west & by west Three hundred and Twenty Perches to another bounded hickory Standing in the Woods, and from thence North west & by North to a bounded white Oake, Standing by a beaver dam Two hundred Perches, & from thence North East & by East by a line of marked trees binding upon Daniell Browns (118) down to the first bounded Poplar Standing by a Pagans Creeke three and twenty Perches, Containing and layd out for four hundred acres of land as by returne of the Survey under the hand of Capt. Edmund Cantwell the Surveyor doth and may appear. Now know yee &c. Quit rent four bushells. Dated the day of   Anno Domini: 167
Ex'd Q. R. 4 bushells
Edward Southeron
Fo 19.

Edmund Andros Esqr. &c. Whereas there is a certaine Tract of land Called Youngshope lying and being upon the Whore kill, The which by vertue of a Warrant hath been layd for George Young the sd. land begining at a small marsh, & Runing up the kill for breadth South East One hundred & fifety perches to a bounded white Oake, and from thence southwest three hundred and twenty Perches, to a bounded red Oake, Standing in the Woods, and from thence with a line of marked trees, running North West two a black wallnut standing by the foresaid Marsh One hundred and fifty Perches bounded upon the Woods, and from thence down the said Marsh to the aforesaid point North East Three hundred & 20 Perches: Containing and layd out for three hundred acres as by returne of the Survey under the hand of Capt. Edmund Cantwell the Surveyor, doth and may appear. Now know yee &c. Quitt rent three Bushells. Dated the   day of   Anno Domini

Ex'd Q. R. 3 bushells
George Young.
Fo 20.

Edmund Andros Esqr. Whereas there is a certaine Tract of land called Locust Neck lying near and upon Rehobath Creeke, the which vertue of a warrant hath been layd out for Henry Peddington the sd. land begining at a bounded pine, Standing by the point of a marsh runing, and bounding up the Said Creeke for breadth west two hundred perches (119) to a bounded Cedar, standing by the side of a Swamp from thence runing and bounding upon the sd. Swamp, North three hundred and twenty Perches to a bounded red Oake, and from thence east by a line of marked trees bound upon the Wood Two hundred Perches, to a bounded hickory standing by the foresaid Marsh, and from thence runing and bounding upon the said Marsh, south three hundred and twenty Perches down to the first bounded Pine Standing upon the point by the Creeke Containing and layd out for foure hundred acres of land as by returne of the Survey under the hand of Capt. Edmund Cantwell the Surveyor doth and may appear. Now know yee & Quitt rent foure bushells, dated the   day of Anno Domini: 167

Ex'd Q. R. 4 bushells
Henry Peddington
Fo 21.

Edmund Andros Esqr. Whereas there is a certaine tract of land lying and being upon, the which was formerly Peter Aldricks, the which by vertue of a warrant hath been layd out for Mr. Wm Tom, the said land begining at a bounded white Oake standing by the killside and from thence South East, runing and bounding upon the kill sixty six Perches to a bounded hickory standing by the sd. kill, from thence by a line of marked trees, South West, to a bounded Red Oake standing by the side of Pagans Creeke Three hundred and twenty perches, bounded upon Hermanus Woolbanck from thence downe the said Creeke north west sixty six perches, to another bounded red Oake and from thence North East by a line of marked trees downe to the first bounded white Oake standing upon the whore kill, Three hundred and twenty Perches bounded upon Alexander Molestody land, Containing and laid out for one hundred thirty and two acres of land as by returne of the survey under the hand of the Survey doth and may appear Now know yee &c.: Quitt rent one Bushell ¼: dated the   day of

Ex'd Q. Rent, 1¼ bushells
William Tom.
Fo 22.

(120)
Edmund Andros Esqr. Examined Q. R. 7 bushells. Whereas there is a tract of land scituate on the Westward side of Delaware River about two miles above Verdrieties hook, in a place called the Bought the which by vertue of a warrant hath been layd out for Olie Fransom, Marcus Lawrenson, and Neils Neilson, the sd. land beginning at a Corner marked white Oake standing at the North East side of the mouth of a small Creeke Called Dogg-Creeke, & from the sd. white Oake runing Northwest by a line of marked trees dividing this from the land of Charles Pieterson three hundred & twenty perches to a corner marked white Oake standing nigh unto the head of a branch of a Creeke Called Stony Creeke and from thence runing North East by a line of marked trees three hundred and ninety perches, to another corner marked white Oake, standing the head of a branch (of the bought Creeke) called Poplar branch & from the sd. Oake, runing down the several Courses of ye sd. branch and creeke to the maine River, and finally downe by the River side to ye first mentioned white Oake at the mouth of Dog Creeke containing and layed out for seven hundred acres of land (besides the Swamp & Sunken ground) viz.: three hundred acres (part thereof) being formerly granted, unto Olie Franson Pieter Mouson & Neils Neilson by Patent bearing date the 7th day of April 1673 (since which time Marcus Lawrenson is invested into the right of Pieter Mouson) and the other foure hundred acres being new land: provided always that inhabitants of Verdrietes Hooke shall have and enjoy the freedom and privilege of Stony Creeke & the Mill they have built in the same manner as formerly Now know yee. Quit rent Seven Bushells dated the   day of   Anno Domini 167
Olie Franson & Co.
Fo 23

Edmund Andros Esq. &c. Whereas there is certain lott of ground below the Fort at New Castle upon Delaware the which by vertue of a warrant hath been layed out for Henry Parker, the Boundaries thereof being as followeth, bounded on the South East with the River, on the West with the Common on the northeast with the James Wallems (121) lott Containing in breadth sixty foot and in length three hundred foot, allowing a pathway from Towne dike that leads into the towne the same to be accepted more or less as by returne of the Survey under the hand of the Surveyor doth and may appear, Now known yee &c. dated the   day of   Anno Domini 167.
Examined.
Henry Parker
Fo 24.

Edmund Andros Esq &c Whereas there is a certain Tract of land lying and being upon the Whorekill, the which by vertue of a warrant hath been layd out for John Kephaven the sd land beginning at a Grad post standing by the kill side running up the kill for breadth South East Three Hundred and twenty Perches to abounded black

Walnut Post and from thence by a line of Marked trees running South
west binding upon Alexander Molestedy to a bounded red Oake standing upon paganes Creeke foure hundred & 80 Perches from thence
north west by the said Creeke to another bounded Oake Three hundred and twenty Perches from thence by a line of marked trees downe
to the first Cedar Post, standing upon the Whore kill North East foure
hundred and eighty perches Containing and layd out for sixty and nine
acres as by the return of the Survey under the hand of Capt. Edmund
Cantwell the Surveyor doth and may appear. Now know yee &c Quitt
Rent $\frac{1}{2}$ bushell Dated the   day of
Anno Domini 167 .

John Kephaven
Fo 25.

    Edmund Andros, Esq. &c. Examined Quitt Rent 3 pecks,
Whereas there is a certain tract of land lying and being upon the
Whore Kill near to the mouth of the kill the which by vertue of a war-
rant hath been layd out for Alexander Molestedy the said land begin-
ning a bounded Cedar runing up to the kill for breadth South East
forty perches to a bounded Red Oake standing by the Kill and from
thence South west binding upon Wm Tom Three hundred and twenty
Perches to a bounded Red Oake standing by the (122) side of Paganes
Creeke and from thence North west down the sd. Creeke, forty
Perches to a bounded white Oake Standing by the Creeke from thence
North East binding upon the Woods three hundred and twenty
perches to the first bounded Cedar Standing by the Whore kill Containing and layd out for Eighty Acres of land as by the return of the
Survey under the hand of Capt. Edmund Cantwell the Surveyor doth
and may appear Now know yee &c Quitt Rent 3 pecks dated the
day of   Anno Domini 167

Alexander Molestedy
Fo 26

    Edmund Andros Esq. &c. Examined Q Rent 1 bushell & a peck
Whereas there is a certaine tract of land lying and being upon the
Whore kill, the which by vertue of a Warrant hath been layd out
for Hermanus Woolbanck the said land beginning at a bounded Red
Oake standing by the kill side runing South East up ye kill for breadth
sixty Seven perches to a bounded white Oake Post standing by the hill
or Creeke and from thence South West Three hundred and twenty
Perches to a bounded Hickarie standing upon Paganes Creeke
from thence North West down the said Creeke Sixty seven Perches
to a bounded White Oake and from thence North East to the first
bounded Red Oake standing by the kill three hundred and twenty
Perches Containing and layd out for One hundred 34 acres of land as
by returne of the Survey under the hand of Capt. Edmund Cantwell

doth and may appear Now know yee &c. Quitt rent one bushell one Peck dated the   day of   Anno Domini 167 .
Hermanus Woolbanck
Fo 27
Ex'd & Comp'd
Thos M. Kean

  Edmund Andros Esq &c. Whereas there is a certaine Tract of land called Rich Neck on the West side of Delaware bay and on the North East side of a branch of Duck Creeke called the Middle Branch the which by virtue of a warrant hath been layed out for Stevan Durdene the said land begining at a marked Poplar, being the last bounded tree of Nicholas Bartlett Runing West up the Creeke (123) two hundred Perches to a marked White Oake by a small branch on the South West with a line drawn West Three hundred and twenty Perches, then North two hundred Perches, till it interseates with the land of the said Bartlett, three hundred Perches to the first bounded Poplar, containing and layd out for foure hundred acres of land as by return of the Survey under the hand of Capt. Edmund Cantwell the Surveyor doth and may appear. Now know yee &c. Quitt rent four bushells dated the day of   Anno Domini: 167.
Ex'd Q. R. 4 bushells
Stevan Durdene
Fo 28

  Edmund Andros Esq. &c. Whereas there is a certaine Tract of land Called Walnut Plaine, on the West side of Delaware Bay, and on the South side of a Creeke of the sd Bay Called Duck Creeke the which by virtue of a warrant hath been layd out for Henry Bowen, the said land begining at a mark White Oake by the Creeke Side runing down the Creeke East two hundred Perches, then with a line drawn South three hundred and twenty perches & with a line drawn West two hundred Perches to a marked Oake, then by a line drawn North three hundred and twenty perches to the first bounded Oake, Containing and layd out for foure hundred acres more or lesse with all the marsh thereto adjoyning as by the Return of the Survey under the hand of Cap. Edmund Cantwell the Surveyor, doth and may appeare. Now, know yee, &c. Quitt Rent foure bushells, dated the   day of Anno Domini 167.
Ex'd Q. R. 4 bushells
Henry Bowne
Fo 29

  Edmund Andros Esq. &c. Whereas there is a certaine Tract of land called Mill Bay on the west side of Delaware Bay & on the South side of Creeke called Duck Creeke, the which by virtue of a warrant hath been layd out for Oliver Melinton (124) and George Hartle the sd land begining at a marked White Oake being the bounded tree of Henry Bowen runing south by the land of the said Bowen three hundred and twenty Perches then by a line West two hundred Perches, and by a line drawn North three hundred and twenty perches to the Creeke, and by the Creeke East two hundred Perches to the first bounded Oake Containing and layd out for foure hundred acres of land more or less as by the Return of the Survey under the hand of Capt. Edmund Cantwell Surveyor Doth and may appeare. Now know yee &c. Quitt rent foure bushells, dated the   day of   Anno Domini 167.

Ex'd Q. Rent 4 bushells
Fo 30
Oliver Melinton

    Edmund Andros Esq. &c. Whereas there is a certaine Tract of land Called Poplar Neck on the West side of Delaware bay & on the South East side of a Creeke Called Black Bird Creeke, the which by vertue of a warrant hath been layd out for Thomas Coks, the sd. land beginning at a marked White Oake standing on a Bank by the Water side being the second fast landing above Walter Wharton's plantation, runing up the South South West one hundred and Fifty perches, then by a line Drawne South South East three hundred and twenty Perches then North North west one hundred and fifety Perches, then West North west three hundred and twenty Perches to the first named Oake with all the Marshes thereunto appertaining Containing and now layd out for three hundred acres of land more or less as by return of the Survey under the hand of Capt. Edmund Cantwell doth and may appeare, Now Know yee &c. Quitt Rent 3 bushels dated the   day of Anno Domini 167 .

Ex'd Q. R. 3 bushell
Thomas Cox
Fo 31.

(125)
    Edmund Andros Esq. &c. Whereas there is a centaine Tract of land called Woodases Choice on the west side of Delaware bay & on the South East side of a Creeke of the sd. Bay Called Black Bird Creeke the which by vertue of a warrant hath been layd out for John Woodars the sd. land begining at a marked red Oake by the Creeke and runing downe the Creeke North two hundred Perches to another Red Oake, then by a line drawn east three hundred and twenty Perches to a Cedar Swamp then by a line drawn South to the land of Mr. Walter Wharton two hundred perches and by the sd. Wharton's land three hundred and twenty Perches to the first bounded Oake Containing and layd out for foure hundred acres as by the Return of the Survey under the hand of Capt. Edmund Cantwell, the Surveyor doth and may appeare. Now know yee &c. Quitt rent foure bushells dated the   day of   Anno Domini 167 .

Ex'd Q. Rent 4 bush.
John Woodars
Fo 32.

Edmund Andros Esq. &c. Whereas there is a Tract of land Called South side, on the west side of Delaware bay and on the south side of a Creeke called Drayers creeke the which by vertue of a warrant hath been layd out for Bryan Omella the sd land begining at a marked Oak by the Creeke side runing South one hundred Perches to a bounded Oake in the woods, then by a line west three hundred and twenty Perches to another bounded tree in the Woods, and by a line north one hundred Perches to the Creeke, then by a line brought by the Creeke to the first bounded Oake Containing and layd out for two hundred acres of land more or less as by the returne of the Survey under the hand of Capt. Edmund Cantwell, the Surveyor doth and may appear. Now know yee &c. Quitt rent two bushells dated the day of   Anno Domini.
Ex'd Q. R. 2 bush.
Bryan Omella
Fo 33.

(126)
Edmund Andros Esq. &c. Whereas there is a certain Tract of land called Tower Hill on the west side of Delaware bay and on the South East side of the Creeke called the Black Bird creeke, the which by vertue of a warrant hath been layd out for Thomas Bromall the sd land begining at a marked Oake Standing upon the bank by the water side being the first fast land above Walter Wharton's plantation, runing south south west one hundred and fifty Perches then by a line drawn south south east three hundred and twenty perches then north North west one hundred and fifty Perches then West North west three hundred and 20 Perches to the first named Oake with all the Marshes thereunto appertaining Containing and layd out for three Hundred acres of land as by the returne of the Survey under the hand of Capt. Edmund Cantwell the Surveyor doth and may appeare. Now know yee &c Quitt rent three bushells dated the   day of Anno Domini 167 .
Ex'd Q. R. 3 bushells
Thomas Bromall
Fo 34.

Edmund Andros Esq. &c. Whereas there is a certaine Tract of land called Marrietes Hooke lying and being on the West side of Delaware River the which by vertue of a warrant hath been layd out for Charles Janson Olle Rawson Olle Nielson, Hans Hopman John Hendrickson & Hans Olleson the sd land being bounded as followeth (viz) begining at a small point of high land within the mouth of Naaman's Creeke, and from thence runing North & by West one hundred twenty & three Perches and North two hundred Perches, bounded with the Creek to a corner marked White Oake by the Creeke side at the mouth of a small branch & from thence East and by North, (bounded with the sd Branch & with a line of marked trees from the head of the branch to a corner mark'd Spanish oake (127) standing by a small Run) Three hundred and eight Perches from thence North North East (along the Run) thirty two perches to a corner marked White Oake standing at the side of Marites Creeke at the lower side of the mouth of the sd Run, & from thence downe the several courses of the Creeke to the Maine River side, and from thence downe along the River side to the place of beginning, at the mouth of Naaman's Creeke, containing and layd out for one thousand acres of land, as by the return of the Survey under the Surveyor doth and may appeare Now Know yee &c. Quitt rent ten bushells dated the   day of   Anno Domini.

Ex'd Q. Rent 10 bush.
Charles Jansen & Company
Fo 35.

Edmund Andros Esq. &c.   Exa'd. 5½ bush.   Q. R.   Whereas there is a certaine Tract of land Called Groeningen lying and being on the West side of Delaware River, and on the South East side of St. Augustine's Creeke, the which by vertue of a warrant hath been layd out for Mr. Peter Alricks and sd land begining at a corner marked Black Oake standing on the nearest point of Woodland unto the said Creeke by the River side, and from thence runing North East ninety four Perches North Easterly thirty degrees,—seventy eight Perches North Northeast fifty two Perches North Easerly fifteen degrees, seventy two Perches, North North east eighty six perches and North East and by North one hundred eighty and six perches (bounding upon the main river) unto the mouth of a small sprout or Creeke, called Little St. Georges Creeke which divideth this from the land of Mrs. Ann Waale, and from thence West fourty Perches South West and by West one hundred fifety and three Perches, and North westerly seventy three degrees one hundred fourty and six Perches (bounding upon the said Creeke or Sprout) to Mrs. Waale's line of marked trees crossing the sd Branch and from thence West South West, along the said (128) Mrs. Waale's line of marked trees one hundred fourty and two Perches, to her upper corner tree being a White Oake standing nigh unto the head of a swamp which proceedeth out of the Northern branch of St. Augustine's Creeke and from thence downe along the several Courses of the said branch & Marsh to the first mentioned black Oake Containing and layd out for five hundred and sixty acres of land as by the return of the Survey under the hand of the Surveyor doth and may appeare. Now know yee &c. Quitt rent five bushells and a halfe dated the   day of   Anno Domini 167 .

Peter Alricks
Fo 36

Edmund Andros Esq. &c. Exa'd, Q. R. 1½ bushells.
Whereas there is a certaine small tract of land Called Abrahams delight lying and being on the West side of Delaware river and on the North side of St. Augustine's Creek next adjoining to Peter Alricks, the which by vertue of a warrant hath been layd out for Abraham Enloes, the sd land beginning at a corner marked White Oak Standing on a

point in the first forke of the sd Creeke, and from the said Oake runing North east sixty eight Perches North sixty four perches Northwesterly fifety eight degrees—two hundred twenty and three Perches bounding on the Northern Branche to a corner marked White Oake, standing on a small point between the two head branches of sd Northern branch from thence south and by West by a line of Mark'd trees sixty and two Perches to a corner mark'd White Oak standing at the East side of the head of a Swamp which proceedeth out of the maine branch of St. Augustine's creeke and from thence down the severall Courses of (129) the said Swamp, & Creek to the first mentioned White Oak, Containing the lay'd out for one hundred and seventy acres of land as by the returne of the Survey under the hand of the Surveyor doth and may appear, Now know yee &c. Quitt Rent 1 bushell and a half. dated the day of Anno Domini 167 .
Abraham Enloes
Fo 37.

Edmund Andros Esqr &c. Exam'd. q. Rent 2 Bush.

Whereas there is a certain parcell of land Called Drumers' Neck lying and being on the West side of Delaware river,. & on the North and West side of Appoquemini Creeke, the which by vertue of a warrant hath been laid out for Morris Daniel the said land begining at a Corner marked White Standing on a point by the sd Creeke at the upper side of a branch which at the mouth of thereof divideth this from the land of Bernard Hendrickson, & from the said Oake runing up the branch North Northwest forty perches, & then Northwest by the sd Bernard's line of marked trees, four hundred & Eighty perches to a corner marked Hickory, from thence Southwest by a line of Marked trees sixty perches to a corner marked Red Oake being the upper corner of a parcell of land formerly granted to Jacob Tiaen from thence South east by the said Jacob's line of marked trees four hundred perches into a swamp and then downe the swamp South South East sixty perches to ye aforesaid Creeke, & finally downe along the Creeke to the first mentioned White Oake containing and layd out for one hundred and ninety acres of land as by the returne of the Survey under the hand of the Surveyor, doth and may appeare. Now know yee &c. Quitt Rent 2 Bushell. Dated the day of Anno Domini, 167 .

The sd land having been formerly granted by Patent unto John Bradburn, bearing date June 17th, 1671, & by him diserted.
Maurice Daniel
Fo 38-39.

(130)
Edmund Andros, Esqr. &c. Exa'd. Q. R. 3 Bush.

Whereas there is a certaine tract or parcell of Called the good Neighborhood lying and being on the West side of Delaware River, and on the North East side of St. Augustine's Creek, the which by vertue of a warrant hath been layd out for Casparus Herman the sd land begining at a corner marked Oake Standing on a Point at the Upper side of the mouth of a branch or swamp and from thence runing North by East up the sd Swamp & from the head thereof by a line of marked trees one hundred and fifety perches to the land of George Axton nigh unto a corner marked hickory, standing a little out of the lyne by the head of a small swamp, & from thence West North West, by a line of marked trees three hundred and seventy perches, to a corner marked White Oak, standing on a levell, and from thence South West & by South by a line of marked trees three hundred Perches to a corner marked Maple Standing at the North Side of the Maine branch of St. Augustine's Creek, & from thence down along the sd branch and Creeke, to the first mentioned White Oak, containing and layed out for three hundred and thirty acres of land, as by returne of the Survey and under the hand of the Surveyor, doth and may appear. Now know yee &c. Quitt Rent 3 bushells.　　Dated the　　day of　　Anno Domini.

Casperus Herman
Fo 40.

Edmund Andros, Esqr. &c. Exa'd. Q. R. 2 Bush.

Whereas there is a certaine parcell of land Called Calton lying and being on the West side of Delaware river & on the North side of a branch of Black Bird Creek that divideth this from the sd land, the which by vertue of a warrant hath been laid out for John Barker, the said land beginning at a corner marked Hickory (131) standing at the side of the sd branch by a beaverdam, it being the upper corner tree of John Hartop, & from thence runing North by the sd Hartop's line of marked trees two hundred forty and six perches to a Corner marked White Oake, from thence West by a line of marked trees one hundred and fifety Perches to a Corner marked Gumme Tree standing on the side of a Poquoson from thence South by a line of marked trees two hundred and thirty Perches to a corner marked Maple Standing at the side of the sd branch, & from thence down along the run of the said branch to the first mentioned corner tree containing and layd out for two hundred and twenty acres of land as by return of the Survey under the hand of the Surveyor doth and may appear　Now know yee &c. Quitt Rent 2 bushells　　dated the　　day of　　Anno Domini 167.

John Barker
Fo 41.

Edmund Andros Esqr. Whereas there is a certain parcell of land Called Wandsor situated on the Westward side of Delaware River & on the South side of St. George's Creeke, opposite to Mr. Jacob Young's Plantation, the which by vertue of a warrant hath been layd out for George Moore, being bounded on the East North East with a line of marked trees runing S. S. E. from a corner marked Black Oake being the bounded tree of James Crawford dividing this from the land of the said Crawford on the N. N. W. with the main Creek on the W. S.

W. with a line of marked trees runing (from a corner marked White Oak on a point by the Creek side) S. S. E. three hundred and fourteen Perches to a corner marked Maple standing, in a branch of the Doctor's swamp & on the S. S. E. with the sd Swamp containing and laid out for two hundred and eighty acres with all the marshes thereunto (132) adjoyning, as by returne of the Survey under the hand of the Surveyor doth and may appeare. Now know yee &c. Quitt rent 2 bushells three quarters, dated the   day of   Anno Domini 1676.
Ex'd Q. Rent 2 bushells ¾.
George Moore
Fo 46.

Edmund Andros, Esqr. &c. Whereas there is a tract of land scituate lying and being upon the North side of the great Creeke called Collison's Delight, the which by vertue of a warrant had been layd out for John Collison begining at a marked White Oake, standing by a branch at the Creeke side runing from thence West North West up the sd Creeke to a marked White Oake One Hundred and Two perches and from the said White Oake into the Woods runing North Northeast four hundred and eighty Perches and from thence East South East one hundred and two perches and from thence South South West to ye first bounded White Oake 480 Perches containing and lay'd out for three hundred acres as by the Return of the Survey under the hand of the Surveyor doth and may appear. Now know yee &c. Quitt Rent Three bushell.
Ex'd Q. R. 3 bushells
John Collison
Fo 48

Edmund Andros Esq. &c., Whereas there is a certaine tract of land situate lying and being at the North Side of the Great Creek (called Bernard his hope) the which by vertue of a warrant hath been lay'd out for Charles Bernard begining at a marked Poplar binding upon Thomas Gillye, and Robert Murday runing up the sd Creeke West North West to a marked Red Oake one hundred and two Perches and from thence runing into the Woods North North East 480 Perches, from thence South South East one hundred and two Perches and from thence runing to the first bounded Poplar South South West (133) four hundred and eighty perches containing and laid out for three hundred acres of land as by the return of the Survey under the hand of the Surveyor doth and may appeare. Now know yee Quitt rent three Bushells: dated the   day of Anno Domini, 167 .
Ex'd Q. R. 3 bush
Charles Bernard
Fo 49

Edmund Andros, Esqr. &c. Whereas there is a certain tract of land situate lying and being at the North side of the Great Creek, (called Murdey his Choice & Gilley his lott) the which by vertue of a warrant hath been layd out for Thomas Gilley and Robert Murdey begining at a marked White Oake Binding upon John Collison runing up the said Creeke, west North West to a marked Poplar one hundred fifety and three perches from thence runing into the woods North North East four hundred and eighty perches and from thence South South East one hundred fifety and three Perches and from thence runing South South West to the First bounded White Oake four hundred and eighty Perches containing and layd out for   hundred and fifty acres as by return of the Survey under the h

Ex'd Q R 4½ bush
Thomas Gilley
Fo 49.

Edmund Andros, Esqr. &c., Whereas there is a certain parcell of land called Gad's Delight lying and being on the West side of Delaware Bay upon the head of a smal creek called Gad's Creek, proceeding out of Misspam Creek lying and being at the North of the sd Misspam Creeke, the which by vertue of a warrant hath been layout for Thomas Gadd's begining at a marked White Oake standing by the sd Gadd's Creek, and runing North from the sd White Oake twenty six Perches and from the North East by North Fifety six Perches, from thence North and by East thirty seven Perches and from thence N. N.W. forty Perches to a marked White Oak standing by a branch side and from the sd. White oak up the said branch North two hundred thirty and four (134) perches, from thence South East by East two hundred Perches, from thence South by West two hundred and seventy Perches, from thence West Sixty Perches, and from thence West by South fourty foure Perches unto the first bounded White Oake containing and layd out for three hundred acres as by return of the Survey under the hand of the Surveyor, doth and may appear. Now know yee &c. Quitt rent three bushells dated the   day of   Anno Domini, 167.

Ex'd Q R. 3 bushells
Thomas Gadds
Fo 50

Edmund Andros, Esqr. &c. Whereas there is a certaine tract of land called Little Boulton, lying and being on the West side of Delaware bay upon the south side of a creeke called Cedar Creeke, the which by vertue of a warrant hath been lay'd out for Alexandre Draper, and dred and thirty perches to a marked White Oake standing upon a branch side and running down the said Creek North East three hundred and twenty perches to a marked White Oake standing upon a point by a marshside and from thence South South East four hundred Perches, and from thence South West five hundred and seventy perches, and from thence down the said Branch North five hundred

and fourty six Perches, unto the first bounded white Oake, containing and layd out for nine hundred ninety and six acres, as by the return of the Survey under the hand of the Surveyor doth and may appear, Now know yee &c. Quitt Rent, Ten bushells, Dated the   day of   Anno Domini, 167 .
Ex'd Q R. 10 bushell
Alex. Draper &c
Fo 51.
(135)

Edmund Andros Esqr. &c. Whereas there is a parcell of land on the West side of Delaware bay on the South West side of a creeke called St. Jones Creeke, next to the land formerly layd out for John Johnson the which by vertue of a warrant hath been layd out for Francis Neals begining at a marked red Oake by a branchside runing South W. for breadth two hundred perches, to another marked Oake then N. W. for length three hundred and twenty perches then N. E. Two hundred perches to the Creek, and by the Creeke to the first bounded Oake containing and layd out for four hundred acres of land as by return of the Survey under the hand of the Surveyor doth and may appeare. Now Know yee &c. Quitt rent 4 bushells Dated the   day of Anno Domini, 167.
Ex'd Q. R. 4 bushells
John Johnson.
Fo 52

Edmund Andros Esq. Whereas there is a certaine tract of Land called Black Smith Hall on the Westard side of Delaware river & on the Southward side of St. George's Creeke, toward the Head of a branch that extended itself W. S. W. out of the maine Creeke, the which by vertue of a warrant hath been layd out for Bernard Egberts being bounded on the N. N. W. with the said branch on the E. N. E. with a line of marked trees, dividing this from the land of John Ogleton, the W. S. W. with a line drawne S. S. E. for a Corner marked White Oake, on a low point at the mouth of a small swamp, & on the South South East with the main Woods, containing and layd out for three hundred acres of land, as by return of the Survey under the hand of the Surveyor, doth and may appear. Now know yee &c. Quitt rent three bushell. Dated the   day of   Anno Domini, 167.
Bernard Egberts
Ex'd Q Rent 3 bushells
Fo 53

(136)
Edmund Andros Esqr. &c., Whereas, there is a certaine tract of land called Hampton, scituate on the Westward side of Delaware river & on the   side of St. George's Creek, the which   tue of a warrant hath been lad out for John Ogle being bounded on the   with a branch of the sd Creek n   itselfe W. S. W. out of the sd Creeks

E. N. E. with a line of marked trees S. S. E. dividing this from the land
W. S. W. with a line of marked runing S. S. E. from a corner marked White Oake, at the mouth of a small swamp dividing this from a parcell of land now Surveyed for Bernard Egbert, and on the South South East with the maine woods, containing and layd out for three hundred acres of land as by return of the survey under the hand of the surveyor doth and may appeare. Now know yee &c. Quitt rent, three bushells, dated the   day of   Anno Domini, 167.

Ex'd Q. R. 3
John Ogle
Fo 53

Edmund Andros, Esqr. &c. Whereas there is a certain parcell scituate lying an being on the Westward side of Delaware bay upon the North side of the Great Creeke, called Roaseberry, the which by vertue of a warrant hath been layd out for William Davids, begining at the Red Oake, standing a little below the Indian bridge runing up the said Creeke, West North West to a marked Red Oake, one hundred and two Perches, from thence into the woods North North East four hundred and eighty Perches, from thence East South East, one hundred and two Perches, and from thence South South West to the first bounded Red Oake, four hundred and eighty perches, containing and layd out of three hundred acres of land as by return of the Survey, under the hands of the Surveyor, doth and may appear. Now know yee &c. Quitt rent three bushell, dated the   dayof   Anno Domini, 167.

Ex'd Q R 3 bushells
William Davids
Fo 54

(137)
Edmund Andros, Esqr. &c. Whereas there is a Tract of land scituate lying and being at the North side of Cedar Creek, (called Hart's Delight) the which by vertue of a warrant hath been laid out for Robert Hart begining at a marked White Oake, standing upon a point of a neck by a marsh side, runing from thence into the Marsh to the mane Cedar Creeke, south East by East twenty Perches and from thence South West by West, through the said Marsh to another neck at a marked Red Oake sixty Perches and from thence runing South West by South One hundred and Nine perches, and from thence East twenty Perches from thence South South West fifety three Perches, and from thence West by South One hundred and three Perches, from thence South One Hundred and eighty Perches and from thence North Northwest into the woods four hundred and eighty Perches. And from thence North North east One hundred and twenty perches and from thence East by North Five hundred and twenty perches and from thence South West by west, three hundred and four Perches, and from

thence North East by East three hundred and sixty four perches, to a marked Red Oake, and from the sd Red Oake through the marsh North North east to the first bounded White Oake sixty two perches, containing six hundred acres of land as by the return of the Survey under the hand of the Surveyor doth and may appeare. Now know yee &c. Quitt Rent six Bushell, dated the   day of   Anno Domini, 167.
Ex'd Q. R. 6 bush.
No 2, Fo 3.

Edmund Andros, Esqr. &c., Whereas there is a certain tract of land situate on the westward side of Delaware river on the North side of Verdities hooke, the which by vertue of a warrant hath been layd out for Charles Peterson, (138) beginning at a Corner Red Oake standing by the river side running North & by East along the river 138 Perches or Poles, to a corner White Oake which parts the land of Walle Franson and Company runing Northwest on both sides 320 Perches, Containing and layed out for two hundred sixty six acres of land with all the marshes thereunto belonging as by return of the Survey under the hand of the Surveyor, doth and may appeare. Now know yee &c. Quitt rent two bushells, a halfe, dated the   day of   Anno Domini, 167.
Ex'd Q Rent 2½ bush
Fo 4

Edmund Andros, Esq. &c. Whereas there is a certain tract of land situate on the West side of Delaware River in a Creeke called Scillpades kill which kill or creeke extendeth out of Christiana Creeke, Northerlerly, which by vertue of a warrant hath been layd out for Hans Peterson; begining at a White Nutton Tree which tree divides the sd land and Andrew Fursen's land runing from the sd tree W. S. W. fifty six perches to a corner marked White Oake which divides the sd land from Jacob Vandrveer, runing on both sides into the woods, N. W. four hundred and fifety Perches into the woods containing and layd out for 157 acres and ½ of land as by return of the Survey under the hands of the Surveyor doth and may appear. Now know yee &c. Quitt rent one bushell ½, dated the   day of   Anno Domini, 167.
Ex'd Q. R. 1½ bushells
Fo 4

Edmund Andros, Esqr. &c. Whereas there is a certain parcell of land on the West side of Delaware bay and on the South side of a Creeke in the said bay called Duck Creeke, the which by vertue of a warrant hath been layd out for Edward Man, the sd land beginning at a bounded red Oake, (139) one a point by the Creeke, and runing South cross a small marsh to another point two hundred and fifty Perches, then by a line West three hundred and twenty Perches, then by a line North two hundred and fifety Perches to a marsh and by the marsh East three hundred and twenty perches to the first bounded Red

Oake containing and layd out for five hundred acres of land with the
marsh hereto adjoyning, as by return of the Survey under the hands of
marsh thereto adjoyning, as by return of the Survey under the hands of
the Surveyor, doth and may appear. Now know yee &c., Quitt rent
five bushells, dated the   day of   Anno Domini, 167.
Ex'd Q. R. 5 bush.
Fo 6.

  Edmund Andros, Esqr. &c. Whereas there is a certaine tract of
land scituate on the West side of Delaware river and on the South side
of St. Georges Creeke, between two branches of a swamp called the
Doctors Swamp the which by vertue of a warrant hath been layd out
for Wm Marriott, beginning at a corner marked White Oake standing
at the head of a branch of the said Swamp (being the upper most corner tree of the land of Bernard Egbert) and from the sd Oake runing
Northeast by a line of marked trees, dividing this from the land of the
said Bernard one hundred & sixty perches to another corner marked
White Oake, standing at the South side of another branch of the said
swamp, and from that Oake, running down the banks south Easterly,
fifety degrees, Ninety perches, & North Easterly: Eighty three degrees sixty five perches to the points of the fork at the dividing of the
aforesaid two branches, and from the sd point up the Western branch
which divideth this from the land of George Axton, to the place of
begining containing and layd out for one hundred acres of land as by
of the return of the survey (140) under the hand of the Surveyor, doth
and may appeare Now know yee &c. Quitt Rent one bushell dated the
day of   Anno Domini.
Ex'd Q. R. 1 bushell
Fo 11.

  Edmund Andros Esqr. &c. Whereas there is a certain tract of
land scituate on the West side of Delaware River and on the South
East side of the South west branch of St. Georges Creeke, the which
by vertue of a warrant hath layd out Richard Scaggs, begining at a
corner marked White Oake, standing at the said Branch side on the
North East side of the Mouth of a small run, and from the sd Oake
runing South east by a line of marked trees dividing this from the land
of Barnard Egberts three hundred and twenty perches to a corner
marked White Oake, standing by the head of a branch of a swamp
called the Doctor's Swamp, and from the said Oake South West
by a line of marked trees one hundred and fifety Perches to a corner
marked Hickory and from the sd Hickory Northwest by a line of
marked trees three hundred and thirty Perches to a corner marked
White Oake, standing at the head of a small branch, from thence
downe the branch North Fifety perches, Northeasterly 8 degrees thirty four perches to another Corner marked White Oake,
standing on a point at the side of the main branch and finally downe the
sd maine branch to the first mentioned White Oake containing and

THE DUKE OF YORK RECORD.

layd out for three hundred acres of land as by the return of the survey under the hand of the Surveyor doth and may appeare.
  Now know yee, &c., Quitt Rent three bushells. Dated the day of   Anno Domini,
Ex'd Q. R. 3 bush
Fo 12.

(141)
  Edmund Andros, Esqr. Whereas, there is a certaine Hone lott of grown in the town of New Castle upon Delaware river, the which by vertue of a warrant hath been layd out for Mr. Samuell Land, the sd lott lying and being in the Warmoes Anedtt, having one lott of Mr. John Molls on the South and ye Commons on the North or ye Lotts undeposed of it being in length three hundred foote to the Menquaes, areas, and in breadth sixty foote both before and behind: as by the returne of the Survey under the hand of the Surveyor doth and may appeare. Now know yee &c. Quitt Rent. dated the   day of Anno Domini 167.
Ex'd Q. R.,
Fo 13

  Edmund Andros Esq. &c. Whereas there is a certaine Tract of land scituate on the West side of Delaware river nigh unto the upper end of Bread and Cheese island, and on the North west side of White Clayes Creeke, which divideth this from the land of John Edmonson, the which by vertue of a warrant hath been layd out for Walraven Johnson, Defox, and Charles Rumsey: Beginning att a Corner marked Poplar standing by the Creek side in a piece of low land nigh unto the upper end of the sd island, and from the sd Poplar runing N. W. by a line of marked trees, three hundred and twenty perches, to a corner marked Black Oake, standing on a piece of falling ground, nigh unto a branch of ye sd Creeke, and from the sd Oake South West by a line of Marked Trees, three hundred perches to a corner marked White Oake, standing on the South West side of a small swamp and from that Oake South East by a line of marked trees two hundred thirty & two Perches to (142) a corner marked Poplar standing at the side of the aforesayd Creeke, nigh unto the lower end of a small island in the creeke at the upper end of the land of John Edmundson, and from thence runing downe the severall courses of the sd Creeke to the first mentioned Corner marked Poplar containing and layd out for five hundred and seventy acres of land as by return of Survey under the hands of the Surveyor doth and may appear. Now know yee &c quitt rent five bushells, and halfe. Dated the   day of   Anno Domini, 167.
Ex'd Q. R. 5½ bush.
Fo 15.

  Edmund Andros, Esq., Whereas there is a certain parcell of land called Teckquarasy scituate on the Westward side of Delaware river

being the land where Olle Stille formerly dwelt the which by vertue of a warrant hath been layd out for Mr. Larentius Carolus being bounded as followeth, viz. begining at a corner marked Poplar standing nigh unto the old Landing in Olle Stilles Creeke and from the sd Poplar runing along by the swamps side (which lieth along by the river) North Easterly sixty two degrees 144 Perches N. E. 18 Perches North by East 16 Perches and North Easterly 62 degrees, 98 Perches to a corner marked Maple, standing by the Swamp side, & divideth his from the land of Neels Mattson and from the said Maple North west by a line of Marked trees dividing this from the land of the sd Neels three hundred and thirty and eight Perches to a corner marked Red Oake, standing on a ridge between the aforesaid Creeke and a Creeke called Crumkill and from the sd Oake South West 46 Perches by a line of Marked trees to a corner markt Red Oake standing by a small piece of (143) marsh at the side of Olle Stiles Creeke, and from the thence downe the severall courses of the sd Creeke to the first mentioned Poplar containing and layd out three hundred and fifty acres of land together with the meadow ground thereto adjoyning as by return of the Survey under the hand of the Surveyor doth and may appear. Now know yee &c., quit rent three bushells, ½, dated the   day of Anno Domini, 167. part of this sd land hath been granted unto Mr. Laurentius Carolus by a former patent.
Ex'd Q. R. 3½ bush
Fo 17.

Edmund Andros Esqr. &c. Whereas there is a certain Tract of land on the West side of Delaware river on both sides of a branch of Christiana Creeke called White Clayes Fall the which by vertue of a warrant hath been layed out for John Nomers being bounded as followeth: viz. Beginning at a corner marked Poplar att the side of the maine run being a corner tree of the land of Walraven Johnson de Fox and Charles Rumsey and from the sd Poplar runing Northwest by their line of marked trees two hundred thirty and two Perches, to their upper Corner marked tree (being a whiteoak) and from the sd Oake South west (by a line of marked trees) one hundred fifety and eight Perches to a Corner marked White Oake, standing on a high bank, at the North side of the sd run and from the sd Oake (slanting over the sd run) Southwesterly 4 degrees thirty and two Perches to a corner marked Gumm tree standing at the South side of the sd run and from the sd gum South twenty perches to a corner marked White Oake, and from that Oake South East by a line of marked trees two hundred and seventy perches to a corner marked White Oake, standing (144) on a Barren levell and from that Oake North east by a line of Marked trees one hundred and twelve Perches to another corner marked White Oake and from thence North forty Perches to a corner marked Maple Tree, standing under a high bank by small island by the Creek or run neigh unto the upper corner tree of the land of John Edmundson and from the sd Mapple runing downe the maine Runne to the first mentioned corner poplar (excluding the sd island): Containing and layd out for three hundred and forty acres of land as by return of the Survey under the hand of the Surveyor doth and may appear. Now know yee &c. Quitt rent three bushells. Dated the day of Anno Domini, 167.

Ex'd Q Rent 3 bush
Fo 18.

Edmund Andros Esqr. &c. Whereas there is a certaine tract of land scituate on the west side of Delaware river upon a branch of Christiana Creeke called the White Clays Creeke, above the fall thereof, on the upper side of the land of John Nomers, the which by vertue of a warrant hath been layd out for Peter Thomason being bounded as followeth beginning att a corner marked Gumm tree standing at the South side of the maine run, and from the sd Gumm running south by a line of marked trees, divideing this from the land of John Nomers twenty Perches to a corner marked White Oake, and from the said Oak South West by West by a line of marked trees two hundred perches to a corner marked White Oak, standing between two small Crepples, and from that Oake North West by North by a line of marked trees one hundred and eighty Perches to a Corner marked White Oake standing upon a (145) piece of high ground on the North side of the sd run and from that Oake, North East by east by a line of marked trees, two hundred and twenty perches to a corner Marked Hickory, and from the said Hickory South East and by South by a line of marked trees one hundred thirty and six Perches to a Corner marked White Oake standing on a high bank at the North side of the aforesaid great runne being the upper corner oake of the land of the aforesaid John Nomers, and from thence Southwesterly four degrees (slanting over the runn) and bounding on the lands of the said Nomers, thirty two perches to the first mentioned gumm tree containing and laid out for two hundred and twenty acres of land as by return of the Survey under the hand of the Surveyor doth and may appeare. Now know yee &c. Quitt rent, two bushells. Dated the day of Anno Domini, 167.

Ex'd Q. R. 2 bushells
Fo 19.

Edmund Andros, Esqr. &c. Whereas there is a certaine track of land called Martin Vineyards, lying upon the Whore kill the which by vertue of a warrant hath been layed out for Henry Stritcher, begining at a small brook lying by Kickout begining at the point by the Whore kill runing and bounding upon the sd kill South East for breadth one hundred and fifety perches to a bounded white Oak standing upon the point of a marsh & from thence up the sd marsh S. W. 640 Perches to another bounded white Oak standing by the said Marsh and from thence N. W. boundeing upon the woods to a bounded Hickory standing by the aforesaid creeke one hundred and fifty Perches. Then down the sd creeke, to ye point in the Whorekill N. E. 650 Perches

Containing 600 acres of land as by returne (146) of the Survey &c. Now know yee, &c. Quit rent 6 bushells. Dated the   day of Anno Domini 167.

Fo 25

  Edmund Andros Esqr. &c. Whereas there is a certaine track of land Called Simpson's Choice on the North side of Creeke, called Little Creeke, the which by vertue of a warrant bearing date the twenty second day of May 1675 hath been layd out for William Simpson, beginning at a red Oake being the first bounds of John Stevens runing E. by N. two hundred Perches to ye Bay side, to a marked Oake then up the bay N. by W. 300 Perches, then W & be S. 200 Perches to the land of the sd John Stevens & by the land of the sd Stevens to the first bounded Oake, containing and layed out for foure hundred acres, as by returne of the Survey &c.,

  Now know yee &c. Quit rent four bushells. Dated the   day of Anno Domini, 167.

Fo 26

  Edmund Andros, Esqr., &c., Whereas there is a certaine parcell of land called Bandbury lying and being on ye West side of Delaware Bay and on the South side of the Creek of the sd Bay called Little Creek, The which by vertue of a warrant hath been layd out for John Webb, begining at a marked Oake standing on the Creek side near the Mouth and runing up the Creeke, bounded therewith S. W. for length 320 Perches, thence runing for breadth South East One hundred and fifty Perches, thence runing North East 320 perches, thence North West 150 perches to ye first bounded Oake, with all marshes thereunto belonging containing and layd out for three hundred acres as by return of the Survey &c. Now know yee, &c. Quitt rent three bushells dated the   day of Anno Domini, 167.

Fo 28

(147)

  Edmund Andros, Esq. &c. Whereas there is a certain parcell of Land Called Chester lying and being on the West side of Delaware Bay on the North Side of Branch in a marsh above little Creeke, the which by vertue of a warrant bearing date the first of May 1675 hath been layed out for William Willoughby begining at marked Poplar standing on the branch side and runing up the branch bounded therewith S. W. one hundred Perches to a marked Oak on ye sd branch thence runing North west 320 Perches, thence N. E. One hundred Perches, thence South East 320 Perches to ye first marked Poplar containing 200 acres, as by returne of the Survey &c. Now know yee &c. Quitt Rent two Bushells. Dated the   day of Anno Domini, 167.

Fo 28

Edmund Andros, Esqr. &c., Whereas there is a certaine tract of Land Called London lying and being on ye West side of Delaware Bay on ye North side of a Creek of ye sd Bay called Little Creek, the which by vertue of a warrant (bearing date the first of May 1675) hath been layd out for John Stevens, beginning at a marked Oake standing on the Creek side & running up the Creek bounded therewith. W. S. W. 640 perches to a marked Oake, thence running N. 325 to another marked Oake, thence running E. N. E. 640 perches to a marked Oake thence running South Three hundred and twenty-five perches to the first marked tree with all the marsh thereunto belonging containing and layed out for thirteen hundred acres as by returne of ye survey &c. Now know yee &c. Quit Rent, 13 Bushels. Dated the day of   167.
Fo 29.

(148)
Edmund Andros, Esq. &c. Whereas there is a certaine track of land called Abergany lying and being on ye west side of Delaware bay on the North side of a branch in a marsh above little Creek, the which by vertue of a warrant bearing date the 23rd day of June, 1675, hath been layed out for Peter Perry, beginning at a marked Oake being the Uppermost bounded tree of ye land of William Willoughby, and running up the branch bounded therewith S. W. One hundred Perches. To a marked Oake on the sd Branch thence running N. W. 320 perches thence N. E. ten perches thence S. E. 320 Perches to the first marked Oake containing 200 acres as by the returne of the survey &c.
Now know yee &c. Quitt rent 2 bushells. dated the day of   167.
Fo 30.

Edmund Andros Esqr. Whereas there is a certaine track of land called Gloucester, lying and being on the west side of Delaware bay on the North side of a branch in a Marsh above little Creek, the which by vertue of a warrant bearing date ye twenty third day of June 1675 hath been layed out for Robert Dicke, beginning at a marked Oake, being the uppermost bound of the land of Peter Perry & runing up the branch bounded therewith S. W. by W. 100 and 2 Perches to a marked Oake on ye said branch thence running N. W. three hundred and twenty Perches thence N. E. by E. one hundred and two Perches, thence S. E. 320 Perches to the first marked Oake, containing 200 acres as by returne of the Survey &c. Now know yee &c. Quitt Rent 2 Bushells. Dated the   day of   167.
Fo 31

(149)
(Note.—The page of the Record is here torn off lengthwise on the right hand side.)

    Edmund Andros, Esq. &c. Whereas th
tract of land on the West side of Delaware
& on the S. W. side of St. Jones Creek the whic
of a warrant hath been layd out for Robe
begining at a marked tree the uppermos
James Crawfords runing N. W. 200 per
ded Oake being the first bounds of the
Johnson then S. W. by the land of the sd. Joh
ches, then S. E. 200 perch. to ye land of the
& by the land of the said Crawford to the fi
containing 400 acres as by returne of
Now know yee &c. Quitt rent 4 bush
      day of   16
Fo 33
Believed to be Robt Francis

    Edmund Andros, Esq. &c. Where
certaine tract of land called Kinson
West side of Delaware bay & on ye North si
called St. Jones Creek the which by vertu
hath been layd out for Thomas Phillips
a marked Mulberry tree and Runing
300 perches to a marked Oake by the
then N. N. E. 320 perches then East S
to ye Bay and by the bay to the first b
ry tree containing 600 acres with all
thereunto belonging, as by returne of y
Now know yee &c. Quitt rent 6 bush
the   day of
Fo 34.

(150)
(Note.—The page of the Record is here torn of lengthwise on the left hand side.)

          mund Andros Esq. &c. Whereas there is a
tain tract of land called Violett lyeing on ye West
    of Delaware Bay on the South side of a Creeke
    led St. Johns Creeke the which by vertue of a warr-
      was layd out for Peter Baucom begining at a
      ked Red Oak being the first bounded tree of
        es Crawford runing E. S. E. 320 perches to a
      ked White Oake by muther creek then by a
    drawne E. N. E. 320 perches to the bay, and by
ay North 10 perches to a marked Pokikickory by
ones creek W. S. W. 320 per. to ye first bound-
Oake containing 200 acres as by returne of the

ey &c. Now know yee, &c. Quitt rent 2 bush. ted the   day of   167.
mund Andros, Esq. &c. Whereas there is a ine called Craft on the west side of Delaware and on the South side of a creek of the said Called Duck creeke the which by vertue of a rant hath been layd out for Herbert Craft ing at a marked Oake by a branch and runing branch S. W. 150 perches to a bounded red then by a line N. W. 320 perches then by a line 150 perches then S. E. 320 perches to the first nded Oake containing 300 acres as by returne he survey &c. Now know yee &c. Quitt rent. shells: Dated the   day of
167.

(151)
Edmund Andros, Esq. &c. Whereas there is a certaine parcell of land lying and being upon Slaughters Creeke, near to the Whorekill, the which by vertue of a warrant hath been layd out for Randall Revill, beginning at a bounded white Oake standing at ye point of a marsh running up the Creeke, for breadth W. & by S. 450 Perches, to a bounded Poplar, standing by the Creek, and from thence to a bounded red Oake, standing in the woods North by W. three hundred and twenty Perches from thence East and by North four hundred and fifty Perches to a Bounded Chestnut standing by the side of a marsh, then down the sd marsh south and by E. three hundred and twenty Perches to the first bounded white Oake, standing upon ye point, containing: 900 acres of land, as by return of the Survey &c. Now know yee &c. Quit rent 9 bushells. Dated the   day of   167.
Fo 37

Edmund Andros, Esq., &c. Whereas there is a certaine tract of land called Prime Hooke the which by vertue of a warrant hath been layd out for Mr. Henry Smith, beginning at a bounded White Oake standing upon the point runing up the Creeke, for breadth W. & by S 1000 Perches to a bounded Red Oake standing by the side of a Swampe from thence North and by West foure hundred and eighty Perches to a bounded Red Oake standing by the side of Slaughter Creeke, from thence East and by North one thousand Perches, down the sd Creek, to a bounded Poplar standing by the marsh then down the sd Marsh S & by E foure hundred and eighty Perches to ye first bounded White Oake standing upon the foresd Prime Creeke containing 3000 acres of land as by returne of the Survey under the hand &c. Now know yee &c Quitt Rent: Thirty bushells. Dated the   day of   167.
Fo 38

(152)
June 23, 1676.

Edmund Andros Esqr Seignuer of Saumarez Whereas there is a certaine Pcell of land, called Yorke Lyeing & being on the West side of Delaware bay the which by vertue of a Wart hath been layd out for Wm. Stevens the sd land begining at a marked Poplar tree standing on the South side of a branch in the Marsh, above a certaine Creeke called Little Creeke, & runing up the sd branch, is bounded therewith in length South West & by West foure hundred Perches, to a marked Oake, from thence runing South East & by South is in breadth, Two hundred fourety Perches, thence runing Northeast and by East Four hundred & then Northwest & by North two hundred & fourety Perches to the first bounded Poplar, containing & layd out for six hundred acres be it more or less, as by the returne of the Survey: under the hand of Capt. Edm. Cantwell, the Surveyor, doth and may appeare: Now know yee that by vertue of the comision & authority unto Mee given by his R. H. I have given and granted and by these Pres. doe give & grant unto William Stevens his heyres & Assigns the aforerecited Parcell of land & premises with all & singular the appurtances to have and to be held the sd Parcell of land & premises unto the sd. William Stevens his heyres and Assignes unto the proper use and behoofe of him the sd William Stevens his heyres & Assigns forever, he making improvement on the sd land according to the law, & continueing in obedience, by conforming himselfe according to the laws of the this government and yielding & paying therefor yearly & Every year unto his R. H. use as a Quitt rent six bushells of good winter Wheate, unto such officer or officers in authority there, as shall be empowered to receive the same given under my hand & seale with the seale of the Province in N. Y. the (153) day of   in the   yeare of his Majesty's reign Anno Domini 1676.

Entered in the office of
Records.
No 3, Fo 1

Edmund Andros, Esqr &c. Whereas there is a certaine Parcell of land called by the name of   lyeing & being on the West side of Delaware bay the which by vertue of warrant hath been layd out for William Ford, the sd land being on the North side of Duck Creek, begining at a markt Oake, runing by the Creeke, South West Foure hundred Perches to a branch called Beare branch, thence North West three hundred & twenty Perches, by a Lyne drawne Northeast Foure hundred Perches, with another lyne drawne South East Three hundred & twenty Perches to ye first bounded Oake, containing and layd out for eight hundred acres as by the returne of the Survey, under the hand of Capt. Edmund Cantwell, the Surveyor, doth and may appeare Now know yee &.

The Quitt Rent eight bushell.
End as the former, with blank for date.
Fo 2

Edmund Andros, Esqr. &c. Whereas there is a certaine Parcell of, land called by the name of   lyeing and being on the West side of Delaware bay, the which by vertue of a warrt hath been layd out for Wm Sharpe the sd land being on the North side of Duck Creeke, begining at a marked Oake being ye bounded tree of Will Fords land & runing down the Creek Northeast, two hundred & fifty Perches, then by a line drawn North West three hundred & (154) twenty Perches, with a line drawne South East Two hundred & Fifety Perches so South West by the Creeke to the first bounded Oake, containing & layd out for five hundred acres, as by the returne of the Survey under the hand of Capt. Edmund Cantwell the Surveyor doth and may appear. Now know yee &c.

The Quitt Rent five bushells and end as ye former without putting in Quitt rent.

Fo 3

Edmund Andros Esqr &c. Whereas there is a certaine pcell of land called Golden Grove, lyeing & being on the West side of Delaware bay, the which by vertue of a warrt hath been layd out for John Morgan the sd land lyeing on the North side of Duck Creeke; begining at a marked Oake standing by a Marsh, and runing West & by South one hundred & Fifety Perches to a markt Oake standing in the woods, then North and by West Three hundred and Twenty Perches to another markt Oake, then East and by North one hundred and fifety Perches, to the Marsh and by the River & Marsh to the first markt Oake, with the Marshes thereunto belonging Containing & laid out for Three hundred acres. Bee it more or less, as by the returne of the Survey, under the hand of Capt. Edm. Cantwell, the surveyor. Doth and may appeare. Now know yee &c. Quitt rent 3 bushell.

Fo 4

Edmund Andros, Esqr. &c. Whereas there is a certaine Pcell of land called Thusk, lyeing & being on the West side of Delaware River, & on the South side of the Maine branch of St. George's Creeke, above the land of John Scott (155) the which by vertue of a warrt hath been layd out for Wm. Grant the sd. land being bounded as followeth viz. beginning at a Corner markt White Oake standing on a Point on the West side of the Mouth of a branch or Swamp which proceedeth out of the sd Creeke, & from the sd Oake, runing South & bounding on the sd Swamp One hundred Ninety & Eight Perches to a markt Oake by the head of a dry valley above the head of the sd Swamp & from thence continueing the same course (South) by a line of marked trees One hundred twenty & two Perches to a Corner Marked White Oake, standing nigh unto the head of another dry Valley, and from that Oake West by a line of marked trees Two hundred Perches, to another Corner markt White Oake standing on the South side of the head of another dry Valley, & from thence North (by a line of markt trees) Sixty four Perches, to a small run, & from thence Northerly Downe the severall courses of the sd run, to a Corner markt White Oake, standing on the East side of the Mouth of the sd run by the Creek side & from thence Easterly Downe the sd Creeke to the fires mentioned Corner Oake containing & layd out for foure Hundred Acres of land as by the returne of the Survey under the hand of the Surveyor doth and may appear, Now know yee &c. Quitt Rent foure bushells blank for the date.

Fo 7

(156)
Edmund Andros Esqr. &c. Whereas there is a certaine Parcell of land lyeing & being on the West side of Delaware River & on the South side of St. George's Creeke, betweene the two Maine branches of a Swamp called the Doctor's swamp the which by vertue of a Warrt hath been layed out for George Axton the sd land being bounded as follows: viz. begining at a corner Markt White Oake, standing in the forke at the dividing of the sd Swamp, & from the sd Oake runing up the Westerne branch of the sd Swamp which divideth this from the land of William Marriott, South West Forty Perches, West South West one hundred seventy six Perches, & South South West eighty six Perches, to a Corner markt Hickory standing nigh unto the Easteward side of the head of the sd Branch & from the sd Hickory runing East South East by a line of markt trees one hundred & Thirty Perches to the head of another branch being the Souther most branch of ye aforesd swamp, which divideth this from the land of Thomas Spry, & from thence downe the severall Courses of the sd Swamp to the first mencioned Corner Oake containing & layd out for two hundred acres as by the returne of the Survey under the hand of the Surveyor doth and may appeare. Now know yee &c. Quitt rent 2 bushells, blanke date.

Fo 8.

(157)
Edmund Andros Esqr &c. Whereas there is a certaine Pcell of land called Westmoreland, lyeing & being on the West side of Delaware Bay, the which by vertue of a warrant hath been layd out for John Denne the sd land lyeing on the North side of a certaine Creeke, called Duck Creeke, beginning at a marked Oake, by the marsh & by the land of John Morgan and running West & by South by the sd Morgan's land two hundred Perches then South by East one hundred & Sixty Perches then East by North two hundred Perches & North & by West One hundred & Sixty Perches, to the first bounded Oake, with all the Marsh thereunto belonging, containing and layd out for Two hundred acres, bee it more or less, as by the returne of the Survey under the hand of Capt. Edmund Cantwell, the Surveyor doth and may appeare. Now know yee &c. the Quitt rent two bushell Blanke date.

No. 23.

Edmund Andros Esqr. &c. Whereas there is a certaine Pcell of land Called Bachelers Harbor lyeing & being on ye West side of Delaware bay the which by vertue of a warrant hath been layd out for Henry Stevenson, & John Richards the sd land lyeing on the North side of a certaine Creeke of the sd Bay called Murders Creek begining at a markt Pockickory or Wallnut tree by the land formerly layd out for Jonathan Hopkins & Edward Winckell runing up the Creeke, and bounded by South West three hundred Perches to a marked Oake by the Creeke side, then North West three hundred and twenty Perches into the woods in length, then North East Three hundred Perches to the land of the sd (158) Jonathan Hopkins and Edward Winckell & by their land to the first bounded tree Containing & layd out for six hundred acres with all the marshes thereunto belonging as by the returne of the Survey under the hand of Capt. Edmund Cantwell, the Surveyor doth and may appeare, Now know yee &c. Quitt Rent Six bushells Blank date.
No. 24.

Edmund Andros Esqr. &c. Whereas there is a certaine parcell of land lyeing and being on the West side of Delaware Bay the which by vertue of a warrant hath been layd out for Robert Francis the sd land lyeing on the South side of St. Jones Creeke, begining at a markt tree being the uppermost bound of James Crawfords land, runing Northwest two hundred Perches to a bounded
No. 28.

Edmund Andros, Esqr &c. Whereas there is a certaine pcell of land lyeing & being on the west side of Delaware river upon a branch of Christina Creeke called White Clay's Creeke, above the fall thereof on the upper side of the land of John Nomers the which by vertue of a warrant hath beene layd out for Pieter Thomason, the sd land being bounded as followeth, viz. begining at a corner markt Gum tree, standing at the South side of the maine run, and from the sd gum runing south by a line of marked trees dividing this from the land of John Nomers, twenty perches, to a Corner marked White Oake, and from the sd Oake South West & by West by a line of Marked trees, two hundred Perches to a Corner marked White Oake, standing between two small Swamps or creuples And from (159) that Oake North West and by North by a line of Markt trees one hundred and eighty Perches to a corner markt White Oake standing on a piece of High ground on the North side of the sd run & from that Oake N. East & by east by a line of marked trees two hundred and twenty Perches to a corner marked Hickory, and from the sd Hickory South East and by South by a line of marked trees one hundred and thirty six Perches to a corner marked White Oake, standing on a high bank at the North side of the aforesd great run, being the upper Corner Oake of the land of the aforesaid Nomers, & from thence Southwesterly foure   slanting over the run, and bounding on the land of the sd Nomers, thirty two Perches to the first mentioned Gum tree Contening and layd out for

Two hundred & Twenty acres of land as by the returne of the Survey under the hand of the Surveyor doth and may appeare. Now know yee &c. Quitt Rent two bushells, blank date.
No 19.

  Edmund Andros, Esqr. &c. Whereas there is a certaine parcell of land Calton lyeing and being on the West side of Delaware river and on the North side of a branch of Black bird Creek that divideth this from the land of   the which by vertue of a warrant hath been layd out for John Barker, the sd land begining at a corner markt Hickory standing at the side of the sd branch by a Beaver dam, it being the upper corner tree of the land of John Hartop, & from thence running North by the sd Hartops line of marked trees Two hundred forty and six perches to a corner markt White Oake, from thence west by a line of markt Trees one hundred & fifty perches to a corner (160) markt Gumme tree standing on the side of a   from thence South by a line of marked trees two hundred and thirty perches to a corner marked Maple standing at the side of the sd branch & from thence downe along the run of the sd branch to the first mentioned corner tree containing a layd out for two hundred and twenty acres of land, as by the return of the Survey under the hand of the Surveyor doth and may appeare. Now know yee Quitt Rent 2 bushells, blanck date.
Fo. 20.

  Edmund Andros, Esqr. &c. Whereas there is a certaine tract of land called Tillmouth Haven, lyeing and being on the West side of Delaware bay and on the South side of the creek of the said Bay called Fish Creeke, the which by vertue of a warrant hath been layed out for Henry Allison. The sd land begining at a bounded red Oake being the last bounded tree of Mr. Willm. Tom's land & runing up the Creeke South South East One hundred and seventy Perches then South West to a bounded Oake, then by a line East North East three hundred and seventy five perches to a Bever dam, and by the markt Oake, N. North West One hundred seventy one Perches to a bounded tree (being a poplar) by the line of Mr. Will Tom, then by the sd Mr. Tom's line West South West, Three hundred Seventy & five Perches to the first bounded Red Oake, conteyning a layd out for Foure hundred acres with the marshes adjacent as by the return of the Survey under the hand of the Surveyor doth and may appeare. Now know yee &c. Quitt rent foure bushells dated 25th of March 1676.
Fo. 24

(161)
  Edmund Andros Esq. &c. Whereas there is a certaine parcell of land called by the name of St. Gileses, lyeing and being on the West side of Delaware Bay west from the Whore kill about one mile from the Creeke called Pagan Creeke, the which by vertue of a warrant hath

been layed out for Edward Southeran, the sd land begining at a markt Oake, being the bounded tree of Daniel Brown's land from thence runing West South West Two hundred Forty five Perches to a bounded Oake standing by the Beaver damm, & from thence runing downe the Beaver damm two hundred and eighty Perches North North East to a marked Oake, standing out upon a point & from thence runing S. E. two hundred Perches to the first bounded tree in manner of a triangle containg & layd out for one hundred ninety and six acres of land as by the return of the survey under the hand of the surveyor doth and may appear. Now know yee &c. Quitt rent two bushells dated June 24th 1676.
Fo 25.

Edmund Andros, Esqr. &c. Whereas there is a certaine part of land called by the name of Arundel's Content lyeing and being on the West side of Delaware bay about three miles south West from the Whore kill in the woods, the which by vertue of a warrant hath been layed out for Wm. Arundel, the sd land begining at a markt Oake runing South South East One hundred & fifety Perches to a marked Hickroy from thence runing West South West Three hundred & Twenty Five Perches to another marked Hickory from thence running North North West one hundred and fifty Perches to a (162) marked Oake from thence with a paralell line to the first bounded tree three hundred and twenty five Perches Contenying & layd for three hundred and foure acres of land as by the return of the Survey, under the hand of the Surveyor doth and may appeare. Now know yee &c. Quitt rent three one half bushells. Dated June 24th 1676.
Fo 26.

Edmund Andros, Esqr. &c. Whereas there is a certaine tract of land called William's his Folley, lyeing and being on the West side of Delaware bay, and on the North West side of a Creeke called Buckham Briggs Creeke, the which by vertue of a warrant hath been layed out for Thomas Williams the sd land begining at a bounded white Oake, being the lasted bounded tree of the land of Wm Troth runing downe the Creeke North two hundred Perches to a bounded black Wallnut tree by the Marsh & by the Marsh One hundred and sixty Perches to the land Troth and by the land of the sd Troth East to the first bounded Oake, containing and layed out for two hundred acres of land. As by ye return of ye survey under the hand of the Surveyor doth and may appeare. Now know yee, that by vertue &c. Quitt rent two bushells. Dated March 25th 1676.
Fo. 27.

Edmund Andros, Esqr. &c. Whereas there is a certaine tract of land called Poplar Hill lyeing and being on the West side of Delaware bay & on the North side of a creeke of the sd bay called Hangmans Creeke, the which by vertue of a warrant hath beene layed out for (163) Robert Talent, the sd land begining at a bounded Oake, & being the

uppermost bounded tree of Robert Morten's land runing North and by West, by the land of the sd Morton Two hundred Perches to a bounded tree, and in the woods, then west and by South one hundred and sixty Perches, then by a lyne South and by East Two hundred Perches to a beaver dam and by the Beaver dam, one hundred and sixty Perches, to the first bounded tree, Conteyning and layd out for two hundred acres of land, as by the returne of the Survey under the hand of the Surveyor doth and may appeare. Now know yee &c. Quitt rent, 2 bushells. Dated March 25th 1676.
Fo. 28.

 Edmund Andros Esqr &c. Whereas there is a certain tract of land called the Exchange lyeing and being on the West side of Delaware river between the sd river and a great Swamp called the Dragon swamp and next adjoyning to the land of Mr. Henry Ward, the which hath been layed out for Mr. John Moll, the sd land beginning at a Corner marked Spanish Oak, standing at the North East side of a branch of the sd Dragon Swamp, it being the upper Corner tree of the land of the sd Ward, and from thence runing North Easterly Forty Seven Along the sd Ward's lyne, one hundred sixty and two Perches, to a Corner marked White Oake, (standing by the side of a swamp or crupple which lieth between this land and the river) & is also another Corner tree of the land of the sd Ward, and from thence following the severall courses of the sd Swamp or creuple to a corner marked White Oake, standing at the head of a beaver (164) Dam Branch, and from thence runing West by a line of marked trees, foure hundred and fourty Perches to a Corner marked White Oake standing at the East side of the head of a branch of the said Dragon Swamp, and from thence following the severall courses of the said branch and Dragon Swamp to the first mentioned Spanish Oake, conteyning and layd out One Thousand acres of land, six hundred acres (part thereof) being formerly granted by patent unto Wm Currer, and William Goldsmith, since which time Mr. John Moll is invested in their right, & the other foure hundred acres being new land as by the return of the survey under the hand of the Surveyor doth and may appeare. Now know yee &c. Quitt Rent ten bushells. Dated July 15th 1676.
Fo. 29.

 Edmund Andros, Esqr., Whereas there is a certain tract of land called the Chops, lyeing and being on the West side of Delaware bay, on the head of a creeke, called Hangman's Creek, the which by vertue of a warrant hath beene layed out for John Street the sd land begining at a bounded Spanish Oake by the head of the Beaver dam, being the upper tree of Robert Talents land, runing North and by West One hundred and Sixty Perches, then West and by South one hundred and Sixty Perches, then South and by East Two hundred Perches, then East and by North one hundred and sixty perches then North and by West Twenty two Perches, to yee first bounded Oake, Conteining and layed out for Two hundred acres of land, as by the return of the Surveyor under the hand of the Surveyor doth and may appeare.: Now know yee &c. Quitt rent 2 bush; dated March 25th 1676.

Fo. 30.
(165)
Book of Patents, N. 2,
Part the 2d, Fo. 77.

A Confirmacon Graunted to Hendrick Jansen for a house and lott of Ground at New Castle upon Delaware.

Richard Nichols Esqr. &c. Whereas Jacob Alricks had heretofore a graunt & by vertue of his purchase was in actual possession of a certaine house and lott of ground at New Castle upon Delaware scituate lyeing and being towards yee strand or water side, between Hobb Jansen's and William Mouritts containing in length on both sides three hundred foot Amsterdam wood measure, in breadth behinde it hath as the other lots are and were at first layed out about sixty foot, and before it is in breadth ye length of that aforesaid Wm. Mouritts house and garden as it lay within the old fence now Hendrick Jansen's Van Jeveren having since lawfully bought the house and lott of ground afore mentioned whereby the right and interest in the premises is devolved upon him for a confirmacon unto him the sd Henry Hendrick Jansen Van Jeveren in his possession and enjoyment of ye premises. Know yee that by vertue of ye comision and authority unto me given I have ratified the patent. Ye eighth day of January 1667.

Delaware,
Hendrick Jansen

A Confirmacon graunted to Johan Hendricks, Neils Neilson Sr., Hendrick Neilson, Mattijs Neilsen, and Neils Neilson, Jr., for each of them a plantation at New castle upon Delaware.

Richard Nicholas Esqr. &c. Whereas there waas upon ye fifth day of March 1663 a Graunt made unto Johan Hendricks, Neils Nielson, Sr., Hendrick Neilson, Mattijs Neilson, and Neils Neilson, Jr. for each of them to have a plantation with a proporcon of meadow ground for hay for their cattle on a certain piece of land at Delaware scituate lyeing and being on the Verdrietige hooke, or corner of land so extending to ye stone hooke upon such condicion as other lands were there given and graunted as also obliedging them to build their houses neare unto one (166) another and ye grant afore mentioned, being afterward that is to say, on ye fifteenth day of June, 1664 confirmed unto the persons aforenamed by those then in authority. Now for a further confirmacon unto them in their possession and enjoyment of ye premises know yee by vertue of ye comision and authority unto me given I have ratified confirmed and graunted and by these presents do ratify confirme and graunt unto Johan Hendricks, Neils Neilson Sr. Hendrick Neilson, Mattijs Neilson and Neils Neilson Jr their heirs, and

assigns the afore recited plantacons and proporcon of meadow grounds
and premises with all and singular the appertances to have and to hold
ye said plantacon meadow ground and premises unto ye sd Johan
Hendricks Neils Neilson Sr., Hendrick Neilson, Mattijs Neilson and
Neils Neilson Jr., their heirs and assigns unto ye proper use and behoofe of the sd Johan Hendricks, Neils Neilson, Sr., Hendrick Neilson,
Mattijs Neilson, and Neils Neilson Jr. their heirs and assigns forever,
rendering and paying and &c. The patent is dated the eighth day of
January 1667.

Five bushells of wheat acknowledgment.

Fo. 78
Delaware
Johannes Hendricks & al.

A Confirmacon Graunted unto Capt. John Carr for
a piece of land and Platacon upon Delaware Ryver.

Whereas there is a certaine piece of land with a plantacon thereupon at New Castle upon Delaware heretofore belonging to Alexander
Boeijr scituate lyeing and being upon ye first hook or corner of land
above ye Fort betweene ye first meadow ground or valley and ye land
of Frans Smith and Jan Willer, from whose sd land strentching to ye
valley South West and By West it Conteins sixty rods, further along
by ye side of the sd valley North West and by West Fifety two rods,
West and by North Forty six rods, North east Sixty one rods, N. W.
and By West One hundred and five rods, then from the meadow or
valley to the opening of ye woods by the land of Smith and Willer
aforenamed North East and by North, one hundred rods, and so from
ye opening of ye woods to ye first desent amounting in all to about
fifty (167) acres or twenty five morgen, and whereas there is at New
Castle upon Delaware aforesaid another piece of land with a bowery
heretofore belonging to Frans Smith and Jan Willer lyeing and being
also upon the first hook or corner of land adjoyning unto tother and
being above ye Fort on the North East side thereof and stretching from
ye land heretofore appertaining to Alexander Boeyer alongst ye strand
Northeast somewhat more Easterly to ye meadow or valley it containes
sixty rods, further along by ye side of the sd valley, northwest and by
north Forty rods, North Northwest sixty five rods, East and by North
somewhat more Easterly twenty five rods, North and by West twenty
six rods, West and by North something more Northerly one hundred
twenty eight rods. Then from the side of ye valley into ye woods
South South West somewhat more Southerly one hundred and fourteen rods and so from ye opening of ye woods to the first desent
amounting to about one hundred acres or fifty morgen. Now both the
sd pieces of land with the plantacon, bowery and appertances having
beene purchased from the Owners by Anthony Bryant and by him
since sould for a valuable consideration under Captain John Carr in
whose tenure and occupation it now is for a confirmacon unto him the
sd Capt. John Carr in his possession and enjoyment of the premises
know yee that by vertue of the comision and authority unto me given I

have ratified confirmed and graunted &c. the patent is dated the eighth of January 1667. Two bushells of Wheat acknowledgment.
Fo. 79
Delaware
C. John Carr.

A Confirmacon graunted to Matthias Nicolls,, Esqr. for a tract of land at Delaware.

Richard Nicolls, Esqr. &c. Whereas there is a certaine tract or parcell of land at Delaware called by the Indian name of Chiepiessinge scituate lyeing and being on the West Syde of the Ryver up above Peter Alricks Islands stretching out into ye sd river and bending like a halfe moone, conteyning by estimacon 3000 acres or thereabouts be they more or less which (168) said tract or parcell of land lies unmanured and unplanted. Now to the end some good improvement may be made thereupon and for divers other good reasons and considerations mee thereunto especially moving know yee that by vertue of the comision and authority to me given I have thought fit to give and graunt and by these presents do give ratifye confirme and grant unto Matthias Nicholls his heirs and assigns the afore recited piece or parcell of land and premises called Chiepiessing as aforesd together with all ye lands soils, woods, meadows, pastures marshes creeks, waters, lakes fishing hawking hunting and fowling, and all other profits comoditys, emoluments and hereditaments to ye sd tract or parcell of land and premises belonging or in any wise apperteyning with their and every of their appertances and of every part and parcell thereof, to have and to hold ye sd tract and parcell of land and premises unto ye sd Matthias Nicolls, his heirs, and assigns unto ye proper use and behoof of ye sd Matthias Nicolls, his heirs and assigns forever. The patent is dated ye 15th of January 1667.

Two Otter skins acknowledgement.
Fo. 80
Delaware
M. Nicolls, Esq.

A Confirmacon graunted to Peter Alricks for two certain Islands in Delaware Ryver.

Richard Nicolls Esqr. &c. Whereas there are two certain islands in Delaware Ryver scituate lyeing and being on ye West side of ye sd River and about South West from ye islands commonly called Matini Conck. The which is the biggest of the two islands haveing been formerly knowne by the name of Kipps Island and by the Indian name of Koomenakineknock Conteining about a myle in length and halfe a mile in breadth, and the other island lyeing somewhat to the North of ye former being of about half a mile in length and the quarter of a myle in breadth, And there being also a small Creeke near unto ye lesser of ye sd islands fitt to build a mill thereupon now to ye end of ye best improvement may be made of ye sd island and Creeke to which there appeare no other lawful pretenders and for divers other good reasons and

(169) consideracons me thereunto especially moving know yee that by vertue of ye comission and authority unto me given have thought fitt to give & grant & by these presents do ratify, confirme, & graunt unto Pieter Alricks his he   assigns the afore recited two islands with all ye soyle, meadow ground woodland, pastures, marshes, waters, creeks, fishing, hunting and fowling, and all other profits comidityies and emouluments to ye sd islands and premises belonging or in anywise apperteyning, as also ye small creek afore menconed near unto ye lesser islands runing up a myle within land to have liberty to erect and build a mill thereupon where shall be found most convenient as also a convenient proportion of land on each side of ye sd creeke, for egresse and regresse to and from ye mill and for other necessary accommodations thereunto belonging. to have and to hould all and singular the sd two islands creeks and proportions of land on each syde thereof and premises with their and every of their appertances to ye sd Pieter Alricks, his heirs and assigns unto ye proper use and behoofe of ye sd Peter Alricks, his heirs and assigns forever, yielding and paying therefore yearly and every yeare unto his Ma'ties use foure Otter skins as a Quitt rent when it shall be demanded by such person or persons in authority as his Ma'tie shall please to establish and empower in Delaware Ryver or ye Parts and plantacons adjacent given &c. The patent is dated ye 15th of February, 1667.
Fo 81.
Delaware
Pieter Alricks.

A Patent graunted unto James Crawford for a piece of land in Cristeene kill in Delaware river.

Richard Nicolls, Esqr. Whereas there is a certain piece or parcell of land scituate lyeing and being in Christine kill or Creeke, adjoyning unto Swarten Nutten island bounded on yee North with ye kill or creek of ye sd island on ye West with Cristeene kill, on ye South is with main land, and on ye East with ye meadow ground or valley belonging to ye sd Swarten Nutten Island, conteyning by estimation One hundred acres or thereabouts and whereas there is also a small tenement or cottage house with a back side there unto belonging being in ye Towne of New Castle (170) upon Delaware bounded by ye river on the South West on ye North by ye house of Martin Gerritts, on ye Northwest by ye land taken up on ye backside of ye town and by ye highway on ye south West. Now know yee, that by vertue of ye comision and authority unto me given in consideracon of the good service performed by James Crawford, a souldier,
Fo. 82
Delaware
James Crawford

Whereas Mr. William Beckman of Esopus did heretofore by way of exchange make purchase of a certaine house or lott of ground at Delaware scituate and being upon ye strand as in ye bill of sale and

transport, is sett forth, these are to certifye all whom it may concerne that ye sd Mr. Beeckman hath liberty either by himselfe or his attorney to see alleyn lett or otherwise dispose of ye same for his best advantag wherein no person is to molest hinder or disturbe him upon any pretense whatsoever. given under my hand at fort James in New Yorke this seventh day of August 1668.
Book of Patents No. 3.
Part the 1st.
Fo 92

A Confirmacon Graunted unto Thomas Wollaston, for a certain house and backside in the Towne of New Castle upon Delaware.

Richard Nicolls, Esq. &c. Whereas there is a certain (171) messuage or tenement with a back side thereunto belonging scituate lying and being upon or near the strand in the town of New Castle, upon Delaware, lately in the tenure of occupacon of Rayner Ravens bounded on the North with a house belonging to Isaack Slein, on the West with the woodlands on the South with a house of Michale Bawn, and on the east with the River. Now it being sufficiently knowne, that the sd Rayner Raven was in hostility against his ma'tie for which reason all his estate stands confiscated, and is in his ma'tie's disposal Know yee that by vertue of the comision and authority unto me given I have thought fit to give and graunt and by these presents do give ratifye confirme and graunt unto T   his heirs, and assigns the af   tenement together with the backside and premises with all and singular their appertances to have and to hold the sd messuage or tenement to the back side and premises unto the sd Thomas Wolliston his heirs, unto the proper use and behoof of the sd Thomas Wolliston, his heirs, and assigns, forever yielding and paying therefore, yearly and every year one bushell of Wheate as a Quitt rent unto his Ma'ties use when it shall be demanded by such person or persons in authority as his ma'tie shall to establish and empower in Delaware Ryver and the parts and plantacons adjacent. Given under my hand and seals, at Fort James, in New York., on the island of Manhattans, the first day of January, in the 19th year of his Ma'ties reigne Anno Domini, 1667.
Same Book, Part the 2d.
Fo 3.

A Confirmacon Graunted unto John Erskin, Thomas Bowne, and Martin Gerrits, a certain parcell of land and meadow at Delaware.

Richard Nicolls, Esq., &c. Whereas there is a certain piece or parcell of land and meadow ground or valley scituate lyeing and being in Delaware river in Christeen Creeke, or kill between (172) Swarten Nutten Island, and the Fyren Hook which is upon the sd kill contayning by estimacon five hundred acres or thereabouts be they more or less bounded on the North with Christeen Creek aforemencioned on the West with Nutten Island, on the South with a little Spring called Bessie's and on the East with the sd Fyran Hook. Now the sd piece or parcell of land and meadow ground being in his Ma'tie's disposall, know yee that by vertue of the comision and authority unto me given I have thought fitt to   nt and by these presents doe give ratifye   ant unto John Erskin, Tho. Brown and Martin Gerritt's their heirs and assigns to be divided equally between them the afore recited piece or parcell of land and meadow ground or valley and premises with all and singular their appertances to have and to hold the sd piece or parcell of land and meadow ground and premises unto the sd John Erskin, Tho. Browne and Martin Gerrits their heirs, and assigns unto the proper use and behoof of the sd John Erskin Tho. Brown and Martin Gerritts their heirs and assigns for ever yielding and paying therefore yearly and every year unto his Ma'te's use five of bushells of Wheate as a Quitt rent when it shall be demanded by such persons in authority as his Majtie shall please to establish and empower in Delaware river and the part and plantatons adjacent. Given under my hand and seale at Fort James, in New Yorke on the Island of Manhattans, the first day of January in the 19th yeare of his Majestie's Raigne Anno Domini, 1667.

Fo 4.

A Confirmation Graunted unto George Whale and George Moore of a certain Parcell of land called by the name of the old Minquas plantation at Delaware.

Richard Nicolls, Esq., Principal Comisioner for his (173) Majesty in New England, Governor General under his Royall Highness James Duke of York and Albany, &c., of all his territories in America and commander in Chiefe of all the forces employed by his majesty to reduce the Dutch nation and all their usurped land and plantatons under his majesty's obedience. To all to whome these presents shall come sendeth greeting: Whereas there is a certain piece or parcell of land commonly called or known by the name of the old Minquas Plantaton scituate lyeing and being in Christeen kill at Delaware contenying by estimacon two hundred acres or thereabout be it more or less, bounded on the North with   Bush or woodland, on the West with a Plantation of Andries Bonus, on the South with the kill and on the East with the plantacon of Andries Andries. Now to the end the sd land may be manured improved and planted Know yee that by vertue of the commission and authority unto me given I have thought fitt to give and grant and by these presents doe give ratifye confirm and grant unto George Whale and George Moore, their heirs and assigns the afore recited piece or parcell of land and premises with all and singular their appertances to have and to hold the sd piece or parcell of land and premises unto the sd George Whale and George Moore, their heirs and assigns unto the proper use, and behoof of the sd George Whale and George Moore their heirs and assigns forever, yielding and paying therefore yearly and every yeare unto his Majesty's use two bushells of

wheat as a quitt rent when it shall be demanded by such person or persons in authority as his Majesty shall please to establish and empower in Delaware river, and the parts and plantacons adjacent. Given under my hand and seal at Fort James in New Yorke, on the island Manhattans the first day of January in the 19th year of his Majesty's Raigne. Anno Domini 1667.
Fo. 5.

(174)
A Confirmacon Graunted unto Capt. John Carr for a Parcell of land at Delaware,

Richard Nicolls, Esqr., &c. Whereas there is a certaine parcell of meadow valley or marsh ground scituate lyeing and being in Delaware river near the fort conteyning by estimacon one hundred and fifty acres or thereabout either more or less not long since in the tenure or occupacon of Alexander D'Hiniosa butted and bounded upon the South by the river, upon the North and North East by the land and Meadow and valley lately in the possession of Gerritt Van Sweering upon the Northwest by the plantacon commonly called the landey and upon the South and South West by the land lately belonging to John Weeber, Now it being sufficiently knowne that the said Alexander D'Hiniosa then Governor was in hostility against his Majesty for which reason all his estate stands confiscated. Know yee that by vertue of ye comision and authority unto me given, and in consideration of the good service performed by Capt. John Carr, in storming and reducing the fort at Delaware, I have thought fit to give and graunt and by these presents do give ratifye confirme and graunt unto Capt. John Carr, the afore recited piece or parcell of meadow, valley or marsh ground with all and singular the appertances to have and to hold the said piece or parcell of meadow valley or marsh ground unto the sd Capta. John Carr, his heires, and assigns, unto the proper use and behoofe of the sd Capta John Carr his heirs and assigns forever, yielding and paying therefor yearly and every yeare unto his Majesty's use one bushell of Wheate as a Quitt rent when it shall be demanded by such person or persons in authority as his Majesty shall please to establish and empower in the Delaware River and the parts and plantacons adjacent. Given under my hand at Fort James in New Yorke, on the Island Manhattans, the first day of January, in the 19th year of his Majesty's Raigne Anno Domini, 1667.
Fo 7.

(175)
A Confirmacon Granted unto Thomas Wollaston, James Crawford, Herman Otto, And Girard Otto for a certaine island in Delaware River.

Richard Nicolls, Esq., and &c. Whereas there is a certaine island scituate lyeing and being in Christeen kill or Creeke, in Delaware river commonly called or known by the name of Swarten Nutten island, conteyning by estimacon Three hundred acres or thereabouts be it more or less which sd island is now in the tenure or occupation of Thomas Wollaston, James Crawford, Herman Otto, and Girard Otto or their assigns, being bounded on the North with Christine kill, on the East with Sargeant's Erskin's land, on the West by a little Creek, and on the South by the main Land. Now the sd   hav   retofore graunted by Alexander D'Hiniosa, the later Governor, there to some persons who have since appeared in hostility against his Majesty whereby it is forfeited and &c. remains in his majesty's disposall. Know yee that by vertue of the comision and authority to me given, I have thought fit to give and grant and by these presents to give ratifye, confirme, and graunt unto the sd Thomas Wollaston, James Crawford, Herman Otto, and Girard Otto, their heirs, and assigns to be so divided between them as now in stands, and is possessed by them the afore recited islands together with all the land wood, meadow ground and premises, thereupon with all and singular their appertances, to have and to hold the sd island together with all the land wood meadow ground and premises thereupon with all and singular their appertances to the said Thomas Walliston, James Crawford, Herman Otto and Girard Ottoe, their heirs and Assigns unto the proper use and behoofe of the sd Thomas Wollaston, James Crawford, Herman Otto, and Girard Otto, their heirs and assigns unto the proper use and behoofe of the sd. Thomas Wollaston, James Crawford, Herman Otto and Girard (176) Otto, their heirs and assigns forever, yielding and paying therefore yearly and every year unto his Majesty's use three Bushells of Wheate as a Quitt rent when it shall be demanded by such person or persons in authority as his Majesty shall please to establish and empower in Delaware river, and the parts and plantations adjacent. Given under my hand and seal at Fort James, in New York. on the island Manhattans the first day of January the 19th year of His majesty's Raigne. Anno Domini, 1667.

Whereas there is given and graunted in the above written patent unto Thomas Wallaston, James Crawford, Hermann Otto and Girard Otto a certain island called Swarten Nutten Island with the appertances I does likewise grant unto them and their heirs the outlett towards the South with freedom of commonage. Given under my hand at Fort James in New York, the 7th day of August, Anno 1668.
Fo 8.

A Patent granted upon a transport bearing date the 23rd day of January 1665, made by Herman Reynderstsen Bruinje unto Reyner Reynertsen Vandercooley for a certaine lott of ground at Delaware lying and being in the otter Street bounded on the one side with the Governor Jacob Alricks and on the other side with Cornelis Wijnharts conteyning in length on each side one hundred and eighty foot Amsterdam's wood measure and in breadth ninety foot. Now for a conformation unto the sd Reyner Reynersten Vandercooly &c. The Patent is dated the 11th day of February 1667.
Fo 10.

A Confirmation granted upon Capta. John Carr for a certaine house and parcell of land at New Castle upon Delaware River.

Richard Nicolls, Esqr., &c. Principall Commissioner from his Majesty in New England, Governor General under his Royall Highnesse, James Duke of York and Albany &c. of all his territories in America (177) and commander in Chief of all the forces employed by his Majesty to reduce the Dutch nacon, and all their usurped lands, and plantatons, under his Majesty to all to whome these presents now come, extendeth greeting: Whereas, there is a certaine house and parcell of land at New Castle upon Delaware, lying and being next unto Jorgen Kijms land, on the Southwest on the Northeast having the Creeke or kill belong to Olle Stille, on the Southeast the Water side, and on the North West the woodland contayning in breadth one hundred & Fifety rod, or thereabout and in length about one hundred acres or fifety Morgen bee it more or less, which sd house, and parcell of land formerly belonging to Niclas Massen, hath been purchased from him by Capt. John Carr and due satisfaction acknowledge to have been rec'd. for the same, for a confirmation therefor unto him the sd John Carr in his possession and enjoyment of the premises. Know yee that by vertue of the commission and authority to me given, I have thought fitt to give and graunt and by these presents do give, ratifye and grant unto Captain John Carr, his heirs, and assigns, the afore recited house and parcell of land with all and singular the appertances, to have and to hold the sd house and parcell of land and premises unto the sd Capta. John Carr, his heires, and assignes, unto the proper use and behoofe of the sd Capt. John Carr, his heirs and assigns forever, yielding and paying yearly and every year unto   Majesty's use two bushells of Wheate as a Quitt rent when it shall be demanded by such person or persons in authority as His Majesty shall please to establish and empower in Delaware River and the parts and plantations adjacent, Given under my hand and seal at Fort James (178) in New York, on the island Manhattans, the fifteenth July in the 20th yeare of his Majesty's raigne. Anno Domini, 1668.
Fo 11.

A Confirmation Graunted unto Israel Helme for a certaine parcell of land at Delaware.

Richard Nicolls Esqr. &c. Whereas there is a certaine piece or parcell of cleared upland scituate lying and being on the West side of Delaware river above New Castle betwixt Neils Massans two lotts, hee having one on either side of it conteyning about sixteen acres or as much as thirty schiple of corne can sowe, having allso a piece of meadow ground or valley thereunto   ing neer adjoyning to   And Jurian Teunis on the other side being about fifty single paces or tread from the land to the river side which sd piece or parcell of land, and meadow hath been and now still is in the tenure or occupation of Irrael Helme as of right belonging unto him Now for a confirmation unto him the sd Israel Helme in his possession and enjoyment of the premises Know yee that by vertue of the commission and authority to me given, I have thought fitt to give and grant, and by these presents do give ratifye, confirme and graunt unto Israel Helme the afore recited piece or parcell of land and premises to have, and to hold the sd piece or parcell of land and premises unto ye sd Isreal Helme, his heirs, and assigns, unto the proper use and behoofe of the sd Israel Helme, his heirs, and assigns forever, yielding and paying therefore, yearly and every yeare unto his Majesty's use one bushell of wheate, as a quitt rent when it shall be demanded by such person or persons in authority as his Majesty shall please to establish and empower in Delaware river, and the parts and plantatons adjacent. Given under my hand and seale, at Fort James, New Yorke (179) on the Island Manhatans, the 18th day of June in the 20th yeare of his Majesty's Raigne Anno Domini, 1668.

Fo 13.

A Patent granted upon a transport bearing date the 17th day of September 1664, made by Hendrick Kipp unto Reyner Reyniessen for a certain lott of ground at Delaware lying and being in the Bever's street, bounded on the one side, with Harman Reynart's and on the other side with the Haartstreet conteyning in length on each side two hundred and fifety foot Amsterdam wood measure in breadth before Sixty two feet and there being likewise graunted unto the sd Hendrick Kipp by the Governor Alexander D'Hiniosa for part of another lott lying behind the former contenying in length one hundred foot and in breadth four and forty foot butting behind on the Otter street on the side of the Haartstreet which sd patents bare date the 20th July 1659 and the 28th May 1660. Now for a conformacon unto the sd Reijner Reignesse &c. Know yee that by vertue of the commission and authority unto me given I do think fitt to ratifye and confirme, and by these presents do ratifye and confirme unto the sd Reynier Reynessen hisheirs and assigns the afore cited lotts of ground with all and singular the appertences to have and to hold the sd lotts of ground unto the sd Reynier Reynessen his heirs and assigns forever, yielding and paying yearly and every year unto his Majesty's use one bushell of Wheate as a Quitt rent when it shall be demanded by such person or persons in authority as his majesty shall please to establish and empower in Delaware River and the parts and plantations adjacent Given under my hand and seale at Fort James in New York on the Island Manhattans, the 22nd day of June, in the 20th yeare of his Majesty's raigne Anno Domini, 1668.

Fo. 17.

A confirmacon graunted to Hans Bones for a certaine Parcell of land in Christeen Kill in Delaware.

(180)
Richard Nicolls, Esqr. &c. Whereas there is a certaine piece or parcell of land lyeing and being in Christine kill in Delaware river heretofore in the tenure or occupation of Toost Rugger, the Miller, de-

ceased which sd piece or parcell of land was by the officers at Delaware who were empowered by my commission to dispose of implanted land there for the best advantage of the inhabitants granted unto Hans Bones the said Graunt bearing date the 21st day of Feb. 1666. Now for a confirmation unto him the sd Hans Bones, in his possession and enjoyment of the premises Know yee that by vertue of the commission and authority unto me given I have thought fitt to give and grant and by these presents do give ratifye confirme and graunt unto the sd Hans Bones, his heirs and assigns the afore recited parcell of land to have and to hold the sd land unto the sd Hans Bones, his heirs, and assigns, unto the proper use and behoofe of the sd Hans Bones, his heirs and assigns forever, yielding and paying yearly and every year unto his Majesty's use two bushells of Wheate, as a Quitt rent when it shall be demanded by such person or persons in authority as his Majesty shall think fitt to empower in Delaware River, and the parts and plantations adjacent. Given under my hand and seal at Fort James, in New York, on the Island Manhattens the first day of August, the 20th yeare of his Majesty's raigne, Anno Domini, 1668.
Fo 19

A Confirmacon graunted unto Serjeant Tho. Wollaston, Jno. Ogle, John Hendrick, and Herman Johnston, for a certaine pcell of land in White Clay kill in Delaware River.

Richard Nicolls, Esqr. &c. Whereas there is a certaine piece or parcell of land lyeing and being in White Clay kill near unto Christeen kill in Delaware River bounded to the E. with Hans Bones Plantation to the South with James Crawford's, to the North and West by a fresh Creeke or Runne of water at the head of Bread and Cheese Island containing about   acres of woodland (181) as also a piece of valley or meadow ground known by the name of the Muscle crupple runing up the kill about   of a mile which sd piece or parcell of land was by the officers of Delaware who were empowered by my commission to dispose of implanted land there for the best advantage of the inhabitants granted unto Serjeant Tho. Wallison, Jno. Ogle, John Hendrick, and Herman Johnson, the sd grant bearing date   day of Feb. 1666. Now for a confirmation unto them the sd Tho. Wolliston, Jno. Ogle, John Hendrick, and Herman Johnson, in their possession and enjoyment of the premises. Know yee that by vertue of the commission and authority unto me given, I have given ratifyed confirmed and granted unto the sd Thomas Wolliston &c. the afore recited parcells of land and premises &c. yielding and paying therefore yearly and every year unto his Majesty's use eight bushells of Wheat as a Quitt rent when it shall be demanded, by such person or persons in authority as his majesty shall please to establish and empower in Delaware River and the parts and plantations adjacent. Given under my hand and seale, at Fort James, in New Yorke, on the Island Manhatans, the first day of August, in the 20th year of his Majesty's raigne, Anno Domini, 1668.
Fo 20

THE DUKE OF YORK RECORD.

A Confirmation graunted unto Paul Dux and Alice his Wife for a certaine plantation at Delaware.

Richard Nicolls, Esqr. &c. Whereas there is a certaine plantation heretofore belonging unto Moens Andriss lyeing and being upon the second Hook or Neck of land above ye fort at Delaware next to ye valley or meadow ground which is on the South west side of ye sd Hook, stretching alongst ye sd valley through ye woods to a swamp or cruppel bush Northwest and by North three hundred and twenty rod, there being left out a way between ye sd land and valley of three rod in breadth (for drift of cattle) further by (182) ye swamp alongst ye land of Laars Boers two and twenty rod next to ye land of ye sd Laars Boers to ye ryverside south East and by South with ye valley or meadow ground three hundred and twenty rod thence along ye strand to ye first going of South West and by West, thirty three rod, in all amounting to about twenty nine acres or foureteen morgen and four hundred and ten rod, the land belonging to Laars Boots next to Tunan Stiddens striking into ye woods North North West somewhat more Northerly according to ye Surveyors Certificate bearing date ye eleventh day of November 1656, the sd plantation being in tenure or occupation of Paul Duxon and Alice his wife who have ye present right and title thereunto, now for a confirmation unto them ye sd Paul Dux and Alice his wife and &c. The pattent is dated August ye 1st 1668 ye quitt rent one bushell &c. 1668.
Fo 21.

A Confirmaton graunted unto Thomas Jackson and Wooley Poulston for an island in Delaware River called Bread and Cheese Island.

Richard Nicolls, Esq. &c. Whereas there is a certain small island in Christeen kill in Delaware Ryver comonly called and known by ye name of Bread and Cheese island which sd island was by the officers at Delaware who were empowered by my comision to dispose of land there for ye best advantage of ye inhabitants granted unto Thomas Jackson and Wooley Poulson with a reservation of liberty to put in a third person to have equal shares and proportion with them therein. Ye sd grant bearing date ye thirteenth day of February 1666. Now for a confirmation unto them the sd Thomas Jackson and Wooley Poulston. The Quitt rent three bushells Wheate, the Patent is dated August 3, 1668.
Fo 22

(183)

A Confirmation granted to Juriean Jansen for a piece of land at Delaware.

Richard Nicolls, Esq. &c. Whereas there was heretofore a grant made by Alexander D'Hiniosa late Governor at Delaware unto Juryan Janson for a certaine piece or parcell of land there next to ye hook or point of Jan Landemakers, conteyning alongst ye riverside to ye land of Mattys Eschelson twenty five rods and so into ye woods six hundred

rod. Now for a confirmation unto him ye sd Juriaen Jansen &c. The Quitt rent one bushell of Wheate, the Patent is dated August ye 3d, 1668.
Fo. 23.

A Confirmation granted to Mattys Eschelsen for a piece of land at Delaware.

Richard Nicolls, Esr. &c. Whereas the was heretofore a graunt made by Alexander D'Hiniosa late Governor at Delaware unto Mattys Eschelsen for a certaine piece or parcell of land there next unto Juryan Jansens, contenying alongst ye River syde Eastward twenty five rod and from thence going North West into ye woods six hundred rods. Now for a confirmation under him ye sd. Mattys Eschelson &c. The Quitt rent is one bushell Wheate, the Pattent is dated August ye 3d 1668.
Fo. 23.

A Confirmation granted to William Tom for a piece of land at ye Whorekill near Delaware.

Richard Nichols, Esqr. &c. Whereas there was a certain piece or parcell of land scituate lyeing and being at ye Hoer kill near Delaware, stretching from ye sd kill or creeke, into ye woods by a West and by South Line bounded by Pieter Hans Herwards land and so stretching North West and upwards South East by ye land formerly belonging to ye Frenchmen deceased, which sd piece or parcell of land did heretofore belonge to Pieter Alricks but stands confiscated to his majesty. Now know yee that by vertue of ye comision and authority unto me given for and in consideration of ye good service (184) done and performed by Mr. Wm. Tom, at Delaware, I have given and granted and by these presents to give ratifye, confirme and graunt unto ye sd Tom his heires and assigns the afore recited parcell of land &c. The Quitt rent 2 bushells of Corne, the Patent dated August ye 3rd 1668.
Fo. 24.

A Confirmation graunted to Andries Maetsen for a parcell of land called ye Wild Hook at Delaware.

Richard Nicolls, Esqr. &c. Whereas there is a certaine piece parcell of land at Delaware scituate lying and being a   called ye Indians or ye Wild Hook having a small streame of water bounding ye sd land on ye East running by skill paets kill to ye marke tree which is betweene it and Hans Pietersens land being about 100 rods in breadth and in going into ye woods North West on both sides it conteyns in length with ye valley or meadow grounds and swamp six hundred rods which sd piece or parcell of land hath hereto fore been and now is in ye tenure or occupation of Andries Maetsen as of right belonging unto him Now for a confirmation under him ye sd Andries Maetsen, &c. The Quitt rent one bushell &c. The patent is dated ye 14th of November 1668.
Fo 25.

A Confirmation granted to Hans Pieters for a piece of land called ye Wild Hook in Delaware.

Richard Nicolls, Esq. &c. Whereas there is a certaine piece or parcell of land at Delaware scituate lyeing and being at a place called ye Indians or Wild Hook conteyning in breadth from ye markt tree betwixt ye sd land and Andries Maetsens to ye small streame that is to ye West of ye sd land about seaventy five rod in length runing on both sides into ye woods North west together with ye meadow ground for valley and Swamp six hundred rod which sd piece or parcell of land hath heretofore beene and now is in ye tenure of Hans Pieterson (185) as of right belonging unto him Now for a confirmation unto him the sd Hans Pieterson &c. The patent is dated November 14th 1668. The quitt rent is one bushell &c.

Fo 26.

A Confirmation granted to Jan Ericksen, for a piece of land in ye fire hook at Delaware.

Richard Nicolls, Esq. &c. Whereas there is a certain piece of land at Delaware in ye fire hook or neck by Christine kill, lyeing and being on ye East side of ye sd neck stretching from ye kill into ye woods on both sydes upon a South East lyne six hundred rod and conteyning in breadth alongst ye sd kill twenty five rods which sd piece of land is now in ye tenure for occupation of Jan Eerickson as his proper right. Now for a confirmation unto him the sd Jan Erickson &c. The Quitt rent is 1 bushell &c. The patent is dated 24th of March 1668-9.

Fo 26.

A Confirmation graunted to Olle Laerten for a piece of land at the fire hook at Delaware.

Richard Nicolls, Esqr. &c. Whereas there is a certaine piece of land at Delaware on ye fire hook or neck by Christine kill now in ye tenure or occupation of Olle Laerton as his proper right ye sd land stretching from ye kill into ye woods on both sides upon a South East lyne six hundred rod and conteyning in breadth alongst ye sd kill twenty five rod. Now for a confirmation. Unto him ye sd. Olle Laerton, The quit rent is one bushell &c. The patent is dated March ye 24th 1668-9.

Fo 27.

A Confirmation granted to Hendrick Claesen, for a piece of land on ye fire hook at Delaware.

Richard Nicolls Esqr. &c. Whereas there is a certain piece of land at Delaware on ye fire hook or neck by Christine kill now in ye tenure or occupation of Hendrick Claesen as his proper right ye sd land stretching from ye kill into ye woods (186) on both sydes upon a South East lyne six hundred rod and contenying in breadth alongst ye sd kill twenty-five rods. Now for a confirmation. unto him ye sd Hendrick Claesen &c. The Quitt Rent is I bushell &c. The patent is dated March ye 24th 1668-9.

Fo 27.

A Confirmation granted to Pieter Olleson for a piece of land on ye fire hook at Delaware.

Richard Nicolls Esqr. &c. Whereas there is a certaine piece of land at Delaware on ye fire hook or neck by Christine Kill now in ye tenure or occupation of Peter Olleson as his proper right lying and being next and adjoyning to Jans Enricksens stretching in like manner from the kill into ye woods on both sydes upon a South East lyne six hundred rod and conteyning in breadth alongst ye sd kill twenty five rods, Now for a confirmation unto him ye sd Peter Olleson &c. The Quitt rent is 1 bushell &c. The Patent dated March 24th 1668-9.
Fo 27.

A Confirmation granted to Pauls Pousen for a piece of land on ye fire hook at Delaware.

Richard Nichols, Esq., &c. Whereas there is a certain piece of land at Delaware on ye fire hook or Neck by Christeen kill now in ye tenure or occupation of Paul Poulsen as his proper right, ye sd land stretching from ye kill into ye woods on both sides upon a South East lyne 600 rods contenying in breadth alongst ye sd kill twenty five rods, Now for a confirmation unto him the sd Paul Pousen &c. The Quitt rent is one Bushell &c. Ye patent dated March 24, 1668-9.
Fo. 28.

A Confirmation granted to Matijs Jansen for a piece of land on ye fire hook at Delaware.

Richard Nicolls, Esqr. &c. Whereas there is a certain piece of land at Delaware on ye fire hook or neck by Christeen kill now in ye tenure or occupation of Matijs Jansen as his proper right (187) ye sd land stretching from ye kill into ye woods on both sydes upon a south east lyne six hundred rod and conteyning in breadth alongst ye sd kill twenty five rods Now for a confirmation unto to him ye sd Matijs Jansen, &c. The Quitt rent is 1 bushell &c. The pattent is dated March 24th 1668-9.
Fo 28

A Confirmation graunted to Paul Laersen for a piece of land on ye fire hook at Delaware.

Richard Nichols, Esq. &c. Whereas there is a certaine piece of land at Delaware on ye fire hook or neek by Christeen kill now in ye tenure or occupation of Paul Laersen as his proper right, ye sd land stretching from the kill into ye woods on both sydes upon a South East lyne six hundred rods and containing in breadth alongst ye sd kill twenty five rods. Now for a confirmation unto him the sd Paul Laersen &c. The Quitt rent is 1 bushell &c. The patent is dated March 24th, 1668-9.
Fo. 28.

A Confirmation granted to Juryaen Jansen for a piece of land on ye fire hook at Delaware.

Richard Nicolls, Esq. &c. Whereas there is a certaine piece of land at Delaware on ye fire hook or neck by Christeene kill now in the tenure or occupation of Juryen Jansen as his proper right ye sd land stretching from ye kill into ye woods on both sides upon a South East line 600 rod and contenying in breadth alongst ye sd kill twenty five rod. Now for confirmation unto him ye sd Juryean Jansen &c. The quitt rent one bushell &c. The patent is dated March 24th 1668-9.
Fo 29.

A Confirmation graunted to all ye and severall persons before named for ye waste land not mentioned in their severall patents lying and being on ye sd neck.

Richard Nicolls, Esqr. &c. Whereas I have granted severall (188) pattents to ye persons hereafter named, that is to say to Jan Erickson, Peter Olleson, Paul Pousen, Matijs Jansen, Olle Laersen, Hendrick Cleasen, Paul Lersen, and Jaurian Jansen, for the land each of them doth now enjoy at Delaware on ye fire hook or neck by Christeene kill, there p'ticular proportions being in their sd patents sett forth, and whereas ye whole hook or neck of land called Unyren or fire hook lyes between two small creeks or kills on ye East syde whereof there is a small parcell of valley or meadowe ground and on ye west syde a swamp or creupell not comprehended in their pattent which lying in common betweene ye persons aforenamed as now it doth will prove some small advantage to them but is of no use neither doth it belong to any other person or persons for an encouragement unto ye several persons afore mencioned as also for a confirmation to them in their possession and enjoyment of ye premises. Know yee that by vertue of ye comision and authority unto me given by his Royal Highness I have ratifyed, confirmed and graunted and by these presents do ratifye confirme and graunt unto yee sd persons their heirs and assigns all ye waste land not mencioned in their severall patents lying in ye sd neck between the two small kills as afore sd. whether meadow or other ground with all and singular the appertances and premises and every parte and parcell thereof to have and to hold all ye sd waste lands meadow ground and premises in common unto you persons before mentioned their heirs and assigns to ye proper use, the Quitt rent 2 bushells &c. The patent dated March 25, 1669.
Fo 29.

A Confirmation graunted to Jan Sibrantsen for a piece of land at Delaware.

Richard Nicholls Esq. &c. Whereas there is a certain piece of land at Delaware now in ye tenure or occupation of Jan Sibrantsen as of right belonging unto him lyeing and being neare ye horse neck (commonly called ye Paerd Hook) that is to say betweene a certaine (189) small creek or kill and ye sd horse neck stretching from ye sd

creek or kill into ye woods N. W. and by W. and towards ye river S. E. and by E. containing in breadth by ye river syde one hundred & fifety rods or thereabouts reaching to ye lands of Arent Jansen in length into ye woods North W. and by West 600 rods on having within ye sd land much Marshy and Swampy ground, Now for a confirmation unto him ye sd Jan Sibrantsen &c. Quitt rent 1 bushell. Patent dated March 26th, 1669.
Fo. 30.

> A Confirmation graunted to Evert Gertsen for a piece of land at Delaware.

Richard Nicholls Esq. &c. Whereas there is a certaine piece of land at Delaware now in ye tenure or occupation of Evert Gertsen as of right belonging to him lyeing and being in New Castle having before ye Otter street and behind ye Calves street abutting on ye North East syde with the land of Top Puthout and on ye South West side with ye land of Reijner Vander Cooley conteyning in length on both sydes four hundred foot wood measure and in breadth as well behynd as before one and twenty rod Now for a confirmation unto him ye sd Evert Gertsen &c. Quitt rent 1 bushell. The patent dated March ye 26th, 1669.
Fo. 30.

> A Confirmation graunted to Andries Andiresen. Sinick Broers and Walrane Jansen for a parcell of land in Delaware.

Francis Lovelace Esqr. &c. Whereas there is a certaine parcell of land in Delaware now in ye tenure or occupation of Andries Andriesen, Sinick Broers, and Walrane Jansen, as in their proper right, The sd land lyeing on ye N. syde of Christiana kill being bounded on ye East syde with ye land (190) belonging to George Whale ye limitts betweene them being a certain marked tree having upon it ye three names afore mensioned and also that of George Whale so striking into yee woods direct Northwest three hundred rods it's in breadth along the kill three hundred and fifety rod, from the marked tree aforesd it strikes to the mill kill more west than North three hundred rod, also, in all amounting to about foure hundred Morgen haveing by agreement with George Whale ye swamp or crupell lyeing within their lymitts in comon betwixt them all Now for a confirmation unto them ye said Andries Andriesen, Sinick Broers, and Walrane Jansen, &c. Quitt rent eight bushells the patent dated Sept. 1, 1669.
Fo. 31.

> A Patent granted to Andries Andriesen & Company to erect a mill on a creek called Andries ye Fynnes creeke in Delaware ryver.

Francis Lovelace Esqr. &c. Whereas there is a certain creek in Christiane kill in Delaware river comonly called and knowne by ye name of Andries ye Fynnes creeke, whereupon there is a convenient

place to erect a mill the which is recommended by ye officers there to be sett up by Andries Andriesen and nineteen more in company whose names are hereunder written for an encouragement to ye said undertaking, it tending to a publique good know ye that by vertue of ye comision & authority unto me given I have given & granted, an by these presents do give, ratify, confirme & grant unto ye sd Andries Andriesen & Company their heires and assigns liberty to erect a mill in ye most convenient place in ye creek afore menconed to have and to hold &c. The quitt rent is bushell wheat. The patent is dated ye 1st of October 1669.
Fo. 32.

A confirmation graunted to John Askue for a house and garden at New Castle in Delaware.

Francis Lovelace Esq. &c. Whereas there is a certain house and (191) garden at New Castle in Delaware River now in the tenure or occupation of Sarjeant John Askue being in breadth about sixty foot bounded on the east with John Henrye's fence on ye West with Martin Gerritsens and on ye North with ye Mart, having a piece of land belonging thereunto of about seaven acres lyeing to ye West of ye towne bounded to ye West by Capt. Carrs land, to ye East with ye Crupell or Swamp, and to ye South with ye Ryver: as also a small piece of land in ye towne given him by Sir Robert Carr conteyning about six acres bounded by ye East with Garrett Garetsons to ye North with ye Highway and to ye West with ye lands heretofore belonging to Reyner Vander Cooley. Now for a confirmation unto him the sd John Askue, &c. Quitt rent 1 bushell, Ye patent is dated the first of October 1669.

A Confirmation granted to Hans Bons for a house and lott of ground at New Castle in Delaware Ryver.

Francis Lovelace, Esq. &c. Whereas there is a certain house and lott of ground at New Castle in Delaware Ryver now in ye tenure or occupation of Hans Bons lyeing and being in the Otter street bounded on ye one side with Corneyls Wynhurst conteyning in length alike on both sydes being about two hundred foot and in breadth before and behind ninety foot, which sd lott of ground was given unto ye sd Hans Bons by ye late Dutch Governor together with a Parcell of Bon land or planting ground lyeing over against the sd house in ye Otter street having on ye south East and South West sydes ye high street runing from ye Smyths to ye Swamp or crupell and containing about three Morgen or six acres of land Now for a confirmacon &c. The Quitt rent &c. 1 Bushell. The patent is dated ye first of October 1669.
Fo. 33.

(192)
>A confirmation graunted to Andren Carr & Margarite his wife for Matiniconck Island in Delaware Ryver.

Francis Lovelace Esqr. &c. Whereas there is a certaine island in Delaware Ryver now in ye Tenure or occupation of Andren Carre & Margarett his wife heretofore ye widow & relect of Joost de la Grange who purchased ye same for a valuable consideration, comonly called & knowne by ye name of Matiniconck conteyning by estimation three hundred acres bee it more or lesse the sd Island lyeing and being about six Dutch myles up ye ryver from ye towne of New Castle bounded on ye North West with ye Mill kill on ye South with ye ryver & on ye N. East or North & by East with ye Bon Kill Now for a confirmation unto him ye sd Andries and Margarite his wife &c. The patent is dated ye first of October 1669. The Quitt rent 2 bushell.
Fo 33.

>A Patent graunted to Thomas Wollaston for a parcell of land in Delaware Ryver.

Francis Lovelace, Esqr. &c. Whereas there is a certaine parcell of land in Delaware Ryver lyeing and being on ye South Syde of Swarte Nutten Island bounded with a mark't tree on Sargeant Askews land on ye East and on Ye West with a markt tree on James Crawfords land conteyning about one hundred acres of Wood land it being a hook of land comonly called by the name of Beeslye which sd parcell of land lyes unplanted & unmanured having no particular owner to ye end ye sd land may be clared & made fitt for a plantaton. Know yee that by vertue of ye comision, & authority unto me given, I have thought fitt to give and graunt and by these presents do hereby give ratifye, confirme and graunt unto Sargeant (193) Thomas Wollaston who came over into these partes in his Majesty's service ye afore recited parcell of land and premises scituate and lyeing as aforesaid with all and singular the appurteinces with privildg of comonage on ye South unto ye woods to have and to hold &c. Quitt rent 1 bushell. Given under ye Governors hand and seale first of October 1669.
Fo. 34.

>A Confirmation graunted to John Askew for a parcell of Marsh Ground in Delaware Ryver.

Francis Lovelace, Esqr. &c. Whereas there is a certaine parcell of Marsh ground in Delaware Ryver lyeing on ye West syde of Christina Kill bounded with a small Kill or Creeke, towards ye long hooke, & runing downe along Christina Kill one hundred and fifety rod towards John Clawsons plantaton haveing ye fast land to ye West of ye sd Marsh conteyning by estimation one hundred acres, bee it more or lesse. Now ye sd Marsh ground having been disposed of by ye officers at Delaware who had comision to do ye same unto John Askew, Matthew Garretson and Gisbert Dircksen for whose use it lyes comodious, if it shall be improved ye which they undertake to do and

belonging to no other particular person for a confirmation to ye sd John Askew &c. The Quitt rent is 2 Bushells, ye patent dated ye 1st of October 1669.
Fo. 34.

> A patent graunted to Robert Scott, John Marshall, John Cousins and John Boyers for a parcell of land in Delaware Ryver.

Francis Lovelace, Esqr. &c. Whereas there is a certaine parcell of land in Delaware Ryver lyeing and being on the East Syde of Christina Kill bounded on ye West with Ye Creeke or ye Kill comonly called ye Mill kill or Andries ye Finnes Kill on ye East with ye bounds of Christina towne or John Stalcops land conteyning (194) about foure hundred acres bee it more or lesse which sd parcell of land hath been layed out bye ye officers at Delaware for foure souldiers that is to say Robert Scott, John Marshall, John Cousins, and John Boyers, to ye end ye sd land may be manured and planted Know yee that by vertue &c. the Quitt rent 4 bushells. The patent is dated October ye 1st 1669.
Fo. 35.

> A Pattent graunted to Thomas Jackson, Wolley Poulson and Thomas Snelling for 100 acres of land upon ye maine over against Bread & Cheese Island.

Francis Lovelace, Esqr. &c. Whereas my predecessor Coll. Richard Nicholls did heretofore give and graunt unto Thomas Jackson, Wolley Pouson and Thomas Snelling a certaine small island in Christine Kill, in Delaware Ryver, the which they have improved to ye best advantage but are very much straitened for want of forrage and other accommodation for their cattle in regard of ye little quantity of land upon ye sd island and ye sd Thomas Jackson, Wooley Poulson and Thomas Snelling being recommended by ye officers there and having requested my graunt for an adicon of one hundred acres of land upon ye maine over against ye creek, North West from ye sd Bread & Cheese Island adjoyning to Hans Bons land ye which lyes unmanured and hath no perticular proprietor for an encouragement to ye sd persons I have given and graunted and by these presents do give ratifye confirme and graunt unto ye sd Thomas Jackson Wooley Poulston and Thomas Snelling their heirs and assigns the afore recited one hundred acres of land lyeing and being as is related and premises with all and singuler the appertances &c. The Quitt rent 1 bushell. The pattent is dated ye 1st of October 1669.
Fo 35.

(195)
> A Confirmation graunted to Pieter Cowenhoven for a small hooke or corner of land at New Castle in Delaware Ryver.

Francis Lovelace, Esqr. &c. Whereas there is a certaine hooke or small corner of land at New Castle in Delaware Ryver lyeing be-

hinde Pieter Cowenhovens lott by which it is bounded on ye one syde and is on all ye other surrounded with ye meadow ground or valley, and swamp or creupell, conteyning between two or three Morgen or five or six acres at most ye which ye officers at Delaware who have had comision to dispose of land there not improved or belonging to no perticular properietor have graunted to Pieter Cowenhoven; for a confirmation to ye sd Pieter Cowenhoven &c. The Quitt rent one bushell, the patent is dated ye first of October 1669.
Fo 36.

    A Patent graunted to Robert Jones, for a small parcell of land convenient to keep a ferry in Christeen Kill in Delaware.

 Francis Lovelace Esqr. &c. Whereas there is a certaine small parcell of land in Christeen kill at Delaware where formerly ye Fort stood which lyes undisposed of and it lyeing neare to ye Water syde where is a convenient place to keep a ferry for ye generall good of ye inhabitants in that ryver ye which Robert Jones doth undertake to maintaine with a sufficient boate for ye same if it may be graunted him as is recomended to me by ye officers at Delaware for an encouragement to any such undertaking as may tend to ye publique good. Know ye &c. With a clause that whosoever hath ye land shall uphold ye ferry or be obliged to keepe a boate for that purpose he or they taking some reasonable satisfaction for ye ferriage &c. Quitt rent &c. 1 Bushell. The patent dated first of October 1669.
Fo. 36.

(196)
    A Confirmation graunted to Pieter Claesen for a lott of ground at Christeene Kill in Delaware.

 Francis Lovelace, Esqr. &c. Whereas there is a certaine lott of ground in Christeene Kill at Delaware belonging unto and now in ye tenrure or occupation of Pieter Claesen lyeing in breadth South East and North West from ye Crane kill neare unto Laes ways to ye land of Juriaen Boosman eighty eight rods and in length South West and North East behynde ye first creupel Boos or Swamp conteyning together in woodland and valley or meadow about one hundred acres be it more or lesse. Now for a confirmation unto him ye sd Pieter Claesen &c. The Quitt rent 1 bushell Winter wheate. The patent is dated November ye 5th 1669.
Fo. 37.

    A Confirmation graunted to Juryen Juryensen and Olle Clementsen for a piece of land at Delaware.

 Francis Lovelace Esqr &c. Whereas there is a certaine piece of land at Delaware lyeing and being upon a long hook by Christeen Kill belonging unto Juryen Juryensen and Olle Clementsen stretching South into ye woods and bounded on each syde by the small creeke or kill amounting in all both woodland and valley or meadow to about

two hundred acres of land Now for a confirmation unto yee sd Juryen Juryensen and Olle Clemenese &c. The Quitt rent 2 bushells of Winter Wheate, the patent is dated ye 5th day of November 1669.
Fo. 38.

A Confirmation granted to Hans Monsen for a parcell of land in Delaware.

Francis Lovelace Esqr. &c. Whereas there is a certain piece or parcell of land in Delaware being bounded to ye North East with ye Swar Kill and to ye South with Andries Jackhornes kill to ye North with a great Pine tree on ye other syde of Nagency kill over ye creeke runing into ye woods West and conteyning by (197) estimation one hundred acres bee ye same more or less, also another piece or parcell of land being bounded with ye fence of John Eustace on ye North and with ye fence of Jonas Neilson to ye South conteying by estimation ten acres bee the same more or lesse. And likewise another small piece or parcell of land being bounded with Peter Andries fence to ye North and with a little creeke runing into ye land of John Bowles to ye South and conteyning by estimation Tenne acres bee ye same more or lesse, which sd severall pieces or parcells of land are now in ye tenure or occupation of Hans Monsen. Now for a conformacon unto him ye sd Hans Monsen &c. The Quitt Rent 1 bushell and a halfe. The Pattent is dated ye 14th of May 1669.
Fo. 38.

A Confirmation graunted to John Eustas for a piece of land in Delaware.

Francis Lovelace Esqr. &c. Whereas there is a certaine piece or parcell of land in Delaware haveing a house or tenement thereupon scituate lyeing and being by ye land of J. Kinseys being bounded to ye South with ye land of Hans Monsen, to ye North East with ye land of John Bowles runing directly into ye woods North West and haveing ye Scoar kill South East Contayneing by estimation one hundred and fifety acres or thereabouts bee ye same more or less. which said parcell of land house and premises are now in ye tenure or occupation of John Eustas. Now for a confirmation under him ye sd John Eustas &c. The Quitt rent I bushell and a halfe. The patent is dated ye 16th of May 1669.
Fo. 38.

A Confirmation graunted to Robert Jones for a Piece of land at Delaware.

Francis Lovelace Esqr. &c. Whereas there is a certaine piece or parcell of land in Delaware lyeing and being to ye South of Brainwend Kill or Creeke haveing a small run or ryvalett (198) neare thereunto and lyeing adjacent to Jacob Vannivers island conteyning by estimation two hundred acres or thereabouts bee ye same more or lesse, which sd piece or parcell of land was bought and purchased by Robert

Jones (in whose tenure and occupation it now is), of Andren Brainwinde. Now for a confirmacon unto him ye sd Robert Jones, &c. The Quitt rent 2 bushell. patent is dated ye 6th of June 1670.
Fo. 39.

> A Confirmation graunted to Dirck Pieters for a certaine piece of land at Delaware.

Francis Lovelace Esqr. &c. Whereas there is a certaine piece of land at Delaware lyeing and being at ye Whore Kill striking alongst ye kill in breadth Northwest and by West One hundred and five rod Dutch measure then in length goes into ye bush or woodland East, and West by South about a myle on each Syde with a bowery thereunto belonging and a kill behynde it about an English myle haveing on ye south syde Anthony Pieters, and on ye North West syde Wm. Claesens land where he has planted betweene two bowerys which sd piece of land hath been for a valueble consideracon transported and made over by Abraham Clementie unto Dirck Pieters in whose tenure or occupatio it now is. Now for a confirmacon unto him ye sd Dirck Pieters &c. Ye Quitt rent 2 bushells. Ye Pattent is dated ye 25th of May 1670.
Fo. 40

> A Confirmation graunted to Derrick Alberts for a lott of ground neare ye fort in Delaware.

Francis Lovelace Esqr. &c. Whereas there is a certaine lott of ground haveing a small piece of land belonging unto it lyeing and being neare ye fort at New Castle in Delaware bounded to ye South East with ye Ryver and to ye West with Gisbert Dericks fence, and to ye North East with Jacob Vanderveers lott, conteyning in breadth thirty five yards and in length one hundred bee it more or lesse which sd lott of ground is in the tenure or (199) occupation of Derrick Alberts to whom of right it doth belonge Now for a confirmacon &c The Quitt rent 1 bushell. The Patent is dated ye 11th of August 1670.
Fo 44.

> A Pattent graunted to James Bollen and Peter Jego for a parcell of land on ye West side of Delaware Ryver.

Whereas there is a certaine parcell of land on ye West syde of Delaware ryver lyeing and being on both sydes of a Creeke or kill comonly called Champone kill runing in length alonge ye sd ryver sixty chaine and conteyning in all foure hundred acres of upland and one hundred acres of meadowe ground thereunto adjacent, which sd parcell of land and meadowe grounds lyes unmanured and belongs to no perticular owner. To ye end some good improvement may be made thereupon Know ye that by vertue of ye comision and authority unto me given by his R. Highness I have given and granted and by these presents do give ratifye confirme and graunt the afore recited parcell of land, meadowe ground and premises unto James Bollen and Peter Jegoe their heirs and Assigns with this provisoe that if ye sd land hath not beene purchased of ye Indian proprietors and is lawfully layd claim to by them that then they make purchase thereof ye which they have hereby liberty to do to have and to hold &c.

Dated the 2nd of Aprill 1670. Quitt rent foure schep of wheate.
Fo 45.

A Confirmation graunted to Peter Alricks for a lott of ground at New Castle in Delaware Ryver.

Francis Lovelace Esq. &c. Whereas William Tom did upon ye 12th day of April last transport and make over unto Peter Alricks a certaine lott of ground at New Castle in Delaware (200) Ryver lyeing and being towards ye strand haveing on ye West syde ye house of Wm Sinclaer and on ye East ye fence of Cornelys Wynharts land contayning in breadth before towards ye strand Nynety fower foot Amsterdam wood measure and in length reaching to yee land belonging to deRine bearing date ye 25th day of Julye 1668 with a reserve of one bushell of winter wheat for a quitt rent and whereas John Erskin did on ye 7th day of June last assign and make over unto ye sd Peter Alricks his third part of another certaine lott of ground lyeing to ye west of New Castle haveing on ye West syde Captaine Carrs land on ye East ye Swamp or crupell bush and on ye South ye River for ye which with other two third parts of ye sd lotts there was a pattent graunted unto him ye sd John Erskin and others dated ye first day of October 1669 with a reserve of 1 bushell of Winter Wheate for Quitt rent upon ye whole. Now for a confirmacon unto him ye sd Peter Alricks &c. The Quitt rent is so much as ye sd William Tom and John Esskin were obliged to pay. The Patent was dated ye 16th of August 1670.
Fo. 47.

A Confirmation granted to Peter Alricks for a piece of land at New Castle in Delaware.

Francis Lovelace Esqr. &c. Whereas there is a certaine piece of land at New Castle in Delaware lately purchased by Peter Alricks from Matthys and Annelys de Ringh abutting on ye West syde on ye land graunted to Sargeant Erskin, on ye North syde on ye street on ye Easte syde on ye Merchant street, and on ye South syde on ye lotts of Mr. Tom and ye sd Peter Alricks Now for a confirmation unto him ye sd Peter Alricks &c. The quitt rent is one bushell of wheat, dated August 16th 1670
Fo 49.

A Confirmation of a certaine piece of land at Delaware unto Barent Hendricksen.

Francis Lovelace Esqr. &c. Whereas ye officers of Delaware being empowered soe to doe did heretofore graunt unto Barent (201) Hendricksen a certaine piece of land scituate lyeing and being on ye West side Delaware ryver on ye North West side of Appoqueminy Creek, ye sd land runing from ye sd Creeke North West into ye Woods on ye North East bounded with ye land of Adam Pieters, and on ye

South West with the land of John Breadband, the sd land conteyning by estimacon two hundred acres bee it more or less with a convenient quantity of about one hundred acres of Marsh land on ye south East side of ye Drayers creeke, for meadow ground, Now for a confirmacon unto him the sd Barent Hendricksen in his possession and enjoyment &c. The pattent is date August 14th, 1671. and to pay for quitt rent 3 bushells Winter Wheate.

Fo 61.
Delaware,
Barent Hendricksen

A Confirmacon graunted to John Sherricks for a certaine piece of land at Delaware Bay &c.

Francis Lovelace, Esqr. &c. Whereas ye officers of Delaware being empowered so to doe did herefore grant unto John Sherricks a certaine piece of land scituate lyeing and being on ye West syde of Delaware ryver on ye North West syde of Appoqueminy creck, ye sd land runing from ye sd creeke North West into ye woods, on ye North East bounded with ye land of Garrett Otto and on ye South west with ye land of Roelofe Anderson, ye sd land contanying by estimation two hundred acres bee it more or less with a convenient quantity of about one hundred acres of Marsh land on ye South East syde of ye Drayers creeke for meadowe ground. Now for a confirmacon &c. The Patent is dated August ye 4th 1671. paying 3 bushells winter wheate quitt rent.

Whore Kill,
Jno. Sherricks
Fo. 62.

A Confirmacon graunted unto Hermanus Frederick Wiltbanck for a certaine parcell of land at the Whorekill

Francis Lovelace Esqr. &c. Whereas Hermanus Frederick (202) Wiltbanck stands possest of a certayne parcell of land at ye Whorekill in Delaware Bay, part of which he hath manured, the sd land runing into the woods, begining at Aroskes kill, and stretching South East and North West to Beaver Kill in breadth and in length as it runs into ye woods South West and North East till it comes behinde ye creeke which is by ye common land of ye Whore kill contayning by estimacon about eight hundred acres; Now for a confirmacon unto ye sd Hermanus Frederick Wiltbanck as also (at his request) to his two sons, Cornelys and Abraham in their possession and enjoyment of ye premises &c. yielding and paying as a quitt rent &c. eight bushells winter wheate yearly. The patent is dated July ye 1st 1671.

Whore Kill
Hermanus Wiltbanck
Fo. 63.

A Confirmacon graunted to Leendert Teunijssen for
a parcell of land at ye Whorekill,
 Whereas there was heretofore graunted by ye Dutch Governor at
ye South Ryver unto Wm. Vandiemen, a certaine piece of land at ye
Whorekill, otherwise called Swanendale in Delaware Bay, the sd land
lyeing and being on ye South Syde of Hendrick Bakers, or of that land
then newly broken up by Gelijaem, and on ye North syde of the lott
formerly belonging to   Lavyny deceased which sd land and
premises as he the sd Willem Vandiemen enjoyed the same, hee transported and made over unto Leendert Teunijsse Van Lier, reserving
only a lott of land on the South side thereof, being in breadth one hundred, and in length three hundred foott, the which is afterwards conveyed to Cornelys Wynhart: Nor for a confirmacon unto him the sd
Leendert Teunisse in his possession &c. The Quitt rent is 2 bushells
of winter wheat yearly, the pattent is dated June 1, 1671.
Whore Kill
Leendert Teunisse
Fo 63.

A Confirmacon graunted unto Cornelys (203) Wynhart for a piece of land at ye Whorekill.
 Francis Lovelace, Esqr. &c. Whereas Hendrick Harmens did
upon ye third day of April 1664 transport and make over unto Corneyls Wynhart a certain piece of land at ye Whorekill and Delaware
Bay otherwise called Swannendall lyeing and being to ye South of ye
Block house between ye land of ye Willem Vandiemen and Geluaem, ye
sd land consisting of two lotts each of them conteyning sixty foot in
breadth and whereas Willem Vandiemen did likewise upon ye 17th
day of April in ye yeare aforesd transport and convey unto ye sd Corneyls Wynhart another certain lott of land at ye Whorekill contayning in breadth one hundred foot and in length alongst ye strand by the
ryver three hundred foot the sd lott lyeing and being on ye South syde
of the land granted unto the sd Willem Vandiemen, and reserved by
him when he made over the remainder unto Leendert Teeunisse Van
Lier: Now for a confirmacon unto him the sd Cornelys Wynhart in
his possession and enjoyment of the premises &c. The Quitt rent 3
bushells of Winter wheat yearly. The Patent dated June 1, 1671.
Whore Kill
Cornelys Wynhart
Fo 64.

A Confirmacon graunted unto Mr. George Whale
Sr. for a parcell of land at Delaware Bay
 Francis Lovelace, Esqr. &c. Whereas there hath been graunted
by the officers at Delaware unto Mr. George Whale Sr. a certain parcell
of land containing foure hundred acres of firme land and ye marsh
thereunto adjoyning scituate, lyeing and being on the Westward side
of Delaware Bay, and on the East side of a Creek now called St. Jones
his Creek, about a myle above Murder Creek, and extendeth itselfe

Northwest or neare thereabout from ye sd Bay, bounded as followeth, viz. begining in the middle of the Marsh between a small hummock of trees in the said Marsh and a corner marked White Oake, standing on the (204) North West side of a pointe of woodland about a mile up the sd Creeke, and runing North East into ye Woods three hundred and twenty poles, then North West two hundred poles and South West three hundred and twenty poles to ye sd Creek, and finally downe ye creeke to ye first mencioned place of bgining; now for a confirmation unto him ye sd George Whale &c. The Quitt rent foure bushells. The Patent is dated June 17th 1671.

Delaware,
George Whale,
Fo. 65.

A Confirmation graunted unto Mr. George Wale Sr. and Mr. Robert Jones, for some small hummocks of land at Delaware.

Whereas there hath been granted by ye Officers at Delaware unto Mr. George Wale Sr. and Mr. Robert Jones certaine hummocks or small parcells of land, conteyning by estimation foure hundred acres, bee it more or less with ye Marsh thereunto adjoyning, it being ye lowermost part of ye land called Bombeys hooke on ye Westward side of Delaware Bay bounded on ye East and South East with ye mayne ryver and Bay, on ye west with Duck Creeke, and on ye North with ye Marsh, and so to a small gutt which runns into ye sd Marsh above ye uppermost of ye sd Hummocks of land, which gutt divideth this land from ye land of Mr. Walter Wharton, and Mr. Thomas Meritt: Now for a confirmation &c. Quitt rent foure bushells. The Patent is dated June 17th 1671.

Delaware
George Wale
& Robt Jones
Fo 66.

A Confirmacon graunted to John Bradborne for a parcell of land at Delaware.

Francis Lovelace Esq. &c. Whereas there hath been graunted by the officers at Delaware unto John Bradborne a certaine parcell of land conteyning by estimation two hundred acres, bee it more or less, scituate lyeing and being in Appoquemini on ye North syde, being bounded on Boute ye Baker and on ye West Jacob Fenns, runing into the woods North west and South East, Now for a confirmacon unto ye sd John Bradborne &c. Quitt rent 2 bushells. The patent is dated June 17th, 1671.

Delaware,
John Bradborne.
Fo. 66.
(205)

A Confirmation graunted unto Mr. Thomas Young for a certaine parcell of land at Delaware.

Francis Lovelace, Esqr. &c. Whereas there hath been graunted by ye officers at Delaware unto Mr. Thomas Young a certaine parcell of land conteyning foure hundred acres of firme land and the Marsh thereunto adjoyning scituate lyeing and being on the Westward side of Delaware bay, and on ye North East side of a creek now called St. Joanes his creeke, being about a myle above Murder Creeke, and extendeth itselfe North West out of ye sd Bay, being bounded on ye South West with ye sd Creeke on the South East with ye land of Mr. Thomas Meritt and on the two opposite sides with ye Maine woods, ye sd land extending a mile into ye woods. Now for a confirmation, &c. The Quitt rent is foure bushells, of winter wheat yearly. The Patent dated June 17th 1671.

Delaware,
Mr. Thomas Young
F. 66.

A Confirmation granted unto Mr. Robert Jones for a parcell of land at Delaware.

Francis Lovelace Esqr. &c. Whereas there hath been graunted by the officers of Delaware unto Mr. Robert Jones, a certaine parcell of land contanying foure hundred acres of firme land with ye marshes thereunto adjoyning scituate lyeing and being on ye Westward side of Delaware bay, and on ye North East side of a creek now called St. Jones his creeke, being about a myle above Murder Creeke, and extendeth itselfe North West from ye sd Bay, bounded on ye South West with ye sd Creek and on ye South East with ye land of Mr. George Wale and on ye two opposite sides with ye maine woods, the sd land extending itselfe a mile into the woods. Now for a confirmation &c. The quitt rent foure bushells of winter wheate yearly. The Pattent dated June 17, 1671.

Delaware
Mr. Robert Jones
Fo 67.

A Confirmation graunted unto Mr. Thomas Merritt for a parcell of land at Delaware Bay.

Francis Lovelace Esqr. &c. Whereas there hath been granted by (206) ye officers at Delaware unto Mr. Thomas Meritt a certaine parcell of land containing foure hundred acres of land and the marsh thereunto adjoyning scituate lyeing and being on ye westward side of Delaware bay and on ye North East side of a creek now called St. Jones, his creeke, being about a mile above Murder creeke, and extendeth itself North west out of the sd Bay bounded on the South West with ye sd Creek, on ye South East with ye land of Mr. Walter Wharton, and on ye two opposite sides with ye Maine woods extending a

mile into ye woods. Now for a confirmation &c. The Quitt rent foure bushells of winter wheate yearly. The patent is dated June 17th 1671.
Disposed to another, being not seated.
Delaware.
Mr. Thomas Merritt
Fo 67.

A Confirmation graunted unto John Bell and Peter Pernon for a parcell of land at Delaware.

Francis Lovelace Esqr. Whereas there hath been granted by ye officers of Delaware unto John Bell and Peter Pernon a certaine parcell of land contenying eight hundred acres and ye Marsh thereunto adjoyning scituate on ye Westward side of Delaware Bay and on ye North syde of a small creeke called Beaver Creeke, which extendeth itself Westerly out of the maine South West branch of Duck Creeke, bounded as followeth, viz. on ye South with ye sd Creeke, or a lyne from thence runing West to make this paralell with ye land of Mr. Lane, on ye east with ye Land of Mr. Thomas Lane and on ye two opposite sides with the Maine woods. Now for a confirmation &c. Quitt rent eight bushells. The patent dated June 17th, 1671.
Delaware,
Jno. Bell,
Pet'r Pernon.
Fo 68.

A Confirmation graunted unto Lucas Abell, Cornelius Buijs, and Tunis   for a piece of land at Delaware Bay.

Francis Lovelace Esqr. &c. Whereas there hath been graunted by the officers at Delaware unto Lucas Abell, Cornelijs Buijs, and Tunis   a certaine piece of land scituate lyeing and being in Appoquimeni in ye Westerward side of Delaware Bay, begining from ye green hook and stretching to Sassafras kill, being in breadth South West and North East; in length it runs East into ye woods, and containes by computation nine hundred acres (207) of land. Now for a confirmation &c. The Quitt rent is nine bushells, The patent dated June ye 17th 1671.
Delaware
Cornelijs Buijs & Tunis,
Fo. 68.

A Confirmation granted unto Patrick Carr for a certain parcell of land at Delaware Bay &c.

Francis Lovelace Esqr. &c.
Whereas there hath been granted by the officers at Delaware unto Patrick Carr a certaine parcell of land conteyning foure hundred acres and the Marsh adjoyning, scituate on ye Westward side of Delaware Bay, and on ye Northward side of ye head of a small creeke called Beaver Creeke which extendeth itself Westerly out of ye Maine South West Branch of Duck Creeke, bounded as followeth, viz. On ye South

with the sd Creeke, or a line from thence running West to make this paralell with ye land of John Bell and Pieter Pernon and on ye two opposite sides with ye maine woods; Now for a confirmation &c. Quitt rent foure bushells. The patent dated June 17th 1671.
Fo. 69.
Delaware
Patrick Carr.

      A Confirmacon graunted unto William Eves for a parcell of land at Delaware.

    Francis Lovelace, Esqr. &c. Whereas there hath been graunted by ye officers at Delaware unto Wm. Eves a certaine parcell of land conteyning foure hundred acres with ye marsh thereunto adjoyning; scituate on ye Westward side of Delaware bay, and on the South West side of a creeke now called St. Jones his Creeke, being about a myle above Murder Creek, bounded on ye North East with ye sd Creeke, on ye South East with ye land of Mr. Walter Wharton, and on ye two opposite sides with ye maine woods. The said land extending a mile in length South West into ye woods. Now for a confirmation unto him the sd Wm. Eves &c. The quitt rent to be paid yearly is foure bushells of winter wheat. The patent is dated June ye 17th 1671.
Delaware
William Eves
Fo 69.

      A Confirmation graunted unto Charles Hutchins (208) for a parcell of land at Delaware Bay.

    Francis Lovelace, Esqr. &c. Whereas there hath been granted by ye officers at Delaware unto Charles Hutchins a certain parcell of land contayning five hundred acres and the Marsh thereto adjoyning, scituate on ye Westward side of Delaware Bay, and on ye North East side of a Creek, now called St. Jones, his creeke, bounded upon ye land of Christopher Sentill, and extending Northwest from ye Bay and from ye bound of Christopher Sentill extending fourety furlonges up ye creeke, and bounding on ye upper side upon ye maine woods; now for a confirmation &c. unto him ye sd Charles Hutchins in his possession and enjoyment of ye premises, now know yee &c. yielding and paying yearly &c. as a Quitt rent five bushells of winter wheat. The patent is dated June ye 19th, 1671.
Delaware.
Charles Hutchins,
Fo 70.

      A Confirmation graunted unto James Crawford for a parcell of land at Delaware.

    Francis Lovelace, Esq., &c. Whereas there hath been graunted by ye officers at Delaware unto James Crawford a certain parcell of land conteyning foure hundred and fifty acers with ye Marsh thereto adjoyning scituate on ye Westward side of Delaware Bay, and on ye south west side of a Creek now called St. Jones, His creeke, bounded

on ye North East with ye sd Creek, on ye south East with ye lands of Charles Hutchins, and on ye two upper sides with ye maine woods, ye sd lands extending into the woods South West, now for a confirmation, &c. Ye quitt rent is foure bushells, and a halfe of Winter wheate; the patent is dated June ye 19th 1671.
Delaware
James Crawford
Fo 70

A Confirmation graunted unto Mr. John Johnson, for a parcell of land at Delaware.

Francis Lovelace, Esqr. &c. Whereas there hath been (209) granted by ye officers at Delaware unto Mr. John Johnson a certain parcell of land conteyning five hundred acres with ye marsh thereunto adjoyning, scituate on ye Westward side of Delaware Bay, on ye South West side of a creek now called St. Jones his creek, being about a mile above Murder Creeke, bounded on ye North East with ye Creeke, on ye South East with ye land of Mr. Thomas Young, and on ye two opposite sides with the maine woods, ye sd land extending a myle into ye woods; Now for a confirmation &c. Quitt rent five bushells. The patent is dated June 19th 1671.
John Johnson,
Delaware,
Fo. 71.

A Confirmation graunted unto Christopher Sentill for a parcell of land at Delaware.

Francis Lovelace Esqr. &c. Whereas there hath been graunted by the officers at Delaware unto Christopher Sentill a certaine parcell of land conteyning foure hundred acres and the marsh thereunto adjoyning scituate on the Westward side of Delaware Bay, and on the North East side of a creek now called St. Jones his creeke, being about a mile above Murder Creek, and extendeth itself Northwest from ye bay, bounded on ye south West with ye creeke, and on ye South East with ye land of Mr. Thomas Young, and on ye two opposite sides with ye maine woods, the sd lands extending a mile into ye woods; now for a confirmation, &c. The Quitt rent is foure bushells of winter wheate yearly The Patent dated June 19th 1671.
Delaware,
Christopher Sentills
Fo 71.

A Confirmation graunted by ye Governor unto Wm. Sincleer, for a parcell of land at Delaware.

Francis Lovelace Esq. &c. Whereas there hath been graunted by ye officers at Delaware unto William Sincleer a certaine parcell of land containing foure hundred acres with ye Marsh thereto adjoyning, scituate on ye westward side of Delaware Bay and on the South West side of a creeke now called St. Jones his creeke, being about a myle above Murder Creek, bounded on ye North East with ye sd Creeke, on ye

South East with ye land of William Eves, and on the two opposite sides with ye maine woods,. Now for a confirmation unto ye sd William Sincleer &c. The Quitt rent is foure bushells of Winter wheate yearly. The Patent dated ye 19th of June 1671.

Delaware,
Wm. Sincleer,
Fo. 71.

(210)
A Confirmation of a Parcell of Land at Delaware Granted to Bezaliel Osborne.

Edmund Andros, Esq. &c. To all to whom these presents shall come, sendeth greeting, Whereas Robert Tallant, had heretofore a Pattent from Col. Francis Lovelace, the late Governor, bearing date the 26th day of February, 1671 for a certain parcell or tract of land containing foure hundred acres, scituate lyeing and being on the West syde of Delaware ryver and on the South East Side of Apoquemini Creeke, being bounded on the North West with the sd Creeke; on the South West with the lands of Lewis Johnson, and on the two opposite sides with the maine woods, and the sd Robert Tallant, having made over his right title and interest to the premises, Lewis Johnston, of Apoquemini, who hath transported the same unto Bezaliell Osborne of East Hampton upon Long Island; for a confirmation unto him the sd Bezaliell Osborne in his possession and enjoyment of the premises know ye that by vertue of the comision and authority unto me given by his Royall Highnesse, I have ratifyed, confirmed and granted and by these presents do ratifye, confirme and grant unto Bezaliell Osborne his heires and assignes the afore recited parcell or tract of land and premises with all and singular the appertances: to have and to hold the sd parcell or tract of land and premises unto the sd Bezaliel Osborne, his heirs and assigns unto the proper use and behofe of the sd Bezeliell Osborne, his heirs and assigns forever: Yielding and paying therefore yearly and every year for the same, as a Quitt rent unto his Royall Highness use foure bushells of good winter wheate unto such officer or officers in (211) authority there as shall be empowered to receive the same. Given under my hand and sealed with the seale of the Province in New Yorke, the 26th day of July in the 27th yeare of the Reigne of our Soveraigne Lord Charles the Second, by the grace of God of England, Scotland, France, and Ireland, King, Defender of the Faith, &c. and in the year of our Lord God 1675.

E. Andros.s.

Book of Patents
No. 4. Part No. 1.
Fo. 100.

A Pattent for a Parcell of Land In Delaware Bay granted unto Paul Marsh.

Sir Edmund Andros, Knt. &c. Whereas there is a certain parcell of land in Delaware Bay lying and being about three myles to the West of the Whorekill called by the name of the Souldiers Resolves, the

which hath been layed out for Paul Marsh by the approbation of the Court of the Whorekill and is certifyed to be all ready seated, the sd land begining at a small creeke at the point of the woods dividing it from the land of Hellmanus Willbanck, and from thence runing Southwest up the creeke, three hundred and twenty perches and from the sd creeke, runing South East, three hundred and twenty perches to a Beaver damm dividing it from the land of Edward Southerin and runing down the sd Beaver dam North East three hundred and Twenty perches and from thence runing North West three hundred and twenty perches, containing six hundred acres of land together with six acres of Marsh adjoyning to it as by the returne of the Survey doth and may appeare. Know yee &c. Quitt rent 6 bushells of wheate dated in New Yorke, August 20, 1679.
Fo. 159.

(212)
A Pattent for a parcell of land in Delaware Bay graunted unto Robert Hignat and John Crue.

Sir Edmund Andros, Knt. &c. Whereas there is a certaine parcell of land in Delaware Bay near unto Rehobah Bay about foure miles to the South of it called by the name of West Chester, the which hath been layd out for Robert Hignat and John Crue, by the approbation of the Court of the Whorekill, and is certifyed to be already seated the sd land begining at a White Oake by a creek, that comes out of Rehobah Bay and runs up the sd Creeke, Northwest three hundred and twenty perches to a white Oake standing upon a Branch and from thence runing North East foure hundred and fifty Perches to a marked red Oake in the woods and from thence runing S. E. foure hundred and eighty perches to the first bounded tree containing nine hundred acres of land as by the returne of the Survey doth and may appeare. Know yee &c. Quitt rent 9 bushells of Wheat. Dated in New Yorke, August 20th 1679.
Fo. 159.

A Pattent for a parcell of land on the West side of Delaware Bay graunted unto Robert Bedwell.

Sir Edmund Andros Knt. &c. Whereas there is a certaine parcell of land on the W. side of Delaware Bay scituate lyeing & being on the S. E. side of St. Jones Creek, called by the name of the Folly Neck, the which hath been layd out for Robert Bedwell, begining at a markt black Oake standing by the said Creeke side neare unto a Branch goeing up to a Beaver (213) Damm being at the North side of the sd Branch separating this from the land of Joshua Barkestead and runing from the sd Oake North up the sd St. Jones Creeke, forty perches then North East and by North one hundred and thirty Perches up the sd Creeke to a Narrow point and from the sd Point South West up the sd Creeke, one hundred and eighty perches then North West and by West five degrees Westerly twenty foure perches up the sd Creeke, then North North West twenty foure perches up the sd Creek then North

North East four degrees Easterly to a point by said creeke, and from thence up the sd Creeke North West and by North one hundred and sixty Perches to a marked Black Oake standing on the South East side at the Mouth of a branch proceeding from St. Jones Creeke, aforementioned and comonly called the Cypresse branch and from thence runing South West and by West sixty Perches binding likewise upon the sd branch, then South south East also binding upon the sd Branch one hundred and forty Perches to a marked red Oake standing in the woods about forty perches from the head of the sd Branch, then south east fifety six Perches with a line of marked trees to a bounded black oake standing in ye woods by Chaptanck road and from thence North East to the head of the South Easter most branch of the aforesd Beaver damm and so binding up the sd branch and sd Beaver damm unto the first bounded black oake containing eight hundred acres of land as by the returne of the survey and certificate from the Court at ye Whorekill that the same is already seated by the sd Robert Bedwell doth and may appeare. Know yee &c. Quitt Rent. 8 Bushells of winter Wheate. Dated in New Yorke, the 20th day of August 1679.
Fo. 160.

(214) A Confirmation to Juryen Jans for a piece of land at Delaware.

Francis Lovelace, Esqr. &c. Whereas there is a certain piece of land at Delaware now in ye tenure or occupation of Juryen Jans of right belonging unto him ye sd land lying and being upon the hook or neck above ye towne of New Castle abutting on ye South by Matthys Eschelsons, and on ye N. E. syde by the comon highway containing in breadth both before and behind thirty foure rod stretching into the woods upon a North West lyne foure hundred rod in all amounting to about six and forty acres or 23 Morgen. Now for a confirmation unto him ye sd Juryen Jansen &c. The patent is dated March ye 24th. The quitt rent 1 bushell of winter wheate.

The end of the Same Book
No. 2. Fo. 9.

A Confirmation granted to Jacob Vanderveer for a small island at Delaware.

Francis Lovelace, Esqr. &c. Whereas there is a small island at Delaware lyeing beyond Christeen kill now in ye tenure or occupation of Jacob Vanderveer as of right belonging to him having behind it upon ye maine a piece of land bounded on ye S. W. side by a small ryvolett runing to Hans Petersons land and on ye North East syde by another rivulett going to Andries Andriesen containing in breadth by ye fish kill together with the valley or meadow from one rivulett to another about three hundred rods bee it more or less and stretching on both sides into the woods upon a Northwest lyne six hundred rods

Nok for a confirmation unto him ye sd Jacob Vanderveer, &c. The patent is dated March 25th, 1669. The quitt rent 2 bushells of winter wheat.
Fo. 9.

(215)
A Confirmation graunted to Hans Block for a piece of land at Delaware.

Francis Lovelace Esqr. &c. Whereas there is a certaine piece of land at Delaware now in the tenure or occupation of Hans Block, as of right belonging to him, ye sd land lying and being upon ye second hooke, or neck above the towne of New Castle, containing in breadth by ye riverside fifety two rods and a halfe on ye South West syde abutting on ye land of Paulus Duxon and runing into the woods three hundred rods and on ye North syde by ye land of Gerritt Sanderson till it comes to a swamp ye light length behynde in breadth twenty two rods and a halfe as also behynde ye swamp or creupell bush a hooke or neck of land lyeing between two swamps almost Northwest into ye woods containing about one hundred acres or fifety Morgen, together with a piece of valley or meadow ground lying on ye South West side of Capt. Carrs land and on ye North East syde with Pauls Duxon being about eighteen or twenty acres Now for a confirmation unto him ye sd Hans Block &c. The patent is dated March ye 25th 1668. The quitte rent 2 bushells.
Fo. 10.

A Confirmation graunted to Gerritt Sanderson for a piece of land at Delaware.

Francis Lovelace Esq. &c. Whereas there is a certain piece of land at Delaware now in ye tenure or occupation of Gerritt Sanderson lyeing and being on ye South West syde by Hans Blocks land contayning in breadth before towards ye strand to Olle Toersons twenty-five rods in length on each syde to a certayne swamp or creupell three hundred rods and in breadth behynde about twenty rod together with another piece lying on ye one side of ye land aforesaid (216) with Jan. Hulcks land being in breadth before by ye strand to Arent Jansens, twenty five rod in length on each side into ye woods six hundred rod and in breadth behind about twenty rod, Now for a confirmation unto him ye sd Gerritt Sanderson &c. The Pattent is dated March 25th, 1669. The Quitt rent is 2 Bushells.
Fo. 10.

A Confirmation graunted to Jan Sibrants for a piece of land at Delaware.

Francis Lovelace, Esq., &c. Whereas there is a certain piece of land at Delaware now in ye tenure or occupation of Jan Sibrantse as of right belonging unto him lying and being near ye horse neck (comonly called ye Paeid hook) that is to say between a certain small creek or kill and ye sd horse neck stretching from ye sd creeke or kill into ye

woods North west and by West and towards ye ryver South East and by East containing in breadth by ye ryver side one hundred and fifety rod or thereabout reaching to ye land of Arent Jansen in length into the woods North West & by West six hundred rod, haveing within ye sd land much marshy and Swampy ground Now for a confirmation unto him ye sd Jan Sibrantse, &c. The patent is dated ye 26th of March 1669. The Quitt rent one bushell.
Fo 11.

A Confirmation graunted to Evert Gertsen for a piece of land at Delaware.

Francis Lovelace Esq. &c. Whereas there is a certaine piece of land at Delaware now in ye tenure of occupation of Evert Gertsen as of right belonging to him lyeing and being in New Castle haveing before the Otter street and behind ye (217) Calves street abutting on ye North East syde with ye land of Top Outhout and on ye Southwest side with ye land of Rayner Vander Cooley Conteyning in Length on both sydes foure hundred foote wood measure and in breadth as well behynde as before one and twenty rod, Now for a confirmation unto him ye sd Evert Gertsen, &c. The pattent is dated March 26, 1669. The Quitt rent 1 bushell.
Fo. 11.

A Confirmation granted to Pauls Jaques for a piece of unmanured land at Delaware.

Francis Lovelace Esq. &c. Whereas there is a certain piece of unmanured land at Delaware now in yee tenure and occupation of Jean Paul Jacquett conteyning by estimation in woodland and valley or meadow about two hundred acres stretching from ye neck of land where ye sd Jean Paul Jacques now lives in length South South West and North North East and in breadth alongst Christeen kill, North North West and South South East, behind along by ye land and fence of Pieter Claesen and Jan Claesen from ye mill to a great swamp haveing some valley or meadow on both sydes, Now for a confirmation unto him ye sd Jean Paul Jacques &c. The patent is dated March 26, 1669. The Quitt rent 2 bushells.
Fo 11.

A Confirmation grannted to Harmen Reyners for a lott of Ground at Delaware.

Francis Lovelace, Esqr. &c. Whereas there is a certaine lott of ground lyeing and being at New Castle in Delaware haveing a house and garden thereupon bounded to ye west by Isaack Fynes fence and to South with ye Mayne ryver conteyning in length one hundred and five yards, and in breadth thirty (218) five, which sd lott of ground house and garden is now in the tenure or occupation of Harmen Reyners or his assign as of right belonging unto him, now for a confirmation unto him ye sd Harmen Reyners, &c. The Patent is dated Aprill ye eighth, 1669. The quitt rent 1 bushell.
Fo 12.

A Confirmation granted to Olla Towson, for a parcell of land at Delaware.

Francis Lovelace, Esqr. Whereas there is a certaine parcell of land at Delaware now in ye tenure or occupation of Olla Towson in his owne right containing in breadth by ye ryver syde twenty five rods then runing in length into ye woods three hundred rod. It is in breadth behynde to ye North West twenty rod being bounded to ye East upon Lucus Pieterse and to ye West upon Gerritt Sanders land. Now for a confirmation unto him ye sd Olla Towson &c. The Patent is dated May ye 28th 1669. Quitt rent 1 bushell.

Fo. 13.

A Confirmation granted to Bernard Eken for a house and garden in Delaware.

Francis Lovelace Esqr. &c. Whereas there is a certain house and garden in ye towne of New Castle upon Delaware now in ye tenure or occupation of Bernard Ekon in his owne right the sd garden containing in breadth sixty foote and ye church yard to ye east with Isaack Fynes and to the North with ye Mart. Now for a confirmation unto him ye said Bernard Ekin &c. The pattent is dated May ye 28th 1669. The quitt rent 1 bushell.

Fo. 14.

A Confirmation granted to Bernard Ekon, for a certaine plantation at Delaware,

Francis Lovelace, Esqr. &c. Whereas there is a certaine (219) plantation at Delaware now in yee tenure or occupation of Bernard Eken in his owne right being bounded on ye West with ye land belonging to Pieter Dewitt and on ye East with ye Marsh that runnes to ye Horse neck or Paerden hook and ye woods and inward with Juriaen Johnsons land comonly called ye Hay Makers' Hook, containing in breadth by ye ryver side one hundred rod runing into ye woods North west three hundred rod or thereabout together with ye meadow ground or valley lying before ye sd land or plantation. Now for a confirmation unto him ye sd Bernard Eken &c. The Patent is dated May ye 28th 1669? The Quitt rent one bushell.

Fo. 14.

A Confirmation granted to Simon Jansen and Mattys Berckelse for a Parcell of land at Delaware.

Francis Lovelace Esqr. &c. Whereas there is a certaine parcell of land at Delaware lyeing and being upon ye crane hook on ye south West syde thereof by a chanell falling into ye ryver runing in length into ye woods 600 rod in breadth before to ye land of Laats Toorsen sixty rod and so by ye land of ye said Laats Toorsen, then again into ye woods six hundred rod, being in equal breadth behind as before and containing all ye meadow ground and swamp or creupel Bos within ye compasse before described to ye ryver syde which sd parcell of land belongeth to Simon Jansen and Mattys Berckelsen in

whose tenure and occupation now it is as in their own right, Now for a confirmation unto them ye said Simon Jansen and Mattys Berckelsen &c dated July ye 1st, 1669.
Fo 15

(220)
A Confirmation granted to William Tom, for a piece of land formerly belonging to Peter Alricks.

Francis Lovelace, Esq. &c. Whereas William Tom of New Castle upon Delaware hath heretofore obtained a patent from my predecessor for a certaine parcell of land formerly belonging to Peter Alricks being below ye towne together with ye meadow ground or valley thereunto belonging ye which is now in his tenure or occupation and there lyeing below ye sd meadow ground or valley alongst ye river a certain piece of land, having no perticular owner ye which ye sd William Tom hath requested of mee for his further accommodation for an encouragement to ye settlement of those plantations, Know yee that by vertue &c. the patent is dated ye twenty-ninth of July 1669, Quitt rent 2 bushell.
Fo. 17

A Confirmation granted to Charles Floyd and John Henry for a lott and parcell of land at Delaware.

Francis Lovelace, Esqr. &c. Whereas John Webber an inhabitant at Delaware under ye Dutch Government stood possessed of a certain lott or parcell of land lyeing behinde ye town of New Castle abutting on ye North East upon ye meadow or valley now belonging to Capt. John Carre, Southerly upon ye Kings highway leading into ye wood northerly upon ye wood, and South East upon ye Smiths house, contayning in all about twenty acres be it more or lesse, the which said lott and parcell of land was seized upon and confiscated by order of ye late Governor my predecessor, and granted unto Charles Floyd and John Henry two soldiers who came over into these partes in his Majesty's service. Now for a confirmation unto them ye said Charles Floyd and John Henry. &c. Dated September ye 1st, 1669. Quitt rent one bushell Winter Wheate.
Fo. 18.

(221)
A Confirmation granted unto Mr. Thomas Spry, for a parcell of land at Delaware.

Edmund Andros, Esq. &c. Whereas there is a certain parcell of land called Doctors Commons, scituate and being on ye W. syde of Delaware ryver the which by vertue of a warrant hath been layd out for Thomas Spry the sd land lyeing on the South syde of St. Georges Creeke, bounded as followeth viz. begining at a corner marked white Oake tree standing close by ye creeke syde at ye first Fast landing within the said Creek, dividing this from the land of Anne Whale, and from the sd Oake, runing West, South West by the said Anne Whales

line of marked trees three hundred & eighty perches to a corner markt black Oake, standing by the side of a swamp called the Doctors swamp, nigh unto the head thereof, and from the said Black Oake, downe the severall courses of the maine runn of the sd Swamp unto the aforesaid creek, and then down the several courses of the creek, to the first mentioned white Oake, containing and layd out for one hundred and sixty acres of land, together with the marshes thereunto adjoyning as by the returne of the Survey under the hand of Capt. Edmund Cantwell, the Surveyor, doth and may appeare. Now for a confirmation of the said land, unto the said Thomas Spry, Know yee &c. The Patent is dated ye 5th day of November 1675. The Quitt rent is 1 bushell and a halfe of Winter Wheate.
Fo. 39.

A Confirmation granted unto James Crawford for a parcell of land at Delaware.

Edmund Andros Esquire. Whereas there is a certain parcell of land called Barwick, scituate and being on the West side of Delaware bay the which by vertue of (222) a warrant, hath been layd out for James Crawford, the said land lying on the South Side of St. Georges creeke, being bounded on the North East and North West with the Maine Creeke, on the South East with a swamp called the Doctors swampe and on the South West with a line of marked trees, runing from a corner marked black oake, standing on a pointe opposite to Jacob Youngs Plantation, South South East, to a corner marked Spanish Oake, by a branch of the aforesaid swamp; containing and layd out for two hundred and ten acres of land together with the marshes thereunto adjoyning as by returne of the Survey, under the hand of Capt. Edmund Cantwell, the Surveyor, doth and may appeare, Now for a confirmation unto him the sd James Crawford, in his possession and enjoyment of the premises, know yee &c. The patent is dated the 5th day of November 1675. The Quitt rent is two bushells of winter wheate.
Fo. 39.

A Confirmation granted unto Bernard Egberts for land in Delaware.

Edmund Andros Esq. &c. Whereas there is a certain parcell of land called Black Smiths Hall, scituate and being on the West side of Delaware river, the which by vertue of warrant hath been layd out for Bernard Egberts, the said land lying on the South side of St. George's creek, towards the head of a certain branch which extendeth itself West South West out of the main creek, being bounded on the North North West with the said Branch on the East North East, with a line of marked trees, dividing this from the land of John Ogle, on the West South West, with a line drawne South South East from a corner markt (223) White Oake, on a low point at the mouth of a small swampe and on the South South East with the maine woods; containing and laid out for three hundred acres of land as by the return of the Survey, un-

der the hand of Capt. Edmund Cantwell, the Surveyor, doth and may appeare. Now for a confirmation unto the said Bernard Egberts &c. The patent is dated the 5th day of November 1675. The Quitt rent is three bushells of good winter wheat, yearly.
Fo. 40.

A Confirmation granted unto Jacob Young for land in Delaware River.

Edmund Andros, Esq. Whereas there is a certaine parcell of land scituate and being on the west side of Delaware river the which by vertue of a warrant hath been layed out for Jacob Young the said land lying on the North side of St. Georges creeke, 'begining at a corner white Oake, standing at the creek side, upon the first neck of fast land on that side, runing North in breadth two hundred and sixty perches to a markt Spanish Oake, standing by a swamp side, called Dragon Swampe, from the said Spanish Oake west, two hundred and sixty perches to a small red Oake, standing by a Path side from the said tree, sixty perches, to a markt white Oake, standing by the said Dragon Swamp, west along the said Swamp, three hundred and eighty perches to a corner markt White Oake, south three hundred and twenty perches with a line of markt trees, to a corner markt Spanish Oake, standing by a swamp side, which extendeth itself out of St. Georges Creeke East along the said Creeke to the first markt White Oake, containing and layd out for One thousand two hundred and (224) eighty acres of land, with the marshes thereunto belonging and adjoyning, as by the return of the Survey under the hand of Capt. Edmund Cantwell, the Surveyor, doth and may appeare. Now for a confirmation unto him the said Jacob Young, in his possession and enjoyment of the premises. The patent is dated the fifth day of November 1675. The Quitt rent is 12 bushells and 3 pecks of good winter wheate yearly.
Fo. 40.

A Confirmation granted unto Hermanus Wiltbanck, for land at Delaware.

Edmund Andros, Esq. Whereas there is a certain tract of land near unto the Whorekill in Delaware bay formerly called Wakers Neck lying upon Fish creeke, the which by vertue of a warrant hath been layd out for Hermanus Wiltbanck, begining at a bounded white Oake, standing upon a point of marsh, runing South South West, being in breadth up the said Creek, foure hundred perches to a bounded poplar standing upon the said Creeke, and from thence West North West, three hundred and twenty perches through the woods to a small creeke parting Wm. Canes land & his to another bounded White Oake from thence N. N. E. downe the said Creeke, foure hundred Perches to a bounded pine standing by the point of the aforesaid Marsh, and from thence downe the aforesaid Marsh, to the first bounded White Oake standing by the point of the aforesaid Fish Creek, E. S. E. three hundred and twenty perches, bounded upon the said Marsh; containing

and layed out for eight hundred acres as by the returne of the Survey brought in by Capt. Edmund Cantwell, the Surveyor doth and may appeare. Now for a confirmation unto him the (225) said Hermanus Wiltbanck, &c. The Patent is dated, the fifth day of November, 1675. The quitt rent is eight bushell of good winter Wheate.
Fo. 41.

A Confirmation granted unto Mr. Henry Ward for a neck of land in Delaware.

Edmund Andros Esq. &c. Whereas there is a certain neck of land scituate and being on the West side of Delaware Ryver, the which by vertue of a warrant hath been layed out for Mr. Henry Ward, the said Neck of land being called Reenden Point begining at the Beaver Damme, at a marked White Oake standing by a Thickety Swamp, adjoyning to the river and runing from the said Oake, over the neck south West, one hundred and Sixty perches, to a marked Spanish Oake, standing by a branch of Dragon swamp, runing downe the said Dragon swamp, S. E. one hundred and sixty perches, N. E. one hundred and thirty perches S. E. one hundred and sixty perches S. W. One hundred perches, S. E. Thirty perches, S. W. forty perches, S. E. eighty perches N. E. 160 perches, South East eighty perches, South West sixty eight perches, South east one hundred and eighty perches North East one hundred Perches, or poles, unto the lowermost point of the said neck next to St. Georges creek, and then runing North West, along a great Marsh joyning to the river six hundred eighty five perches to the first marked white oake, containing and layd out for foure hundred forty six acres and a halfe of land, with the marshes thereunto adjoyning, as by the return of the Survey, under the hand of Capt Edmund Cantwell, the Surveyor, doth and may appeare. Now for a (226) confirmation unto the said Henry Ward, in his possession and enjoyment of the premises, &c. The patent is dated the fifth day of November 1675. The quitt rent is foure bushells and a halfe of good winter wheate.
Fo. 42.

A Confirmation granted unto John Roods for land in Delaware.

Edmund Andros, Esq. Whereas there is a certain tract of land at the Whorekill on the West side of Delaware bay called Rehobah lyeing upon Rehobah Bay, the which by vertue of a warrant hath been layed out for Wm. Roods, begining at a bounded Black Walnut standing upon a point at the Sea beech, from thence runing and bounding upon the Bay, West three hundred perches, to a small creeke parting John Averys land and his from thence runing and bounding up the said creeke North Three hundred and twenty perches to a bounded red Oake standing by the side of the Creeke, and from thence East by a line of Marked trees, bounded upon the woods three hundred perches, to another red Oake standing upon the sea beach, and from thence South three hundred and twenty perches, unto the first bounded Black

walnut, standing by the point, containing and layed out for six hundred acres of land, as by the returne of the survey, under the hand of Capt. Edmund Cantwell, the Surveyor, doth and may appeare. Now for a confirmation unto him the said William Roods in his possession and enjoyment of the premises &c. The patent is dated the 5th day of November 1675. The quitt rent is six bushells of Winter Wheate.
Fo. 42.

(227)

A Confirmation granted unto Hans Peterson, for land in Delaware.

Edmund Andros, Esq. Whereas there is a certaine parcell of land scituate and being on the West side of Delaware river, the which hath been layd out for Hanse Peterson, by vertue of a warrant, the said land lying on a creeke called Skilpades Kill, which kill or creek, extendeth out of Christiana Creeke, Northerly begining at a White Nutten tree, which tree divides the said land, and Andries Toursens land, runing from the said tree West South West fifty six perches to a marked Corner White Oake, which divides the said land, from Jacob Vanderveres land, runing on both sides into the woods North West, four hundred and fifty perches, containing and layed out for one hundred fifety seven acres and a halfe of land, with the marshes thereunto adjoyning, as by the returne of the Survey under the hand of Capt. Edmund Cantwell, the Surveyor, doth and may appeare, Now for a confirmation unto him the said Hanse Peterson in his possession and enjoyment of the premises &c. The Patent was dated the   day of   1675. The quitt rent is one bushell and a halfe of good winter wheate.
Fo. 43.

A Confirmation granted unto Charles Peterson for a parcell of land in Delaware.

Edmund Andros, Esq. &c. Whereas there is a certain parcell of land, scituate and being on the West side of Delaware river, the which by vertue of a warrant (228) hath been layd out for Charles Peterson, The said land lying on the North side of Verdrity's hook, beginning at a corner red oake, standing by the river syde, runing North and by East along the River, one hundred thirty eight perches or poles to a corner white oake, which partes the lands of Woolsey Fransen & Company, runing North West on both sydes, three hundred and twenty perches, containing and layed out for two hundred sixty six acres of land, with the meadow or marsh thereunto belong and adjoyning, as by the return of the survey, under the hand of Capt. Edmund Cantwell, the Surveyor doth and may appeare. Now for a confirmation unto the said Charles Peterson, in his possession and enjoyment of the premises &c. The patent is dated the fifth day of November 1675. The quitt rent is two bushells and a halfe of good winter wheate.
Fo. 43.

THE DUKE OF YORK RECORD. 165

A Confirmation granted unto George Moore for some land in Delaware.

Edmund Andros, Esq. &c. Whereas there is a certaine parcell of land called Windsor, scituate and being on the West side of Delaware Ryver, the which by vertue of a warrant hath been layed out for George Moore, the said land lying on the south side of St. Georges Creeke, opposite to Mr. Jacob Young's plantation, being bounded on the East North East with a line of markt trees, runing South South East from a corner black markt oake, being the bounded tree of the land of James Crawford, dividing this from the land of the said James Crawford, on the North North West with the maine Creeke, on the West South West with a line (229) of markt trees runing from a corner markt white Oake, on a point by the creeks side, south South East three hundred and fourteen perches to a corner markt maple, standing in a branch of the Doctors Swamp, on the South South East with the said swamp; containing and layed out for two hundred and eighty Acres of land with the marshes thereunto adjoyning, as by the returne of the Survey, from Capt. Edmund Cantwell, the Surveyor, doth and may appeare. Now for a confirmation unto the said George Moore, in his possession and enjoyment of the premises and &c. The patent is dated the fifth day of November 1675. The quitt rent is two bushell and a halfe of good winter wheate.

Fo. 44.

A Confirmation granted unto Anne Wale for a parcell of land in Delaware river.

Edmund Andros Esq. &c. Whereas there is a certaine parcell of land called Chelsey, lyeing and being on the West side of Delaware River, the which by vertue of a warrant hath been layed out for Anne Wale, the said land lyeing on the South side of St. George Creek, being the first neck of firme land within the said Creeke, and is bounded as followeth viz. Begining at a corner marked White Oake, standing on a point by the North side of a swamp, which divideth this from a parcell of land formerly granted to Mr. Pieter Alricks, and from the said Oake running up the said Swampe, west and by North thirty eight perches, North Westerly twenty five degrees, twenty eight perches; North west eighty eight perches, South West thirty two perches, West and by North, seventy two perches, South and by West (230) thirty foure perches; East South East sixty perches, South West fourty perches; West and by South; twenty foure perches to a corner markt Gumme, standing by the head of a branch of the said Swamp; and from the said Gum, running West South West by a line of markt trees, one hundred thirty three perches, to a corner markt white oake, standing nigh unto the head of a swamp or branch and from ye said White Oake, North N. W., by markt trees, one hundred and fifty perches to a corner markt black Oake, nigh unto the head of a swamp called the Doctors swamp; and from the said Black Oake, East North East by a line of markt trees, three hundred and eighty perches to a corner markt White Oake, standing on the banke of the said creeke, and divideth

this from a parcell of land now surveyed for Thomas Spry, and from the said White Oak, down the severall courses of the creeke, to the river; and from the river westerly, along the afore mentioned branch or swamp, through the marsh, to the first mentioned corner white Oake; containing and layed out for three hundred acres of land, with the marshes thereunto adjoyning, as by the returne of the survey under the hand of Capt Edmund Cantwell, the Surveyor, doth and may appeare. Now for a confirmation of the said land unto the said Anne Wale, in her possession and enjoyment of the premises &c. The patent is dated the fifth day of November, 1675, the quitt rent is three bushell of good winter wheate.
Fo. 45.

(231)
          A Confirmation granted unto John Ogle, for a parcell of land in Delaware.

Edmund Andros, Esq. &c. Whereas there is a certain tract of land on the west side of Delaware river called by the name of Hampton the which by vertue of a warrant hath been layed out for John Ogle the said land lying on the South side of St. Georges creeke, being bounded on the North North West with a branch of the said Creeke, which extendeth itself west South West out of the said Creeke, on the East North East with a line a marked trees running South South East dividing this from the land of George Moore; on the west, South West with a line of marked trees runing South South East from a corner markt White Oake, at the mouth of a small swamp, dividing this from a parcell of land surveyed for Bernard Egberts, and on the South South East with the maine Woods; containing and layed out for three hundred acres, as by the tenure of the Survey under the hand of Capt. Edmund Cantwell, the Surveyor, doth and may appeare. Now for a confirmation unto him the said John Ogle, &c. The Patent is dated the fifth day of November 1675. The quitt rent is three bushells of good winter wheat.
Fo. 46

          A Confirmation of a parcell of land in Delaware river, granted to Morris Listen.

Edmund Andros, Esq. Whereas there is a certain tract of land or parcell of land on the west side of Delaware bay called   the which by vertue of a warrant hath been layed out for Morris Listen; the said land lyeing on a creek called Cedar Creeke, in a forke of the (232) said Creeke, begining at a marked Oake and runing North East seventy five perches, by a line drawn North west, three hundred and twenty perches, then South west seventy five perches, then south East, three hundred and twenty perches to the first bounded Oake; containing and layed out for one hundred and fifty acres, bee it more or lesse, as by the returne of the survey under the hand of Capt Edmund Cant-

THE DUKE OF YORK RECORD. 167

well, the Surveyor doth and may appeare. Now for a confirmation, &c. The patent is dated the fifth day of November 1675. The quitt rent is one bushell and a halfe of good winter wheate.
Fo. 46.

A Confirmation of a parcell of land in Delaware River granted unto Peter Baucom and Richard Blincks.

Edmund Andros, Esq. &c. Whereas there is a certaine parcell of land on the West side of Delaware bay, called Stening the which by vertue of a warrant hath been layed out for Peter Baucom and Richard Blincks; the said land lying on the South side of a creeke, called Baucom Briges; begining at a markt red Oake, by a branch of the Creeke, runing up the creeke in breadth South South West, three hundred perches; then East South East three hundred and twenty perches: then North North West, three hundred perches, West North West three hundred and twenty perches, to the first bounded Oake, containing and layed out for six hundred acres, together with all the marshes thereunto belonging as by the returne of the survey under the hand of Capt. Edmund Cantwell, the Surveyor, doth (233) and may appeare. Now for a confirmation unto them the said Peter Baucom and Richard Blincks in their possession and enjoyment of the premises etc. The patent is dated the fifth day of November 1675. The quitt rent is 6 bushell of good winter wheate.
Fo 47.

A Pattent for a parcell of land at Delaware granted to John Cornelis.

Edmund Andros, Esq. &c. Whereas there is a parcel of land which by my order hath been layed out for John Cornelis scituate lyeing and being in a small creeke called Marches Creek on the West side of Delaware bay to the Northward of yee Whorekill towne, named Casier, beginning at a white Oake and runing N. W. three hundred and twenty perches to a certain bounded hickory, and from thence runing South West one hundred and fifty Pearches, to a White Oake with a line of marked trees and from thence S. E. with a line of marked trees to a small creeke, three hundred and twenty pearches and from thence with a line paralell to the first bounded white Oake, one hundred and fifety perches containing three hundred acres as by ye return of ye survey under the hand of the Surveyor doth and may appeare. Know yee &c. dated.
Fo. 65.

A Pattent for a parcell of land neare Dellaware granted to Cornelius Verhoofe,

Edmund Andros, Esq. &c. Whereas there is a certain parcell of land which by my order hath been layed out by Cornelius Vorhoofe, called New Sevenhoven, situated on ye West side of Delaware bay and on ye North side of a creeke (234) called Mispam creeke, beginning at a

marked white Oake, standing by a little creeke, called Indyan bridge creeke and running from thence South South West three hundred perches binding upon the aforesaid Mispam creeke, unto a White Oake standing by a little creeke called Beaver Damm creeke, and runing from thence West North West binding upon ye said Beaver Damm Creeke, Beaver damm & Branch six hundred & fifty five pearches, and from thence North North East three hundred pearches, unto a branch proceeding from ye aforesaid Indyan Bridge creeke and from thence binding with a course East South East upon the said Indyan Bridge Creeke six hundred and fifty five perches, unto ye first bounded white Oake, containing and layed out for twelve hundred and eighteen acres as by ye returns of ye survey under ye hand of ye Surveyor doth and may appeare. Know yee &c. Dated.
Fo. 65.

A Patent for a parcell of land neare Dellaware granted to Samuel Stills.

Edmund Andros, Esq. &c. Whereas there is a certain parcell of land which by my order hath been layed out for Samuel Stilles called ye Planters Delight scituate upon Masspin Creeke and on ye North side of ye said Creeke in ye woods about a mile from ye creeke side and beginnith at a white Oake standing by a branch and running from thence N. N. E. two hundred pearches to a red Oake and from thence running W. North West three hundred & twenty perches to a hickory tree, and from thence running South South East two hundred pearches to a white Oake bounded and from thence to ye first bounded white Oake East North East three hundred and twenty pearches contayned and laid out for foure hundred acres as by the returne of the survey under ye hand of ye surveyor doth and may appeare. Know yee and &c. Dated.
Fo 66.

(235)

A Pattent for a parcell of land at Dellaware granted unto John Allward.

Edmund Andros, Esq. Whereas there is a certain parcell of land which by my order hath been layd out for John Allward, scituate lying and being in a neck called Cemballs neck joyning to a creeke called Mill Creek, begining at a White Oake being the bounded tree of Abraham Clement and runing south West up ye creeke two hundred pearches to a white Oak, and from thence S. E. with a line of marked trees three hundred and twenty pearches to a white Oak bounded tree and from thence North East two hundred pearches to the bounded tree of Abraham Clement and runing downe Northwest to ye first bounded tree being also ye bounded tree of Abraham Clement, containing and layed out for foure hundred acres, as by ye returne of ye survey under ye hand of ye surveyor doth and may appeare. Know yee &c. Dated.
Fo. 68.

A Pattent for a parcell of Land at Dellaware granted unto Henry Stretcher.

Enmund Andros Esq. &c. Whereas there is a certain parcell of land at Dellaware which by my order hath been layed out for Henry Stretcher called by the name of Plaine Dealing scituated lyeing and being in a neck called Cemballs Neck joining upon a creek called Mill Creek beginning at a white Oake being the bounded tree of Richard Patey and runing up ye said Mill Creek S. W. to a bounded white oake standing by a creeke side two hundred perches from thence into the wood south east three hundred and twenty pearches to a bounded redd Oake, and from thence North East and by North one hundred and fifty perches to a bounded red Oake, and from thence North West three hundred and twenty pearches to the first bounded tree joyning to ye land of Richard Patey containing and layed out for foure hundred acres as by the return of ye survey under the hand of ye Surveyor doth and may appeare. Know ye &c. Dated
Fo. 69.

(236)
A Patent for a parcell of land near Delaware granted to Walter Lewis,

Edmund Andros, Esq. &c. Whereas there is a certain parcell of land which by my order hath been layd out for Walter Lewis called by ye name of Lewis's lott scituate lyeing and being in a neck called Cimball's neck, on the North side of a small creeke and on ye West side of Delaware bay, begining at a White Oke from thence runing W. S. W. 150 perches to a white Oake by a branch and from thence runing with a line of marked trees South South East three hundred and twenty perches to a white Oake, by ye beaver damme, and runing downe ye beaver damme East North East one hundred and fifty perches and from thence with a line parralell to ye first bounded White Oake three hundred and twenty pearches North North West layd out for three hundred acres as by ye returne of ye Survey under the hand of ye surveyor doth and may appeare. Know ye &c. Dated
Fo 66.

A Pattent of a parcell of land at Dellaware granted to Richard Brasie,

Edmund Andros, Esquire, &c. Whereas there is a certaine parcell of land which by my order hath been layed out for Richard Brasie scituate upon Middle Creeke, beginning at a White Oake standing by a Beaver damm and running from thence East three hundred and twenty perches to a red Oake and from thence runing South one hundred and fifty perches along ye Creeke to a red Oake and runing from thence up ye creeke three hundred and twenty pearches to a Hickory and from thence North to ye first bounded white Oake by the head of

the beaver dam containing and layd out for three hundred acres as by
the returne of the Survey under the hand of ye surveyor doth and may
appeare. Know yee &c. Dated.
Fo. 67.

(237)
    A Pattent for a parcell of land at Dellaware granted
      to Abraham Clement.

  Edmund Andros Esq. &c. Whereas there is a certain parcell of
land which by my order hath been layed out for Abraham Clement
called by ye name of Abraham his Content, scituated lyeing and being
in a Neck called Cimballs Neck and bounded upon a Creeke called
Mill Creeke, beginning at a White Oake being ye bounded tree of
Henry Stretcher and from thence runing up ye creeke South West two
hundred pearches to a bounded white Oake standing by ye aforesaid
Creeke side, and from thence runing with a line of marked trees to a
red Oake in ye woods three hundred and twenty perches South East,
and from thence runing North East two hundred Perches to a White
Oake, being the bounded tree of Henry Stretcher and alsoe Henry Harman, and from thence to ye first bounded tree three hundred and
twenty perches N. W. parralell to ye line of Henry Stretcher contained
and layed out for foure hundred acres as by ye returne of ye survey under ye hand of ye surveyor doth and may appeare. Know ye &c.
Dated.
Fo 67.

    A Pattent for a parcel of land at Dellaware granted
      for James Peddy.

  Edmund Andros, Esq. &c. Whereas there is a certaine parcell of
land scituate lyeing and being upon ye west side of Delaware Bay
which by my order hath been layed out for James Peddy in a creek
called Masspillin creek, and on ye North side of ye said creeke and
neare unto ye head of ye said Creeke, begining at a white Oake, and
from thence runing South South West, three hundred pearches to a
side of a Branch and from thence runing (238) West North West, three
hundred and twenty perches to a red Oake bounded tree, and from
thence in a line of marked trees, North North East three hundred
perches to a bounded red Oake and from thence runing East South
East three hundred and twenty perches to ye first bounded tree containing and layed out for six hundred acres as by ye returne of ye survey under the hand of the surveyor doth and may appeare. Know ye
&c. Dated
Fo 68.

    A Pattent for a parcell of land at ye Whorekill
      granted to John Liming.

  Edmund Andros, Esq. &c. Whereas there is a certaine parcell of
land which by my order hath been layed out for John Liming scituated
lyeing and being in ye woods to ye Eastward of ye Whorekill town

called Hopewell, begining at a Hickory tree being ye bounded tree of William Warren and from thence runing South East one hundred and fifty purches to a bounded Hickory and from thence North East to a bounded Red Oake to a line of marked tree three hundred and twenty perches and from thence North West one hundred and fifety perches to a bounded red Oake, and from thence to ye first bounded Hickory alongst ye line of Wm Warren three hundred and twenty perches containing and layed out for three hundred acres as by ye returne of ye survey under ye hand of ye surveyor doth and may appeare. Know yee &c. Dated.
Fo. 69.

A Pattent for a parcell of land at Dellaware granted to Edward Furlong

Edmund Andros Esq. &c. Whereas there is a certain parcell of land which by my order hath been layed out for (239) Edward Furloung called by the name of My fortune scituated upon ye west side of Delaware bay lying in a creeke called Cedar creeke, begining at a marked Poplar and runing along a marsh East North East two hundred perches to a white Oake standing in a branch and from thence runing South South East three hundred and twenty perches to a red Oake with a line of marked trees and from thence runing West South West two hundred perches to a black walnut tree, and from thence runing North North West three hundred and twenty perches to the first bounded tree containing and layed out for foure hundred acres, as by ye returne of ye survey under ye hands of ye surveyor doth and may appeare. Know yee &c. Dated
Fo. 70.

Pattent for a parcell of land At Dellaware Granted to John Otten.

Edmund Andros, Esq. &c. Whereas there is a certain parcell of land which by my order hath been layed out for John Otten called by the name of Ottens Folley scituated lyeing and being in a creek called Cedar Creek on ye west side of Dellaware Bay begining at a white oake from thence runing up ye creeke West South West one hundred and fifety perches to a red Oake, and from thence runing South South East three hundred twenty five perches to a bounded Red Oake, with a line of marked trees, from thence East South East one hundred and fifety perches to a white Oake, with a line of marked trees and from thence North North East three hundred twenty five perches containing and layed out for three hundred acres as by ye returne of the survey under ye hand of ye surveyor doth and may appeare. Know yee &c. Dated
Fo 70.

(240)

A Pattent for a parcell of land at Dellaware granted unto Thomas Davis

Edmund Andros, &c. Whereas there is a certaine parcell of land which by my order hath been layed out for Thomas Davis called by the

name of Good luck, lying in a creeke called Cedar creeke, on ye West side of Delaware bay, begining at a bounded white Oake standing in a branch dividing it from the land of Edward Forlonge and runing East North East one hundred and fifty perches to a bounded white Oake, and from thence South South East three hundred and twenty perches to a marked white Oake and from thence West South West one hundred and fifty perches with a line of marked trees to a red Oake, and from thence North North West, three hundred and twenty perches to ye fiist bounded tree containing and layed out for three hundred acres as by ye returne of ye survey under ye hand of ye surveyor doth and may appeare. Know yee &c. dated.
Fo 71

  A Pattent for a Parcell of Land Granted to Robert Brasey, Senior.

 Edmund Andros Esq. &c. Whereas there is a certain parcell of land which by my order was layed out for Robert Brasey called by the name of. Robert Brasey his Pleasure lyeing in ye woods near Rehoboth bay begining at a white Oake standing at a head of ye branch and from thence runing West North West three hundred and twenty perches to a White Oake, and from thence South South West foure hundred perches to a white oake standing by the Indyan path, and from thence runing East North East three hundred to a certaine Bever Dam, and from thence up ye said (241) Bever dam, North North West foure hundred perches to ye first bounded white Oake, cantaining and layed out for eight hundred acres as by ye returne of ye survey under ye hand of ye surveyor, doth and may appeare. Know ye &c. Dated
Fo 71

  A Pattent for a lott of land att Dellaware granted unto Richard Hill.

 Edmund Andros, Esqr. &c. Whereas there is a certaine parcell of land which by my order hath been layed out for Richard Hill scituate lyeing and being upon a Creek called Mispilin Creeke, and on ye west side of Delaware bay, called by the name of Hills Content begining at a white Oake, being ye bounded tree of Josias Cowdrey, and runing from thence West North West three hundred and twenty perches to a white Oake, standing upon Mispilin creeke side, and from thence South South West six hundred and thirty perches to a Spanish Oake, from thence with a line of marked trees into ye woods three hundred and twenty five perches, to a red Oake, and from thence with a line of marked trees North North East five hundred and seventy perches to ye first bounded tree containing and layed out for one thousand acres, as by ye returne of ye survey under ye hand of ye surveyor doth and may appeare. Know yee &c. Dated
Fo. 72.

A Pattent for a parcell of land at Delaware granted
unto Thomas Davis Taylor.

Edmund Andros, Esq. &c. Whereas there is a certaine parcell of land which by order hath been layd out for Thomas Davis Taylor called by the name of the Taylors delight, scituate lyeing and being upon Maspillin creeke (242) and on ye East side of ye said Creek, beginning at a Spanish Oake being the bounded tree of John Field, and runing from thence East South East foure hundred and sixty perches to a red Oake bounded tree, and from thence runing South South West two hundred and fifty perches to a bounded red Oake, by the side of ye creeke, and from thence runing downe the creeke North West foure hundred and sixty perches to a bounded tree by ye Marsh and from thence North East to ye first bounded tree containing and layed out for five hundred acres as by ye returne of ye survey under ye hand of ye surveyor doth and may appeare. Know yee &c. Dated
Fo. 72.

A Pattent for a parcell of land at Delaware granted
unto John Kirke.

Edmund Andros, Esq. &c. Whereas there is a certaine parcell of land which by order hath been layed out for John Kirke scituate upon ye West side of Dellaware Bay anl lyeing in ye woods South west from ye Whore kill towne about five miles begining at a white Oake being the bounded tree of Jacob Seth, and from thence runing South South East, foure hundred perches to a certain branch in ye woods proceeding from ye Rehoboth bay to a marked red Oake by ye aforesaid branch and from thence runing up ye said branch three hundred and twenty perches to a bounded red Oake, West South West and from thence runing North North West foure hundred and ten perches to another branch proceeding from Delaware bay, and from thence East North East, three hundred and ten perches to ye first bounded tree, contayning and layed out for eight hundred acres as by ye returne of ye survey under ye hand of ye surveyor. Know ye &c. Dated.
Fo. 73.

(243)

A Pattent for a parcell of land near ye Whorekill
granted to Wm. Prentis.

Edmund Andros, Esq., &c. Whereas there is a certaine parcell of land which by my order hath been layed out for William Prentis called by ye name of Hope Well, scituate lyeing and being in ye woods five miles south West from the Whorekill towne, at ye head of a branch, begining att a White Oake, and runing downe the branch North North East three hundred and twenty perches to a red Oake, standing by a branch side, and from thence runing East South East two hundred perches to a white Oake bounded and from thence runing South South West three hundred and twenty perches and from thence

runing to ye first bounded tree contayning and layed out for foure hundred acres as by ye returne of ye survey under ye hand of ye surveyor doth and may appeare. Know yee &c. Dated.
Fo. 73.

A Pattent for a parcell of land near the Whorekill granted unto Wm. True.

Edmund Andros, Esq. &c. Whereas there is a certaine parcell of land which by my order hath been layed out for William True called by ye name of Trues fortune, scituate lyeing and being in ye woods five miles distance south West from ye Whorekill, begining at a White Oake, being the bounded tree of William Prentis, and from thence runing East South East one hundred and fifty perches to a red Oake, and from thence runing South South West three hundred and twenty perches to a bounded red Oak, and from thence running West North West one hundred and fifty perches to a marked White Oake, and from thence runing North North East three hundred and fifty perches to ye first bounded tree contanying and layed out for three hundred (244) acres as by ye returne of the survey under ye hand of ye surveyor doth and may appeare. Know ye &c. Dated.
Fo. 74.

A Pattent for a parcell of land at Delaware Granted to Christopher Jackson.

Edmund Andros, Esq. &c. Whereas there is a certain parcell of land which by my order hath been layed out for Christopher Jackson called Jackson's lott, scituated on the West side of Delaware Bay, and on ye North side of a Creek, called Mispam Creeke, some certain distance from the creeke, begining at a marked Oake runing by a branch and runing from thence three hundred twenty perches, and from thence North East one hundred and fifty perches and from thence South East three hundred and twenty perches and thence South West one hundred and fifty perches unto ye first bounded White Oake, contayning three hundred acres of land as by ye returne of ye survey, under the hand of ye surveyor doth and may appeare Know yee &c. Dated.
Fo. 74.

A Pattent for a parcell of land at Dellaware granted to Jno. Johnson,

Edmund Andros, Esq. &c. Whereas there is a certaine parcell of land which by my order hath been layed out for John Johnson called Johnsons purchase, scituated upon Rehoboath Bay, upon a creeke called Lowes Creeke, begining at ye said Creeke, by ye mouth of a little creeke, and runing up ye little Creeke, West South West three hundred and twenty perches and from thence two hundred perches to a marked White Oake, and from ye said White Oake, by severall courses unto ye mouth of ye aforesaid Lowes Creeke, three hundred and twenty perches unto a point and from ye sd. (245) poynt North-

west unto the first bounded Oake, by ye aforesd little creeks mouth, containing foure hundred acres of land as by ye returne of ye survey under ye hand of ye surveyor doth and may appeare. Know ye and &c. Dated
Fo. 75.

    A Pattent for a parcell of land att Dellaware granted to Jacob Seth.

 Edmund Andros, Esq. &c. Whereas there is a certaine parcell of land which by my order hath been layed out for Jacob Seth called by ye name of Timber Ridge scituate upon ye west side of Delaware Bay S. W. from ye Whorekill Towne distance about foure miles begining at a white Oake, standing by a branch of Rehobath Bay, & from thence North North West two hundred and fifty perches to a bounded white Oake standing by a small meadow, and from thence runing West North West three hundred forty and five pearches to a bounded white Oake standing by a branch proceeding out of Dellaware Bay and from thence South South East two hundred and fifty perches to a bounded red Oake and from thence runing East South East three hundred and forty five pearches to ye first bounded tree contayning and layed out for five hundred acres as by ye returne of ye surveye under ye hand of ye surveyor doth and may appeare. Know yee &c. Dated:
Fo. 75.

    A Pattent for a parcell of land At Dellaware granted to Hubardus Francis.

 Edmund Andros, Esq. &c. Whereas there is a certain parcell of land which by my order hath been layed out for Hubardus Francis, lyeing in a creeke, called St. Johnsons Creeke and on ye West side of ye said creeke, scituate on ye west side of ye Dellaware Bay, called by ye name of Plane Dealing begining at a head of a small creek, and runing (246) downe ye creek, North East three hundred and twenty perches, to a red Oake, standing by ye side of ye said small creeke, and from thence along ye side of ye marsh two hundred perches to a red Oake bounded tree and from thence into ye woods with a line of marked trees three hundred and twenty perches to a white Oake, and from thence with a line paralell to ye first bounded tree of ye said small creeke, two hundred perches as by ye returne of ye survey under ye hand of ye surveyor doth and may appeare. Know yee &c. Dated
Fo. 76.

    A Pattent for a parcell of land at Dellaware granted unto John Field.

 Edmund Andros, Esq. &c. Whereas there is a certaine parcell of land which by my order hath been layed out for John Field called by the name of Fields Hope, scituate lyeing and being in a creeke called Maspilin creeke, and on the east side of the said creeke, and on ye west side of Dellaware bay, beginning at a corner tree of Richard Hills and runing from thence S. South West one hundred & seventy perches to a

Spanish Oake by ye creek side and from thence runing East South East three hundred and five perches to a white Oake in ye woods, and from thence North North East one hundred and seventy perches to a red Oake and from thence with a line of marked trees West North West parallell to ye first bounded tree contayning and layed out for three hundred acres as by ye returne of ye survey under ye hand of ye surveyor, doth and may appeare. Know yee &c. Dated
Fo. 76.

     A Pattent for a Parcell of land at ye Whorekill granted unto James Wells.
 Edmund Andros, Esq. &c. Whereas there is a certaine parcell of land which by my order hath been layed out for (247) James Wells, called Sunn Dyalls and begining by Beaver dam proceeding from a Creeke, called Lowes Creeke, begining at a marked white Oake, and runing South East and by East two hundred and eighty perches from ye said Beaver Damm, and part downwards ye said Lowes Creeke, unto a marked Red Oake, standing by ye said creeke, and from thence North East by North forty perches then North East one hundred and ninety eight unto a red Oake, then West North West three hundred and seaventy perches unto a White Oake, and from thence unto ye first bounded White Oake, contayning foure hundred acres as by ye returne of ye survey under ye hand of ye surveyor doth and may appeare. Know ye &c. dated
Fo. 77.

     A Pattent for a parcell of land at Delaware granted unto James Lille.
 Edmund Andros, Esq. &c. Whereas there is a certaine parcell of land which by my order hath been layd out for James Lille, scituate upon a branch of Slaughter creeke on ye west side of Delaware Bay, begining at a white Oake, upon ye side of ye branch, and runing down the branch East three hundred and twenty perches to a White Oake, standing by ye path and from thence runing North one hundred and fifty perches to a red Oake, with a line of marked trees and from thence runing West three hundred and twenty perches to a red Oake, and from thence runing South one hundred and fifty perches to ye first bounded White Oake, contayning and layd out for three hundred acres as by ye returne of ye Survey under ye hand of ye Surveyor doth and may appeare. Know ye &c. Dated
Fo. 77.

(248)
     A Pattent for a parcell of land at Dellaware granted unto Sanders Mollistin.
 Edmund Andros, Esq. &c. Whereas there is a certaine parcell of land which by my order hath been layd out for Sanders Mollistin, lyeing on the back of his own land and bounded on ye East with ye lyne

of Otto Woolgast and on ye South with ye line of Jeffery Sommerford and William Arrundall, begining at a poplar and runing twenty-five perches South West to ye lyne of Jeffery Sommerford, and from thence runing North West three hundred and twenty perches to ye lyne of William Arrundall and from thence uning North East twenty five perches, contayning fifety acres as by ye returne of ye survey under ye hand of ye surveyor doth and may appeare. Know yee &c. Dated
Fo. 78.

A Pattent for a parcell of land at Dellaware granted unto William Warrin.

Edmund Andros, Esq. &c. Whereas there is a certaine parcell of land which by my order hath been layd out for William Warrin called Warrins choice scituate & lyeing in a creek, called Potocks creek, and on ye east side of ye Whorekill towne begining at a White Oake, being ye bounded tree of Abraham Clement, and from thence runing South West three hundred and twenty perches to a hickory and from thence runing South East one hundred and fifety perches to a Hickory with a line of marked trees, and from thence with a line of marked trees to a red Oake, three hundred and twenty perches North East, and from thence to the first bounded White Oake, one hundred and fifety perches N. W. contayning and layd out for three hundred acres, as by ye returne of ye survey under ye hand of ye surveyor doth and may appeare. Know yee &c. dated.
Fo. 78.

(249)

A Pattent for a parcell of land at Dellaware granted unto Wm Burton.

Edmund Andros, Esq. &c. Whereas there is a certaine parcell of land which by my order hath beene layd out for Wm Burton called ye Loving Neck, scituated on ye South Side of Rehobath Bay, and on ye North side of ye great ryver, begining at a point of woods, and runing West up ye great ryver one thousand perches to a White Oake, at the head of a small creeke, called Indyan Cabin Creeke, and from thence North three hundred and fifty perches to a White Oake standing by a Creeke side called Middle Creeke with a lyne of marked trees, and from thence bounded upon ye aforesaid bay to ye first bounded point South East one thousand Perches, contayning and layd out for one thousand acres as by ye returne of ye survey under ye hand of the Surveyor doth and may appeare. Know yee &c. dated
Fo. 79

A Pattent for a parcell of land at Dellaware granted to Robert Hart, Jun.

Edmund Andros, Esq. &c. Whereas there is a certaine parcell of land which by my order hath been lay'd out for Robert Hart Jun. called by the name of Harts choyce, scituate lyeing and being upon a creeke called Cedar Creek, begining at a White Oake, and runing from thence

West along ye line of trees of James Totten, two hundred and fifety perches to a White Oake, and from thence North West and by North three hundred and twenty perches to a bounded red Oake, and from thence North East and by East two hundred and fifety perches to a White Oake, and from thence South East and by South three hundred and twenty perches to ye first bounded tree being a White Oake, contayning and layed out for five hundred acres as by ye returne of ye survey under ye hand of ye surveyor doth and may apeare. Know yee &c. dated
Fo. 79.

(250)
A Pattent for a parcell of land at the Whore Kill granted unto Cornelius Verhoofe.

Edmund Andros, Esq. &c. Whereas there is a certaine parcell of land which by my order hath been layd out for Cornelius Verhoofe, called by ye name of the Carpenters Yard, scituate upon ye Whorekill creeke, at ye mouth of ye said creeke, begining at ye point of ye said creeke, and from thence runing south and by West two hundred and eighty foure perches to a White Oake, & from thence runing North East two hundred and eighty foure perches to a bounded cedar tree, & from thence runing West North West seventy eight perches to a White Oake bounded tree, containing and laid out for one hundred and twelve acres as by ye return of the survey under ye hand of ye surveyor doth and may appeare. Know yee &c. dated
Fo. 80.

A Pattent for a parcell of land at Dellaware granted unto John Deprey,

Edmund Andros, Esq. &c. Whereas there is a certaine parcell of land which by my order hath been layd out for John Deprey scituate lyeing and being in ye West side of Dellaware Bay near unto a Creeke, called Slaughter Creek, begining at a White Oake standing by a branch and from thence runing South East two hundred and fifety perches to a white Oake, standing by a marsh, and from thence runing South West six hundred and fourty perches to a Red Oake tree with a line of marked trees, and from thence runing North West two hundred and fifety perches to a White Oake tree being the bounded tree of Richard Forlound, and from thence runing North East six hundred and forty perches to ye first bounded White oake containing and layed out for one thousand acres, as by ye returne of ye survey under ye hand of ye surveyor, doth and may appeare. Know yee &c. dated.
Fo. 80.

(251)
A Pattent for a parcell of land Granted joyntly for Samll. Styles and Robt. Trayly.

Edmund Andros, Esq. &c. Whereas there is a certaine parcell of land which by my order hath been layed out joyntly for Samll Styles

and Robert Trayly called by the name of Styles his delight, scituate on the west side of Delaware bay and on ye North side of a creeke, called Mispann creeke, begining at a marked White Oake standing by the edge of a marsh proceeding from ye aforesaid bay and by a pond in ye said Marsh, and runing from thence west and by South two hundred and thirty perches up ye said Mizpann creeke, and from thence North West two hundred and forty perches, then North East one hundred and eighty five perches, then South East two hundred forty five perches, then North East one hundred and fifety perches, then North West two hundred and fourty five perches, then North East one hundred and seventy perches, & from thence South East two hundred and fifety perches unto ye aforesaid Marsh, & from thence by severall courses unto ye aforesaid first bounded white Oake three hundred fourty eight perches, contayning seaven hundred and fourty foure acres as by the returne of the survey under ye hand of ye surveyor, doth and may appeare. Know ye &c. dated.
Fo. 81

A Pattent for a parcell of land At Dellaware granted unto Josias Cowdery.

Edmund Andros, Esq. &c. Whereas there is a certaine parcell of land which by my order hath been layd out for Josias Cowdery called by the name of ye lott of Bengman, scituate lyeing and being upon a creeke, called Cedar Creeke, and on ye North side of ye said Creeke, and from thence begining at a red Oake, and runing West South West one (252) hundred perches, & from thence runing North West and by North three hundred and twenty perches to a white Oake, with a lyne of marked trees dividing it from the land of Robert Hart, & from thence North East & by East with a lyne of marked trees to a White Oake, and from thence South East & by South three hundred and twenty perches to a White Oake, and from thence South West and by West three hundred and twenty perches to a Hickory, and from thence East North East one hundred perches to a bounded red Oake tree, and from South South East one hundred pearches to ye first bounded red Oake, contayning and layd out for seven hundred acres, as by ye returne of ye survey under ye hand of ye Surveyor doth and may appeare. Know yee &c. dated.
Fo. 81.

Granted unto John Stevens.

Edmund Andros, Esq. &c. Whereas there is a certaine parcell of land which hath been certifyed by the Court at the Whorekill & layd out for John Stevens scituate lyeing and being in a creeke called Little Creeke, near unto a creeke called St. Johns creeke, lyeing on ye west side of Delaware bay, & on ye North syde of ye said Creeke, called by ye name of Content, begining at a Poplar adjoyning upon a branch of Duck Creeke, and runing from thence North West three hundred and seventy five perches with a lyne of marked trees, to a red Oake, bounded tree, and from thence runing South West three hundred and

fifety perches to a bounded white Oake, & from thence runing South South East two hundred and fifety perches to a bounded red Oake, and from thence with a lyne of marked trees, runing South and by West one hundred and seventy perches to a bounded Redd Oake, and from thence runing West and by South one hundred and eighty two perches to a bounded hickory, and from thence runing South and by West one hundred and fifety perches to a bounded White Oake, standing at ye head of ye said little Creeke, and from thence runing North East eight hundred perches to ye first bounded Poplar ye said land is bounded upon ye land formerly layd out for (253) John Stevens and on ye East with the land of William Stevens, layd out for one thousand two hundred acres, as by ye returne of ye survey under ye hand of ye surveyor doth and may appear. Know yee &c. Dated Septr. 29, 1677.
Fo. 82

A Pattent for a parcell of land neare the Whorekill granted unto Robert Brasey, Junyo.

Edmund Andros, Esq. &c. Whereas there is a certaine parcell of land which by my order hath been layed out for Robert Brasey, Junior, called by ye name of Robert his Fortune, scituate upon Rehoboth Bay distant from the Whore Kill about tenn myles and on ye west side of ye said Bay begining at a redd Oake, dividing it from ye land of Richard Brasey, and runing downe ye Creeke, East three hundred twenty perches, to a bounded white Oake, and from thence runing into ye woods North one hundred and fifty perches to a white Oake tree & from thence runing West three hundred and twenty perches to a bounded red Oake, and from thence runing South, to ye first bounded tree, contayning and layd out for three hundred acres as by ye returne of ye survey under ye hand of ye surveyor doth and may appeare. Know ye &c. dated
F. 82.

A Pattent for a parcell of land At D granted unto John Antrey,

Edmund Andros, Esq. &c. Whereas there is a certaine parcell of land which by my order, hath been layd out for John Antrey, called by ye name of Fortune, scituate lyeing and being in a creeke, called St. Johns creeke, on ye west side of Delaware Bay, begining at a branch dividing it from the land of Daniell Whitly, and runing down ye maine creeke, South Easte one hundred perches, to a redd Oake bounded tree and from thence runing South West and by South three hundred and twenty perches to a white Oake bounded tree & from thence runing North west two hundred pearches to a white Oake (254) standing by ye branch, and from thence runing downe ye branch North East three hundred perches to ye lower poynt of ye branch being ye first bound contayning and layed out for three hundred acres, as by ye returne of ye survey under ye hand of ye surveyor doth and may appeare. Know yee &c. Dated.
Fo. 83.

A Pattent for a parcell of land Att Dellaware granted unto Daniell Whitly.

Edmund Andros, Esq. &c. Whereas there is a certaine parcell of land which by my order hath been layd out for Daniell Whitly called by the name of ye Grove, scituate lyeing and being in a creeke, called St. Johns Creeke, by ye head of ye said creeke, and on ye west side of Delaware bay begining at a Poplar marked tree, and runing South East along ye creeke side one hundred and fifety perches to a black Wallnut marked tree, and from thence South West three hundred and twenty perches to a bounded redd Oake, and from thence runing North West one hundred and fifety perches to a bounded redd Oake, and from thence to ye first bounded Poplar, by the creeke side three hundred and twenty perches North East contanying and layd out for three hundred acres as by ye returne of ye survey under ye hand of ye surveyor, doth and may appeare. Know ye &c. dated
Fo. 83.

A Pattent for a parcell of land granted to Ephraim and Casper Hermans.

Edmund Andros, Esq. To all to whom these presents shall come, sendeth greeting: Whereas there is a certaine tract of land on ye west side of Dellaware ryver called St. Augustine, being on the N   side of Apoquemini creeke, opposite to ye lower end of Reed I   the which by vertue of a warrant hath been layd out for Augustine Herman, the said land being bounded with the Ryver on the East (255) on the South with Apoquemini creeke, and land of Dirck Williamson and Dirck Lawrenson, & also w   land of Clas Kirston on ye North with a small creeke called St. Augustine creeke dividing this from a tract or parcell land granted to Mr. Peter Alricks, on the west with the maine woods, contayning and layd out for foure hundred acres, with the marshes thereunto belonging as by the returne of the survey brought in by Capt. Edmond Cantwell, the Surveyor doth and may appeare. And the Said Augustine Herman having transfered his rights and interests in the premises unto his two sons Ephriam and Casper Hermann, Now know ye &c. quitt rent foure bushells wheate. dated December first, 1675.
Omited to be entered in due course.

A Pattent for a parcell of land at ye Whorekill granted to Francis Whitwell

Edmund Andros, Esq. Kt. &c. Whereas there is a certaine tract of land called Whitwells Chance the which hath been granted by the Co'rt at the Whorekill, unto Francis Whitwell, the same lyeing and being on the West side of Delaware Bay and on the North side of the Southermost branch of a creeke called Duck Creeke, begining at a White Oake, being   westermost bounded tree of a tract of land called Whiteha   from thence runing west up the Creeke, five hundred   another bounded white Oake, standing by the creeke side, from thence North by a line of marked trees, three hun-

dred and twenty perches to another bounded white Oake, standing in ye woods by a small proson, from thence East by a line of marked trees to a bounded white gumme standing by a great swamp or creuple five hundred perches from thence South by a line of marked trees to the first bounded tree contayning one thousand acres of land as by the returne of the Survey under the hand of the surveyor doth and may appeare. Know yee &c. The Quitt rent ten bushells. Dated August 14, 1678.
Fo. 84.

(256)
      A Pattent for a parcell of land Whorekill granted unto John Briggs.

 Sir Edmund Andros, Kt. &c. Whereas there is a certaine parcell of land called Poplar ridge the which hath been layd out by vertue of a warrant from the Court at Whorekill for John Briggs, scituate lyeing and being on the West side of Delaware Bay, about two miles above St. Jones Creeke, being bounded as follows, vizt. begining at a corner marked White Oake, standing at the South East side of a Swamp which divideth this from a piece of land called Poplars Neck and from the said Oake runing downe the said Swamp, North Easterly fifty five degrees ninety and two perches East South East seventy and foure perches. and North Easterly seventy five degrees, one hundred fourty and two perches, to another corner markt White Oake, standing on a point, at the South East syde of the said Swamp, from thence South by a lyne of marked trees, one hundred ninety and eight perches to a corner markt black Oake, standing on a Barren Swell, from thence South West by a lyne of markt trees, seventy and two perches, to a corner markt black Oake, standing in the Head line, of the land of Robert Jones, from thence North West, along the said Jones line of markt trees, one hundred and twelve perches, to the upper corner of the sd Jones land being markt with a post in the ground, from thence South West thirty and three perches to a corner markt white Oake, of the land layd out for Walter Wharton and from thence by his lyne of marked trees, North west one hundred and eighty perches to the first mentioned white Oake, contayning and layd out for two hundred and sixty acres of land as by returne of the Survey under the hand of the Surveyor doth and may appear. Know yee &c. Quitt rent two bushells, ½. dated August 14, 1678.
See the Platt & Survey
Page 35.

(257)
      A Pattent for a parcell of land at Dellaware granted unto John Briggs, and Mary Phillips

 Sir Edmund Andros, Kt. &c. Whereas there is a certaine tract of land called Kingston, upon Hull, the which hath been layd out by vertue of a warrant from the Court at the Whorekill for John Briggs and Mary Phillips scituate lyeing and being on ye west side of Delaware

bay, and on ye North syde of St. Jones creeke, being the land and plantation whereon they now dwell, & is bounded as followith viz: Beginning at a corner marked Black Oake, standing by ye side of a Marsh, which lieth between the land & the creeke, right unto the upper side of ye cleared ground and from ye said Oake, runing North East by a line of marked trees dividing this from the land of Robert Jones, three and seventy perches to the side of a marsh which proceedeth from the maine bay, & from thence South East two hundred perches, and then South West by a line of marked trees dividing this from the land belonging to the towne point, two hundred fifety eight perches to a corner marked black oake, standing at the head of a great marsh branch which divideth this from the towne point and from thence following the severall courses of the marsh and creeke, to the first mentioned corner black Oake, contayning foure hundred and fifety acres of land and about forty acres of marsh lyeing between this land the aforesaid creeke, &c. Know yee &c. Quitt rent five bushells. Dated August 14, 1678.
Fo 86.
See the Platt & Survey,
Page 37.

A Pattent for a parcell of land at Delaware granted unto John Briggs.

Sir Edmund Andros, Esq. Knt. &c. Whereas there is a certaine parcell of land called by the name of Aberdeen, lyeing and being on the South West side of Delaware bay, the which by vertue of a warrant hath been layed out for John (258) Briggs, the said land lyeing on the South Side of a certain creek, called Boucom Bridge creeke, begining at a marked red Oake, runing East South East in length three hundred and twenty perches then North North East two hundred perches to the bay, and by the bay and marsh, West North West, three hundred and twenty perches to a marked White Oake, by the Creek side, then up the creeke, South South West two hundred perches, to ye first bounded tree contayning and layd out for foure hundred acres as by the returne of the survey; under the hand of Capt. Edmund Cantwell, the Surveyor, doth and may appeare. Now know ye that by vertue of his Majesty's letters patents and the comision and authorite derived unto me under his Royall Highnesse I have given & granted & by these presents do hereby give an graunt, unto John Briggs, his heires & assigns the afore recited parcell of land & premises with all & singular, the appertances to have and to hold the said parcell of land and premises unto the said John Briggs, his heires and assigns unto the proper use and behoofe of him the said John Briggs, his heires and assigns for ever: he making improvement on the said land according to law, and yielding and paying therefore yearly and every yeare, unto his Majesty's use as a Quitt rent foure bushells of good winter wheate unto such officer or officers as shall be empowered to receive the same in the whorekill. Given under my hand, and sealed with the seale of the

Province in New Yorke, the twenty fifth day of March, in the twenty eighth year of his Majesty's reigne, Anno Domini, 1679.

A Transport of the above said land to John Curtis of the Whorekill.

Know all men by these presents: that I John Briggs of St. Jones in Delaware for a valuable consideration to me in hand paid or secured to be payd before the sealing and delivery hereof by John (259) Curtis of the Whorekill the receipt whereof I acknowledge and by these presents transport, assign and set over unto ye said John Curtis, his heirs and assigns forever, all my right title and interest to the within mentioned parcell of land and premises. In testimony whereof I have hereunto set my hand and seale in New York, this fifth day of May, 1679.

Sealed and Delivered in presence of.

No. 87.

A Pattent for a parcell of land at Delaware granted unto Walter Dickinson.

Sir Edmund Andros, Knt. &c. Whereas Thomas Merritt, obtayned a patent from the late Governor called Francis Lovelace, bearing date the 17th day of June, 1671, for a certaine parcell of land contayning foure hundred acres scituate lyeing and being on the Westward side of Delaware Bay, and on the North East side of a creeke, called St. Jones Creeke, being about a mile from Murder Creek, and extendeth itself North West out of the said Bay, bounded on the South West with the said Creeke, on the South East with the land of Mr. Walter Wharton, and on the two opposite sides with the maine woods, extending itselfe a myle into the woods which said land haveing not been settled or improved by the said Thomas Meritt, who hath not appeared ever since and is supposed to be dead, the same granted to Mr. Walter Dickinson. And there being another certaine parcell of land adjoyning, heretofore belonging unto Mr. Walter Wharton, who having likewise a patent from Governour Lovelace, had in part ceded it but since sold for debt by vendue at New Castle, it being also scituate on the Westward side of Delaware Bay, and on the North East side of the Creeke, called St. Jones creeke, being about a mile above Murder creeke, and extendeth itself (as the former) North West (260) from the said Bay bounded on the South West with the land of Mr. Robert Jones, & on the two opposite sides with the maine woods contayning the like quantitie of foure hundred acres of the which the said Walter Dickinson hath for some years been in possession by vertue of the said Vendue not performed by John Ogle, the whole complement of land aforedescribed being eight hundred acres. Now know yee &c. Quitt rent eight bushells of winter: Date the 15th day of September 1676.

Fo. 88.

A Pattent for a parcell of land at Delaware granted to Bryan Omalle.

Sir Edmund Andros, Knt. &c. Whereas, there is a certaine parcell of land on the West side of Delaware ryver lyeing and being on the N. side of Apoquemini creek being the first hooke or point of land in a small creeke, called the Drawers creeke, and bounded with a swamp or creuple bush North and with another swampe between the creeke, and the firme mainland South, runing into the woods North West containing foure hundred acres of land, which said land together with a portion of hay land for cattle in Apoquemini creeke, having been seated and manured by Claes Kerson, and Bernard Brand the first settlers and had a pattent for the same, was purchased by Bryan Omalle, who as is certified by the Court hath made improvement thereon likewise and is in possession thereof. Know yee &c. Quitt rent 4 bushells of wheate. Dated in New Yorke, November 20th, 1679.
Fo. 88.

A Pattent for a parcell of land at Delaware granted unto Morris Daniell.

Sir Edmund Andros, Knt. &c. Whereas there is certaine (261) parcell of land on the west side of Delaware Bay called Drummers neck lyeing and being on the North West syde of Apoquemini creeke, the which by vertue of a warrant hath been layed out for Morris Daniel, the said land begining at a corner markt white Oake, standing on a point by ye said Creeke, at the upper side of a branch which at the mouth thereof divides this from the land of Bernard Hendricksen, and from the said Oake runing up the Branch North North West fourty perches and then North West by the said Bernards line of markt trees, foure hundred and eighty perches to a markt corner hickory from thence South West by another line of markt trees sixty perches to a corner markt red Oake, being the upper corner tree of a parcell of land formerly granted to Jacob Taien, from thence South South East by the said Jacobs line of markt trees foure hundred perches into a swamp and so downe the swamp South South Easte sixty perches to the aforesaid creeke, and finally downe along ye creeke to ye first mentioned white Oake, contanying and layed out for one hundred and ninety acres of land as by the returne of the survey under the hand of the surveyor doth and may appeare. Know yee &c. Quitt rent two bushells of wheate. Dated in New Yorke the 20th day of November 1679.
Fo. 89.

A Patent for a parcell of land granted unto Mr. John Moll.

Sir Edmund Andros, Knt. &c. Whereas there are three lotts of ground in the towne of New Castle in Delaware River the which did formerly belong to Capt. John Carr and being since exposed to sale at publick outcry or open vendue, in the same place by order of the court to pay the debts of the said Capt. Carr, were bought by John Moll one of the Justices (262) there. The said lot lyeing as followeth vizt. The

one to the East of Warmoes Street having the lock of Johannes De Haes at ye front to the water side, the Harte Street on the South ye lott of Edmund Cantwell on the North the said lott being in length on both sides two hundred thirty three foot in breadth behinde at the Warmoes now called the Lands streete, and before next to Johannes De Haes sixty foot. The other two lotts haveing the Warmoes street to the east the Minquas streete to the West, the lott of Samuel Lands, to the North and the Hart Street to the South, the said two lotts being in length on both sydes three hundred foot, and in breadth at both ends one hundred twenty foot, which said three lotts were layed out by the surveyor for the aforesaid John Moll, and are now in his possession. Know yee Quitt rent two bushells of good winter wheate. Dated in New Yorke, the 20th day of November 1679.
Fo. 90.

A Patent for a parcell of land granted unto Peter Teschenmacker.

Sir Edmund Andros, Knt. &c. Whereas there is a certaine piece of land at New Castle in Delaware River, lyeing and being at ye West end of the towne haveing a piece of land belonging to Peter Alricks, to the east of it and to the West the lott of Matthias and Amilius De Ring containing in length on both sydes, three hundred foot and in length before and behinde foure hundred and eighty foot of land the which was layd out by the Surveyor the 22nd day of July last for Mr. Peter Teschenmaecker by vertue of a warrant from the Court of New Castle bearing date the fourth day of June before. Know yee &c. Quitt rent one bushell of wheate, dated in New Yorke, November 20th, 1679.
Fo 90

A Patent for a parcell of land at New Castle granted unto Matthias & Amilius De Ring.

Sir Edmund Andros, Knt. &c. Whereas there is a certaine piece of land at New Castle in Delaware River (263) lying and being at the West end of the towne, having the land or lott of Mr. Pieter Teschenmaeccker to the east and the little valley or marsh to the west containing in length next to Mr. Teschenmaeckers to the East three hundred foot and in breadth to the waterside six hundred and one foot. thence to the marsh sixty six foot, so along and by the edge of the Marsh five hundred seventy foure foote and to the corner of Mr. Teschenmaeckers land one hundred and twenty foot, the which was layd out by the Surveyor the 22nd day of July last for Matthias and Amilius De Ring by vertue of two warrants from the Court of New Castle, bearing date the 5th day of June 1678 and third of July 1679. Know yee &c. Dated in New Yorke, November the 20th, 1679. Quitt rent
Fo. 91.

A Patent for a lott of land in the towne of New Castle granted unto Hendrick Vanderburgh.

Sir Edmund Andros, Knt. &c. Whereas there is a certaine lott of ground at New Castle in Delaware River lyeing and being in the street

called the Land streete, haveing the lott of John Boyer,. on the South West, and the Comon not as yet taken up on the North East, being in breadth before and behind sixty foot, and in length on both sides three hundred foot, the which was layd out by the Surveyor, the third day of July last for Hendrick Vanderburgh by vertue of a warrant from the Court of New Castle, dated the first day of the said Month. Know yee &c. Dated in New Yorke the 20th day of November 1679. Quitt rent one bushells of Wheate.
Fo 91.

> A Patent for a parcell of land granted unto Thomas Jacobson, Olle Paulsen, and Arent Johnson at Delaware.

Sir Edmund Andros, Knt. &c. Whereas there is a certaine parcell of land on the West syde of Dellaware River called Red Clayes Point lyeing and being on North and (264) Northwest side of Bread and Cheese Island, and is more than halfe compassed with a branch of Christiana creeke, called Red Clays Creeke, the which by vertue of a warrant hath been layd out for Thomas Jacobson, Olle Paulsen and Arent Johnson, begining at a corner marked White Oake, standing at the Mouth of a small branch of red Clayes Creeke, called Herring branch, which divides this from the land of Jacob Johnson, and from the sd Oake runing North Easterly seven degrees up the said Branch or rivulett one hundred and sixty perches, then from the same rivulet North by a line of marked trees one hundred and sixty perches to a corner marked white Oake, standing on a levell from thence west by a line of marked trees one hundred perches to a corner marked White Oake, standing under a high bank by a small swamp nigh unto the side of Red Clayes creeke, and from thence runing downe the severall courses of the said creeke, to the first mentioned white Oake at the mouth of Herring branch contayning two hundred & forty eight acres of land, as by the returne of the survey made in the year 1675 since certifyed by the Court of New Castle doth any may appeare. Know yee &c. Quitt rent two bushells of Wheate and halfe Dated in New Yorke, November 20th, 1679.
Fo 92

> A Pattent for a parcell of land in Delaware Bay granted unto Andries Du Pre.

Sir Edmund Andros, Knt. &c. Whereas there is a certaine parcell of land in Delaware Bay lyeing and being near to Rehobath Bay on the North side thereof, called by the name of the Timber neck the which hath been layed out for Andries Du Pre by the approbation of the Court at the Whorekill and is certifyed to be seated allready in part the said land begining at a white Oake bounded tree from thence runing North and by East two hundred perches to a red Oake bounded tree and from thence runing East and by South three hundred and twenty perches to a redd Oake, standing by a branch and from thence runing downe the Branch South South West two hundred perches to

(265) the land of John Avery and from thence runing West and by North three hundred and twenty perches to the first bounded tree, containing foure hundred acres of land as by the returne of the Survey doth and may appeare. Know yee. Quitt rent foure bushells of Wheate, dated in New Yorke, the twentieth day of August 1679.
Fo. 98.

A Pattent for a parcell of land on the West side of Delaware Bay. Granted unto Joshuah Barkstead.

Sir Edmund Andros, Knt. &c. Whereas there is a certaine parcell land on ye west side of Delaware bay scituated lyeing and being on the S. E. side of St. Jones Creeke, called by the name of Caroone Manor, the which hath been layed out for Joshuah Barkstead by the approbation of the Court at the Whorekill as is certifyed by them The said land begining at a markt red Oake, being the head bounded tree of the land where the said Joshuah Barkstead now dwells runing from the said Red Oake with a line of marked trees South West five hundred and sixty perches, to a markt Black Oake, standing by a branch proceeding from the Murder Creeke, and commonly called the Island Branch, and from thence North West up the said branch binding sixty perches, then North West and by North binding also up the said branch eighty foure perches, then North North West also binding up the said branch one hundred and six perches, to a marked white Oake, standing by the said branch and a valley proceeding from the said branch and from thence North East with a line of markt trees five hundred thirty two perches to a markt hickory standing near the head of a branch proceeding from a Beaver Damm, separating this from the land of Robert Bedwell, and from the said Hickory South East thirty nine perches to the North West head bounded tree of the sd land the sd Joshuah (266) Barkstead now dwells on as aforesaid. Containing eight hundred acres of land as by the returne of the Survey doth and may appeare. Know yee &c. Quitt rent 8 bushells of wheate. Dated in New Yorke, the twentieth day of August 1679.
Fo 99.

Sir Edmund Andros, Knt. &c. Whereas there is a certaine parcell of land in Delaware bay lying and being in the woods neare unto Rehobah bay distant from the Whorekill about ten miles called by the name of the Exchange, the which hath been layed out for Francis Meggs and John Crolley by the approbation of the Court at the Whorekill as is certifyed by them. The sd land begining at a marked white Oake, from thence runing downe a branch South three hundred twenty five perches to another marked white Oake, standing by a Beaver Dam from thence runing East three hundred twenty five perches to a markt Redd Oake, from thence runing North three hundred twenty five perches to another marked Redd Oake, and from thence runing west three hundred twenty five perches, with a line parallell to the first bounded tree containing six hundred acres of land as by the returne of

the Survey doth and may appeare. Know yee &c. Quitt rent six bushells of good winter wheate. Dated in New Yorke, the 20th day of August 1679.
Fo 99
   (Note.—The bottom of page 266 is torn off.)

(267)
from thence with a line drawn East North East to a markt Oake, standing by a small creeke three hundred and twenty five perches and from thence runing up the said creeke North North West two hundred perches to the first bounded tree containing foure hundred Acres of Land as by the Returne of the Survey doth and may Appeare, Know yee &c. Quitt rent foure Bushells of good winter wheate. Dated in New York, the 20th day of August, 1679.

        A Confirmation granted to William Tom for a House and lott at Delaware.
   Francis Lovelace Esq. &c. Whereas there is a certaine house and lott at New Castle upon Delaware formerly belonging to Peter Alricks and now in the tenure or occupation of William Tom, butted on ye North with James Crawfords on ye East wth ye River wth ye house of Cornelys Wynlin, on ye South and ye land of De Ringe, on ye West and there being also a halfe a lott of ground in ye said Towne where formerly the said mill stood, having a small house standing thereupon the wch. is bounded on ye North wth a lott belonging to ye said William Tom, wth. a river bounded on ye East wth a house of William Breakman on ye south and ye Mart on ye West. Now for a confirmation unto him ye said William Tom, &c. The Patent Dated New Yorke 1669, The Quitt Rent 1 bushell.
   (The page is here torn off.)

CERTIFICATE.

I, James Lord, Recorder of Deeds in and for Kent County and State of Delaware, do hereby certify that the within and foregoing is, to the best of my knowledge and belief, a true copy of the original record of the Dutch grant of lands from the year 1646 to the year 1657 inclusive and the Duke of York grant of lands in Delaware from the year 1667 to 1680 inclusive as now lodged in the office of the Recorder of Deeds in and for said Kent County and State of Delaware except as to the part thereof recorded in Dutch, which said part so recorded as aforesaid, I do hereby certify to the best of my information and belief to be a true and correct translation thereof.

In Witness Whereof I have hereunto set my hand and seal of office this third day of January in the year of our Lord One thousand nine hundred and three.

JAMES LORD,
Recorder.

INDEX.

A
	Pages
Andriesen, Jan, grant to	5
Andros, Sir Edmund, commission to	31
Andros, Sir Edmund, confirmations and patents	85 to 123
Andros, Sir Edmund, confirmations and patents	160 to 188
Avery, Capt. John, survey	69
Ashman, John, confirmations	89, 90
Alricks, Peter, confirmations	100, 125, 146
Axton, George, confirmation	118
Allison, Henry, confirmation	120
Arundel, William, confirmation	121
Andirensen, Andries, confirmation	139
Andries Andirensen & Co., confirmation	139
Askue, John, confirmations	140, 141
Alberts, Derrick, confirmation	145
Abell, Lucas, confirmation	151
Allward, John, patent	168
Antrey John, patent	180

B
Boyer, Alexander, grant to	6
Broen, Thomas, grant to	6
Briggs, John, surveys	44, 47
Bodell, Edward, survey	49
Butlar, William, survey	65
Breacy, Robert, survey	71
Browne, Daniell, confirmation	85
Barbary, Sam'll, confirmation	86
Barker, John, confirmations	87, 102, 120
Bartlett, Nicholas, confirmation	92
Bowen, Henry, confirmation	97
Bromall, Thomas, confirmation	99
Bernard, Charles, confirmation	103
Baucum, Peter, confirmations	114, 167
Bowne, Thomas, confirmation	127
Bones, Hans, confirmations	132, 140
Broers, Sinick, confirmation	139
Boyer, John, confirmation	142
Bollen, James, patent	145
Bradborne, John, confirmation	149
Bell, John, confirmation	151
Buijs, Cornelius, confirmation	151
Bedwell, Robert, patent	155

INDEX.

	Page
Block, Hans, confirmation	157
Blincks, Richard, confirmation	167
Brasie, Richard, patent	169
Brasey, Sr., Robert, patent	172
Burton, Wm, patent	177
Brasey, Jr., Robert, patent	180
Briggs, John, patents	181, 183
Barkstead, Joshuah, patent	188

C

Crabbe, Jacob, grant to	14
Carr, Robert, commission to	22
Carr, Robert, instructions to	22
Carr, Robert, agreement between, and Burgomasters	23
Carr, Capt. John, patents to	25
Carr, Capt. John, certificate	27
Clifford, Thomas, survey	38
Certificates of Land	54
Chambers, Michael, survey	67
Caning, Jr. William, survey	80
Currer, William, confirmation	91
Coks, Thomas, confirmation	98
Collison, John, confirmation	103
Carolus, Larentius, confirmation	110
Craft, Herbert, confirmation	115
Carr, Capt. John, confirmations	124, 129, 131
Crawford, James, confirmations	126, 129, 152, 161
Claesen, Hendrick, confirmations	136, 138
Carr, Andren and wife, confirmation	141
Cousins, John, confirmation	142
Cowenhoven, Pieter, confirmation	142
Claesen, Pieter, confirmation	143
Carr, Patrick, confirmation	151
Crue, John, patent	155
Cornelis, John, patent	167
Clement, Abraham, patent	170
Cowdery, Josias, patent	179
Curtis, John, transport	184
Crolley, John, patent	188

D

De Hinst, Jacob, grant to	7
De Haas Roeloff, widow of, grant to	10
Dircksen, Luke, grant to	10
Dominicus, Rynier, grant to	13
Duke of Yorke, grant to the	17
Duke of Yorke, commission of	31
Daniel, Maurice, survey	34
Dawson, John, survey	57

INDEX. 193

	Page
Dawson, Richard, survey	59
Durdene, Stevan, confirmation	97
Daniel, Morris, confirmation	101
Draper, Alexander, confirmation	104
Davids, William, confirmation	106
Defox, confirmation	109
Dicke, Robert, confirmation	113
Denne, John, confirmation	118
Dux, Paul, and Alice his wife, confirmation	134
Davis, Thomas, patent	171
Deprey, John, patent	178
Dickinson, Walter, patent	184
Daniell, Morris, patent	185
De Ring, Matthias, patent	186
De Ring, Amilius, patent	186
Du Pre, Andries, patent	187

E

Ebel, Pieter, grant to	13
Eckhoff, Jan, grant to	15
Enloes, Abraham, survey	33
Ematt, William, survey	68
Enloes, Abraham, confirmation	100
Egberts, Bernard, confirmations	105, 161
Erskin, John, confirmation	127
Eschelsen, Mattys, confirmation	135
Ericksen, Jan, confirmations	136, 138
Eustas, John, confirmation	144
Eves, William, confirmation	152
Eken, Bernard	159

F

Fritcher, William, survey	75
Fransom, Olie, confirmation	95
Ford, William, confirmation	116
Francis, Robert, confirmation	119
Floyd, Charles, confirmation	160
Furlong, Edward, confirmation	171
Francis, Hubardus, patent	175
Field, John, patent	175

G

Groenenburg, Constantinus, grant to	9
Gerritsen, John, grant to	14
Gumly, Benjamin, survey	33
Garvess, Thomas, survey	37
Groenendyck, Peter, survey	42
Gollege, Thomas, survey	84
Goldsmith, William, confirmation	91
Gilley, Thomas, confirmation	104

	Page
Gadds, Thomas, confirmation	104
Grant, Wm., confirmation	117
Gertsen, Evert, confirmations	139, 158

H

Harmensen, Pieter, grant to	5
Hudden, Andries, grant to	7
Hermens, Pieter, grant to	12
Hodges, Barnard, order for survey	39
Hodges, Barnard, survey	40
Hanson, Peter, surveys	41, 43
Harrmen, Henry, survey	48
Hart, Jr., Robert, survey	50
Hermans, Augustine, confirmation	85
Hopman, Hans, confirmation	99
Hendrickson, John, confirmation	99
Herman, Casparus, confirmation	101
Hart, Robert, confirmation	106
Hendricks, Johan, confirmation	123
Helme, Israel, confirmation	131
Hendrick, John, confirmation	133
Hendricksen, Barent, confirmation	146
Hutchins, Charles, confirmation	152
Hignat, Robert, patent	154
Henry, John, confirmation	160
Hill, Richard, patent	172
Hart, Jr., Robert, patent	177
Hermans, Casper, patent	181
Hermans, Ephraim, patent	181

I

J

Jacobson, Thomas, survey	34
Johnson, Arent, survey	34
Johnson, Cornelis, survey	48
Jackson, Sammuel, confirmations	89, 90
Janson, Charles, confirmation	99
Johnson, Walraven, confirmation	109
Johnson, Herman, confirmation	133
Jackson, Thomas, confirmations	134, 142
Jansen, Juriean, confirmations	134, 138
Jansen, Matijs, confirmations	137, 138
Jansen, Walrane, confirmation	139
Jones, Robert, patent	143
Juryensen, Juryen, confirmation	143
Jones, Robert, confirmations	144, 150
Jego, Peter, patent	145
Johnson, John, confirmation	153
Jans, Juryen, confirmation	155

INDEX.

	Page
Jaques, Pauls, confirmation	158
Jansen, Simon, confirmation	159
Jackson, Christopher, patent	174
Johnson, Jno., patent	174
Jacobson, Thomas, patent	187
Johnson, Arent, patent	187

K

Kieft, William, grant of	5
Kipshaven, John, surveys	41, 43
Kipshaven, John, confirmation	95
Kirke, John, patent	173

L

Laurense, Pieter, grant to	12
Leenderson, Sander, grant to	15
Lourensen, Pieter, grant to	16
Letter of Thanks to Magistrates	27
Letters Patents to Duke of Yorke	27
Loten, James, survey	51
Lester, Morris, confirmation	87
Lawrenson, Marcus, confirmation	95
Land, Samuel, confirmation	109
Laerten, Olle, confirmations	136, 138
Laersen, Paul, confirmations	137, 138
Listen, Morris, confirmation	166
Lewis, Walter, patent	169
Liming, John, patent	170
Lille, James, patent	176
Lovelace, Francis, Esq., confirmations and patents,	139 to 160

M

Moe, Ryer Lammersen, grant to	11
Mills, James, orders for	25, 47
Minutes of Council, 1668, 1678	27
Molestady, Alexander, survey	52
Morilson, Thomas, survey	62
Marsh, Capt. Paul, survey	66
Molestady, Alexander, confirmations	85, 96
Melinton, Oliver, confirmation	97
Moore, George, confirmations	102, 128, 165
Murdey, Robert, confirmation	104
Man, Edward, confirmation	107
Marriott, William, confirmation	108
Morgan, John, confirmation	117
Moll, John, confirmation	122
Maetsen, Andries, confirmation	135
Marshall, John, confirmation	142
Mousen, Hans, confirmation	144

INDEX.

	Page
Merritt, Thomas, confirmation	150
Molistin, Sanders, patent	176
Moll, John, patent	185
Meggs, Francis, patent	188

N

Nichols, Richard, appointment of	20
Nielsen, Niels, orders for	24, 95
Nielson, Olle, confirmation	99
Neals, Francis, confirmation	105
Nomers, John, confirmations	110, 119
Nielson, Sr., Neils, confirmation	123
Nielson, Hendrick, confirmation	123
Neilson, Mattijs, confirmation	123
Neilson, Jr., Neils, confirmation	123
Nichols, Matthias, confirmation	125
Marsh, Paul, patent	154
Nichols, Richard, Esq., confirmations and patents	123 to 139

O

Olleson, Olle, order for	24
Order vindicating Magistrates	27
Omella, Bryan, confirmations	88, 99
Olleson, Hans, confirmation	99
Ogle, John, confirmations	105, 133, 166
Otto, Herman, confirmation	129
Otto, Girard, confirmation	129
Olleson, Pieter, confirmations	137, 138
Osborne, Bezaliel, confirmation	154
Otten, John, patent	171
Omella, Bryan, patent	185

P

Planck, Abraham, grant to	5
Piecolet, Jan, grant to	8
Pietersen, Claes, grant to	11
Paulson, Olie, survey	34
Philips, Mary, survey	47
Peaty, Richard, survey	48
Palmer, Henry, confirmation	88
Pitt, John, confirmation	93
Peddington, Henry, confirmation	94
Parker, Henry, confirmation	95
Peterson, Charles, confirmations	107, 164
Peterson, Hans, confirmations	107, 164
Perry, Peter, confirmation	113
Philips, Thomas, confirmation	114
Pieters, Hans, confirmation	136
Pousen, Pauls, confirmations	137, 138

INDEX.

	Page
Paulson, Wolley, confirmation	142
Pieters, Dirck, confirmation	145
Pernon, Peter, confirmation	151
Peddy, James, patent	170
Prentis, Wm., patents	173
Philips, Mary, patent	181
Paulsen, Olle, patent	187

Q

R

Root, Symon, grant to	5
Ringo, Philip Jansen, grant to	8
Roades, John, survey	58
Rowles, Bryand, survey	60
Richardson, Robert, survey	70
Rawson, Olle, confirmation	99
Rumsey, Charles, confirmation	109
Revill, Randall, confirmation	115
Richards, John, confirmation	119
Reynersten, Reyner, confirmation	130
Reynessen, Reyner, confirmation	132
Reyners, Herman, confirmation	158
Roads, Jacob, confirmation	163

S

Stuyvesant, Petrus, grants from	6 to 16
Steenwyck, Cornelis, grants to	13
St. Gaggen, John, grant to	16
Snelling, Thomas, survey	33
Stiles, Samuel, survey	49
Surveys returned by Capt. Edm. Cantwell	55
Sharrett, William, survey	56
Showlster, Richard, survey	72
Southrin, Edward, surveys	81, 93
Stephens, Richard, survey	82
Street, John, confirmation	87
Salisbury, Evan, confirmation	89
Swandall, Edward, confirmation	90
Scott, John, confirmation	91
Scaggs, Richard, confirmation	108
Stretcher, Henry, confirmation	111
Simpson, William, confirmation	112
Stevens, John, confirmation	113
Smith, Henry, confirmation	115
Stevens, William, confirmation	116
Sharpe, Wm., confirmation	117
Stevenson, Henry, confirmation	119
Southron, Edward, confirmation	121

	Page
Street, John, confirmation	122
Sibranteen, Jan, confirmation	138
Scott, Robert, confirmation	142
Snelling, Thomas, confirmation	142
Sherricks, John, confirmation	147
Sentill, Christopher, confirmation	153
Sincleer, Wm., confirmation	153
Sanderson, Gerritt, confirmation	157
Sibrant, Jan, confirmation	157
Spry, Thomas, confirmation	160
Stills, Samuel, patents	168, 178
Stretcher, Henry, patent	169
Seth, Jacob, patent	175
Stevars, John, patent	179

T

Taillor, Willem, grant to	15
Tom, William, patent to	26
Trale, Robert, survey	49
Tom, William, surveys	53, 94
Troth, W., confirmation	89
Tallant, Robert, confirmations	90, 121
Thomason, Peter, confirmation	110
Tom, William, confirmations	135, 160, 189
Teunijssen, Leendert, confirmation	148
Towson, Olla, confirmation	159
Taylor, Thomas Davis, patent	173
True, Wm., patent	174
Tragly, Robert, patent	178
Teschenmacker, Peter, patent	186

U

V

Vogele Lant (Birds' Land)	5
Van Bronswyck, Hans Albertsen, grant to	9
Van Struckhousen, Jan Hendricksen, grant to	9
Van Swoll, Barent Jansen, grant to	11
Von der Veer, Jacob, grant to	16
Verhoofe, Cornelis, survey	52
Van Jeveren, Henry Hendrick Jansen, confirmation	123
Vanderveer, Jacob, confirmation	156
Verhoofe, Cornelis, patents	167, 178
Vanderburgh, Hendrick, patent	186

W

William, John, survey to	32
Wolgast, Otto, surveys	50, 64
Wilburne, Thomas	50
Wilburne, John, survey	50

INDEX.

	Page
Wilburne, William, survey	50
Walterland, Jonathan, survey	50
Woolbank, Harman, surveys	53, 96
Wiltbanck, Helmanus, surveys	61, 63
Whitman, Stephen, survey	73
Walker, Capt. Nathaniell, surveys	76, 78
Woodhus, John, confirmation	86
Woodersell, Percifell, confirmation	87
Williams, James, confirmation	87
Williams, Edward, confirmation	87
Whittwell, Francis, confirmations	87, 92
Wallem, James, confirmation	88
Wodars, John, confirmation	98
Webb, John, confirmation	112
Willoughby, William, confirmation	112
William, Thomas, confirmation	121
Wollaston, Thomas, confirmations	127, 129, 133, 141
Whale, George, confirmations	128, 148
Wiltbanck, Hermanus Frederick, confirmation	147
Wynhart, Cornelys, confirmation	148
Wale, Sr., George, confirmation	149
Wiltbanck, Hermanus, confirmation	162
Ward, Henry, confirmation	163
Wale, Anna, confirmation	165
Wells, James, patent	176
Warrin, William, patent	177
Whitly, Daniell, patent	181
Whitwell, Francis, patent	181

X

Y

Young, George, surveys	83, 93
Young, Thomas, confirmation	150
Young, Jacob, confirmation	162

Z